THE RECORD S
LANCASHIRE AN̄   ⌐⌐⌐ıKE

FOUNDED TO TRANSCRIBE AND PUBLISH
ORIGINAL DOCUMENTS RELATING TO THE TWO COUNTIES

VOLUME CXXIX

The Society wishes to acknowledge with gratitude the assistance given towards the cost of publication by

The P.H. Holt Trust
Cheshire County Council
Lancashire County Council
Greater Manchester County Council Residuary Body

© Record Society of Lancashire and Cheshire
D.J. Dutton

ISBN 0 902593 18 8

Produced by Alan Sutton Publishing Limited, Gloucester
Printed in Great Britain

ODYSSEY OF AN EDWARDIAN LIBERAL:

the Political Diary of Richard Durning Holt

Edited by
David J. Dutton

PRINTED FOR THE SOCIETY
1989

COUNCIL AND OFFICERS FOR THE YEAR 1989

President

Professor A. Harding, B.Litt., M.A., F.S.A., F.R.Hist.S.

Hon. Council Secretary

Dorothy J. Clayton, M.A., Ph.D., A.L.A., c/o John Rylands University Library of Manchester, Oxford Road, Manchester, M13 9PP

Hon. Membership Secretary

Miss M. Patch, B.A., D.A.A., c/o Greater Manchester County Record Office, 56 Marshall Street, Manchester, M4 5FU

Hon. Treasurer

B.W. Quintrell, M.A., Ph.D., F.R.Hist.S., c/o School of History, Liverpool University, 8 Abercromby Square, Liverpool 7

Hon. General Editor

P. McNiven, M.A., Ph.D., c/o John Rylands University Library of Manchester, Oxford Road, Manchester, M13 9PP

Other Members of Council

Miss E.A. Danbury, B.A.	P.J. Morgan, B.A., Ph.D.
R.N. Dore, M.A., F.R.Hist.S.	M.A. Mullett, B.A., M.Litt., Ph.D.
F.I. Dunn, B.A., D.A.A.	C.B. Phillips, B.A., Ph.D.
K. Hall, B.A., D.A.A.	J.R. Studd, B.A., Ph.D., F.R.Hist.S.
S. Jackson, B.A., Ph.D.	A.T. Thacker, M.A., D.Phil., F.R.Hist.S.
Mrs J.I. Kermode, B.A.	T.J. Wyke, B.A.

CONTENTS

Acknowledgements	vii
Preface by George Holt	ix
Introduction	xiii
Richard Durning Holt's Diary	1
Appendix One: Biographical Notes	104
Appendix Two: R.D. Holt – Electoral Career	125
Appendix Three: Holt Durning Family – Simplified Family Tree	126
Index	127

ILLUSTRATIONS

(with acknowledgements to contributors)

Richard Durning Holt as a young man (*Liverpool Daily Post and Echo*)	*viii*
A modern photograph of 54 Ullet Road (*Mr George Sewell*)	*between pp.16&17*
A debate in the Commons in 1907, when R.D. Holt first took his seat as member for Hexham (*Walker Art Gallery, Liverpool*)	*between pp.16&17*
Punch's view of the 'Holt Cave', 15 July 1914 (*Punch*)	*p. 32*

For my Mother

ACKNOWLEDGEMENTS

Richard Holt's diary is held by Liverpool City Library to which body I am grateful for permission to reproduce material of which it owns the copyright. Mr George Holt has supported the publication of his uncle's diary throughout the project and I owe him a debt of thanks for his many kindnesses. I am particularly pleased that he has written a preface to this edition. Generous financial support to underwrite the costs of publication has been given by Ocean Transport and Trading plc (P.H. Holt Trust).

Among those who helped in the early stages of this book's preparation I should like to record my thanks to Dr H.B. Chrimes, Dr P.N. Davies, Professor P.E.H. Hair and Professor A. Harding. The staff of the Liverpool City Library, particularly Miss Janet Smith, greatly facilitated my tasks of transcription. Miss Lesley Gordon of the Library of the University of Newcastle-upon-Tyne helped me to uncover valuable references to Holt's career in the papers of Walter Runciman and Charles Trevelyan. I am most grateful that the Council of the Record Society of Lancashire and Cheshire accepted my edition of the diary for publication and I owe a particular debt to Dr Peter McNiven, the Society's General Editor. My friends and colleagues Dr Patrick Buckland and Mr Philip Bell have given me the benefit of their advice and learning, particularly in relation to the introductory essay. Mrs Peggy Rider typed the entire work with the expert efficiency which I have come to take for granted from her, while Dr Helen Jewell gave freely of her time to check the proofs.

Notwithstanding the genuine debt which he owes to all of the above, the editor accepts sole responsibility for the opinions expressed in the introduction and for all decisions of editorship.

D.J. DUTTON
Liverpool, March 1988

Richard Durning Holt as a young man.

PREFACE

I regard it as a privilege to have been asked by Dr David Dutton to write a preface to his edition of my Uncle Richard Holt's diaries, accompanied by his fascinating introduction to it.

I knew Uncle Dick, as we nephews and nieces called him, from my early childhood. My father, Philip, was the third of five sons of Robert Holt. Unlike his eldest brother Richard, but following the next one (also Robert), he went to work in what was then the senior family business, the cotton brokers, George Holt and Co., which had been founded by my great grandfather, George Holt, a younger son of Oliver, who owned a small dyeing works in Rochdale. Oliver had business connections with the Liverpool cotton merchant, Samuel Hope, whom he persuaded to take George on as an apprentice. Having arrived in Liverpool with a guinea in his pocket, George served his apprenticeship so well that he was made a partner when he came out of it. Eventually he gained control of the firm, which became George Holt and Co. It flourished considerably for nearly a hundred years, but finally perished in the great slump of the early 1930s.

When the First World War was imminent, the Hon. Ferdinand Stanley raised a battalion, the twentieth, for the King's Liverpool Regiment from the commercial community of the city, which became known as the 'Liverpool Pals', the directors and partners being officers and the clerks and office workers other ranks. My father was one of the officers, and they did some early training at Croxteth Park near Liverpool. Our own family home was then in the country south of Chester, whence my father commuted to Liverpool. My mother, no doubt wishing to be near her husband before he faced the ordeal of continental warfare, was kindly invited by Aunt Eliza, Uncle Dick's wife, with her two children, my sister and myself, plus our nurse. 'Fifty-four', as we always called it, had been built in the early 1870s by grandfather Robert, a large house with a fine garden. Though I was barely four at the time, I remember enjoying our stay and receiving much kindness from Uncle and Aunt. This was when I first got to know them.

After the War our family were regularly invited to stay with them at Abernethy, a beautiful tract of pine forest, moorland and mountain on the northern slopes of the Cairngorms. This was rented for sporting purposes – deer stalking, grouse, black game and ptarmigan shooting, and loch fishing. It had been taken by grandfather Robert in 1867 and, after an interlude around the turn of the century, was resumed by Uncle Dick. He was a keen shooting man, as was my father, and enjoyed the experience of deer-stalking.

My visits there always gave me great pleasure in a kind and friendly atmosphere with interesting guests, including eminent Liberals. My early activities were mainly trout fishing in the burns, guided by my uncle's butler,

x *Preface*

Stephen Butcher. Stephen also acted as his valet and shaved him every morning with a cut-throat razor. As children we delighted in the company of the serving staff including the Scottish ghillies and Pinnington, the chauffeur, who drove Uncle Dick's limousine Daimler painted Blue Funnel blue. (Uncle Dick never learnt to drive himself.) We were sometimes given lifts in it. My sister and I sat in front with Pinnington and were entertained by his stories and music-hall songs.

However, enough of childhood. I did continue my visits to Abernethy into manhood, and with help and encouragement from Uncle Dick joined in the stalking and shooting. I still have his splendid pair of single triggered guns, which I inherited on his death.

I got to know Uncle Dick best when, having graduated from Oxford in the early thirties, I was accepted into the Ocean Steam Ship Co., of which he was then chairman. Uncle Dick and Aunt Eliza invited me to lodge with them at 'Fifty-four', where I remained for about two years, before doing a spell with our agents in Holland, where some of our ships were based under the Dutch flag. Uncle Dick was then in his early sixties, fit and well. He had given up his political aspirations, though not his adherence to what remained of the old Liberal party and its beliefs. Though the firm was far from prosperous at the time, the early thirties slump having hit the shipping industry as hard as any, living conditions at 'Fifty-four' left nothing to be desired. The indoor staff of domestic servants including Stephen Butcher must have numbered about ten, with the chauffeur Pinnington and at least two gardeners outside. We always dressed for a dinner of at least three courses, accompanied by wine, the port decanter being circulated after it. Uncle Dick never smoked and disapproved strongly if anyone lighted up while the port was being drunk. I used to go to my parents in the country for the weekend and so was unavailable to attend at the Ullet Road Unitarian Church, to which Uncle Dick regularly went.

Guests from various sources came often to dine and stay. I remember on one occasion we had Sir Herbert Samuel and attended a Liberal meeting somewhere in the North end of Liverpool. Uncle Dick was asked to propose a vote of thanks to Sir Herbert in the course of which he gave vent to his old Liberal views. These roused considerable heckling from a Lloyd Georgeite in the audience. I feel fairly sure that if he were alive today, Uncle Dick would be giving full support to the present Conservative government and Prime Minister, whom he would regard as keeping much of the old Liberal doctrine alive and putting it to good use.

Uncle Dick saw to it that I was given good practical training in my job, though things were rather awkward when I started. Strict economy measures had to be taken, which included cuts in pay and redundancies. As the thirties proceeded things got gradually better. I joined the army when Hitler marched into Prague, but returned to work in the office when peace came. Uncle Dick retained the chairmanship until his death in 1941. I remained with the company until retiring as a senior director in my sixty-first year.

Richard Holt was a man of outstanding and determined character, tempered by a keen sense of humour and great kindliness, to whom I owe a large debt. I am therefore glad to have an opportunity of paying this tribute to him.

George Holt
Bala, 1988

INTRODUCTION

Richard Durning Holt was born in 1868 into one of Liverpool's richest and most respected mercantile families. The Holts were prominent Unitarians who had made a substantial philanthropic contribution to their city. Richard was the eldest of a family of eight, five boys and three girls. His father Robert was a cotton broker, leader of the Liberal party on the City Council and Liverpool's first Lord Mayor in 1892–3. His uncle Alfred was the founder of Alfred Holt and Company, managers of the Ocean Steam Ship Company, the world-famous Blue Funnel Line. His mother Lawrencina, usually known as Lallie, was the eldest sister of the Fabian Beatrice Webb (née Potter) and the latter's sometimes embarrassingly frank correspondence and diary, written from a very different political and intellectual perspective from the Holts', throw an interesting light on Dick's early years and the Holt family in general. This often acts as a corrective to and relief from the image which emerges from the Holts' own more discreet family writings.

Lallie was a devoted mother. In fact she lavished so much attention on her children as to incur the criticisms of her sisters including Beatrice Webb. All believed that the family was growing up without sufficient discipline. One commented in 1873 that though the Holt children were 'charmingly dispositioned', they were 'decidedly spoilt little monkeys.'[1] Matters improved when the children, including Dick, were of sufficient age to settle into a routine of lessons, with their mother as teacher. 'He is much better in spirit and temper,' noted Lallie, 'since he has some regular occupation.'[2] Robert, too, was an affectionate father. His own diary reveals his constant interest in and concern for his children's educational progress and general development.[3] Some years before he was old enough to attend, Dick's parents tried to put his name down for Winchester, but no vacancy was then available. Careful preparation for the scholarship examination, however, enabled the boy to win a place as a foundationer.[4] The parents evidently had high hopes for their eldest son. Family correspondence reveals an almost obsessional concern with the boy's progress at school. All Dick's letters home made reference to his position in class and his weekly achievements.[5] Beatrice Webb noted in November 1884: '[Lallie] is a proud mother and believes that Dick will someday be distinguished.'[6]

After Winchester the young Holt moved on to New College, Oxford. On completion of his education it was all but inevitable that he should enter the

1 B. Caine, *Destined to be Wives* (Oxford, 1986), p. 123.
2 Lallie to her mother 1871, cited Caine, pp. 123–24.
3 Caine, p. 137.
4 Ibid., p. 142.
5 Ibid., p. 143.
6 N. Mackenzie (ed.), *The Letters of Sidney and Beatrice Webb* (Cambridge, 1978), i. 29.

family firm, where his progress was rapid. His arrival at Alfred Holt and Company was timely. If the organisation was to continue to grow, changes in management would be required, and during the 1890s control of the firm's policy passed increasingly into the hands of younger men, especially Richard Holt. The latter's powers of leadership helped revive the company's flagging fortunes, inspiring the management with new ideas about the entrepreneurial function of the ship-owner.[7] In December 1892 Holt left Liverpool for an extended tour of the company's Far-Eastern stations. This experience transformed his views about the potentialities for trade in the Far East and the Pacific. He now envisaged the expansion of some of the subsidiary Singapore trades and the possibility of opening up a direct service to Australia.[8] He also began to press the desirability of providing greater depth of water at Birkenhead, by deepening the Albert sills, so that export trades would not be impeded.[9] At the company's Annual Meeting in December 1895 Holt was one of three new directors (known as 'managers') to be appointed, the others being his cousin, George Holt, and Maurice Llewelyn Davies.

In 1892 Sidney Webb had noted:

> Yes, Dick needs a little generous widening of sympathies. I wonder whether love will bring him this. Just at present he is a little too cynical and perhaps too prosperous.[10]

Five years later Holt married an American, Eliza Wells. Within a few years they had three daughters, Grace, Anne and Dorothy, but a much longed-for son was still-born in October 1904. After staying two weeks with her sister in the autumn of 1899, Beatrice Webb noted that 'Dick . . . under the influence of a charming American wife [has] developed into a shrewd, pleasant, public-spirited man.' Yet significantly this most critical of observers continued: 'He retains his parrot-like prejudices against all new ideas; in political intelligence he is still a child.'[11]

Notwithstanding Beatrice Webb's misgivings the new century saw Holt begin to follow his father into political life. Liverpool was not a very hopeful prospect for an aspiring young Liberal, for the local Conservative party, masterminded by Alderman Archibald Salvidge, had cultivated the working-class vote so successfully as to make the city one of the party's strongholds. By contrast Liverpool Liberalism was stagnating. Liverpool's electorate was by no means typical of the country as a whole. The large number of Irish immigrants made it perhaps the most Catholic city in England and the concept of Tory Democracy existed at least in part as a working-class and Protestant reaction against the Irish-Catholic-

7 F. Hyde, *Blue Funnel* (Liverpool, 1957), p. 170.
8 Ibid., pp. 92–93.
9 S. Mountfield, *Western Gateway* (Liverpool, 1965), p. 80.
10 Mackenzie, *Letters of Webbs*, i. 410.
11 Beatrice Webb diary 10 Oct. 1899.

Liberal alliance.[12] When the Liberal Chief Whip, Herbert Gladstone, inspected Liverpool in January 1900 he found that no Liberal candidate had been selected in any of the eight Liverpool constituencies held by the Conservatives. A few months earlier Gladstone had noted that the ageing Robert Holt was a fading force – 'very feeble and good natured' over the problem.[13] Not surprisingly Richard Holt's first attempt to gain a parliamentary seat did not meet with success. A by-election in 1903 in the West Derby division of the city, where his father was President of the local Liberal association, saw Holt contest the seat against William Rutherford.

Rutherford was very much in the Salvidge mould of Toryism, staunchly Protestant and with 'eccentrically democratic views.'[12] Backed also by the forces of freemasonry and the Orange Order, the Conservative candidate appeared to hold all of the cards as the campaign opened. By contrast Holt's appeal seemed to lack bite. In part this may have reflected the fact that he was by no means the party's first choice as candidate.[12] The traditional Liberal cry of 'Peace, Retrenchment and Reform' held little appeal. On imperial questions Holt showed a hesitancy which recalled the recent scars of the Boer War, from which a divided Liberal party had scarcely recovered. Over Ireland he was vague in a way that was unlikely to appeal to the constituency's sizeable number of Catholic voters. The result of the election was a considerable disappointment, not least to Holt's father who recorded:

> We all waited at the Reform Club until the result was known and went home sorrowfully: not so much that Dick had not won, but the majority was a 1000 more than we anticipated. We calculated there would be a Tory majority of 500 to 1000, but it's over and there is very little to be gained by speculating on causes and influences. It's pretty clear that the Liverpool working man is not Liberal.[16]

It was, thought Richard Holt, among the lowest class of electors, who 'must have voted five or even ten to one against us,' that he had been least successful. Rutherford had sought popularity through blatant 'hospitality' following on the years of careful nursing of the constituency by his Tory predecessor, Higginbottom, who had given weekend trips to the Isle of Man to all his supporters.[17]

Liverpool politics in these years moved along paths which bore little relation to concurrent developments at the national level and Holt was unable to benefit from the fissures within the Unionist ranks which followed Joseph Cham-

12 D. Dutton, 'Lancashire and the New Unionism: The Unionist Party and the Growth of Popular Politics, 1906–1914', *Transactions of the Historic Society of Lancashire and Cheshire*, CXXX (1981).
13 P. Clarke, *Lancashire and the New Liberalism* (Cambridge, 1971), p. 232.
14 Ibid., p. 48.
15 P. Waller, *Democracy and Sectarianism* (Liverpool, 1981), p. 197.
16 Robert Holt diary 20 Jan. 1903, Liverpool City Library, 920 DUR 1/8.
17 R.D. Holt to Herbert Gladstone 27 Jan. 1903, Gladstone Papers, British Library, Add MS 46060 fo. 109.

berlain's celebrated declaration on Tariff Reform in Birmingham in May 1903. As an unquestioning exponent of Free Trade – for him it was little less than holy writ – Holt debated the issue with Rutherford in the Sun Hall, West Derby, in April 1905 and acquitted himself well, at least in the judgement of his father.[18] Yet in the General Election of the following year Liverpool's Tory Democracy stood largely immune against the cold winds which devastated the party over most of the rest of the country. In a second contest with Rutherford, Holt laid stress upon the tasks of social reform which would confront the new Liberal government, but his call made little impression upon the electorate. With his wife taking an active role in the campaign, interviewing over a thousand voters, Holt improved on his 1903 performance by 349 votes, while Rutherford's total dropped by eight. But all this still left the sitting member with a majority of 1847 votes. Again, the losing candidate's father recorded the family's disappointment:

> Dick was fighting for Free Trade and Liberal Principles. Everyone appreciated the hard fight in which he was engaged against an opponent like Rutherford who had . . . nursed and treated the electors – wives and families – garden parties and when Ld. Mayor at the Town Hall. Dick and Eliza have worked hard in the constituency since he accepted the position of candidate. . . .[19]

It was becoming clear that Holt's political ambitions were likely to remain frustrated unless he looked outside his native city for a constituency. Little over a year after the Liberals' crushing victory in the 1906 General Election, the local party in Hexham, Northumberland, was 'in search of a rich man' to fight a by-election that was pending following the elevation of the sitting member to the peerage.[20] Holt received an unexpected approach from the local constituency party and was soon selected as Liberal candidate. Though the constituency was quite unlike the West Derby division, Holt responded well to the local party and its agent and he and his wife were soon involved in active campaigning.[21] Holt dealt easily enough with the charges of his opponent concerning the employment of Chinese sailors on the Ocean Steam Ship Company's steamers, a cry which echoed the recent national campaign over 'Chinese slavery' in South Africa, and he was elected to parliament in April 1907 with a majority of 1157 over his Tory adversary. Arriving at Westminster a little over a year after the Liberals' landslide victory in the General Election, Holt joined the mainstream of his party's affairs at what most contemporaries believed to be a high point of its history.

18 Robert Holt diary 17 April 1905, 920 DUR 1/8.
19 Ibid., 16 Jan. 1906, 920 DUR 1/9.
20 W. Runciman to C.P. Trevelyan 13 Feb. 1907, University of Newcastle-upon-Tyne, Trevelyan Papers 17.
21 Robert Holt diary 21 Feb. 1907, 920 DUR 1/9.

* * * * *

Richard Holt began to keep a diary in the year 1900. In this he was following a strong family tradition which included his father and grandfather. Holt meant his diary to provide 'a short historical record of the doings of my particular family.'[22] More than half of the entries in it relate to family, business and social matters and the great bulk of this material has not been included in the present edition. Only occasional entries of a non-political nature have been retained in the published diary in order to give the reader a flavour of the original and to illuminate aspects of Holt's character and attitudes. Moreover, despite his stated intentions, Holt was in fact most discreet in what he recorded about the private affairs of his family and he gives the reader little information about the bitter family feuds which clouded the early years of his married life. The balance of the original diary is, however, an important reminder that politics was never an all-consuming concern for Holt. Even when his political fortunes were at their lowest ebb, he could still find solace in his social and sporting activities:

> Luckily, bad as politics and business are, I see one bright spot – the coming grouse season should be well above the average.[23]

The original document also throws shafts of revealing light on the outlook of a wealthy, upper middle-class businessman at the beginning of the twentieth century. Some of it reads rather uncomfortably to a modern ear. In 1928 Holt recorded:

> We slept at Crawford – the decent looking Murray House proved a whited sepulchre – bad service and teetotal. Evidently meant for the lower middle class en pension.[24]

A quarter of a century earlier Beatrice Webb – with the Holt family in mind – had noted that 'observing the results of the luxurious upbringing of children does not make me less anxious to redistribute wealth.'[25]

Especially in the early years Holt was not a consistent or reliable diary keeper – a fact with which he repeatedly reproached himself.[26] Particularly after his entry to parliament in 1907 the pressure of work led to frequent lapses and it was perhaps only the more diligent example of his forbears which motivated Holt to persevere. As a result the diary provides but a disappointing record of the first years of the Liberal government and momentous events such as the constitutional crisis of 1909–11 are only cursorily mentioned. From around 1914, however, Holt seems to have developed a more consistent habit of diary keeping and the entries made during the First World War are of considerable interest.

22 Richard Holt diary 17 Feb. 1900.
23 R.D. Holt to F.W. Hirst 20 July 1930, Holt Papers 920 DUR 14/27/170.
24 Richard Holt diary 24 Oct. 1928.
25 Beatrice Webb diary 29 April 1903.
26 Richard Holt diary 27 July 1904, April 1906, 31 Aug. 1908, 14 April 1909, 20 May 1910.

xviii   *Introduction*

Holt never became a major force in Liberal politics. In more than eleven years in parliament he failed to achieve even junior ministerial office. His diary should not be expected to contain dramatic revelations of the doings of the great and famous. But on the second rung of the political ladder Holt occupied an important and representative niche in Liberal politics, particularly after the formation of the first coalition in May 1915 – an event which he bitterly resented.[27]

The diary confirms the dramatic suddenness with which the international crisis of July 1914 overtook even the politically well-informed. Holt belonged to that majority wing of the Liberal party which entered the war without enthusiasm, overwhelmed by the tragedy of the situation but convinced by the official explanations of British participation. But as the months went by and the casualty lists mounted, he became increasingly disillusioned with the British war effort. Beatrice Webb recorded in her diary:

> I gather that the foreign policy that Dick would have approved of was war with Germany, but from the first war limited to naval blockade and the complete supersession of Germany on the seas. The domestic policy would have been modernised laisser faire, leaving prices alone but maintaining a firm hand with labour.[28]

In particular Holt could not accept that the necessities of war legitimised political methods which ran counter to his basic philosophy. He would have agreed with W.L. Williams, M.P. for Carmarthen, who told the House of Commons in July 1915 that

> it would be tragedy worse than war if, in order to win the War, England ceased to be the beacon of freedom and liberty which she has been in the past.[29]

Holt failed to recognise that the War had destroyed for all time the Victorian society into which he had been born. He seemed to envisage the recreation of a post-war political and economic structure that had no place in twentieth-century Britain, failing to appreciate that the War had brought about irreversible changes in the way Britain could be governed. As the *Financial News* put it a decade later:

> [Holt] seems to hold that the golden age is not before us, but behind us and that it was at its most roseate between 1850 and 1890.[30]

The *Manchester Guardian* recorded a revealing speech which Holt delivered to the North-Western Counties branch of the Free Trade Union in May 1918:

> Our great danger in the future would come not from an enemy who, whatever happened, would have been terribly punished and weakened, but from

27 C. Hazlehurst, *Politicians at War* (London, 1971), p. 273.
28 Beatrice Webb diary, dated Aug. 1918 but inserted at 8 Dec. 1913.
29 House of Commons Debates, 5th Series, lxxiii, col. 122.
30 *Financial News* 22 April 1931: 'Men of Mark: Mr R.D. Holt'.

oppressive taxation at home and from Government control, which, like a bad drug habit, grew upon the people who indulged in it. We could only cut the danger by making the greatest possible use of the means of production, and we could only reach our maximum of industrial efficiency under the stimulus of free trade and open competition.[31]

Not surprisingly the War saw Holt develop a deeply felt detestation of Lloyd George for what he held to be the latter's prostitution of the Liberal gospel. The hero of pre-war radicals – Robert Holt wrote in 1907 that the Welshman was 'much in the affection and high regard of everyone'[32] – became now a satanic figure for whom no amount of contempt was adequate. Once idolised, Lloyd George had become a threat to the civilised world. *Faute de mieux* Holt became an Asquithian but his conversion was never wholehearted. Acting with the same olympian detachment which had characterised his pre-war leadership, Asquith failed, after the change of government in December 1916, to inspire those Liberals who were looking for a forthright defence of their party's principles against the attacks of Lloyd George and his Tory allies. Asquith's position was a difficult one. In part he was paralysed by his own patriotism, 'unwilling to strike when the war was going badly and unable when it was going well.'[33] Additionally Asquith realised that he would not be able to form a war government even if Lloyd George were defeated in parliament. Thus Asquith failed to give a lead to his followers, including Holt, on such issues as Indian Cotton Duties, Irish conscription and the ban placed on overseas editions of *The Nation*. Holt made a personal appeal to Asquith in April 1918:

> May I – with great respect – urge that any such opposition should receive your open support or better still be led by you[34]

but this went largely unheeded by the former Prime Minister. Research has shown that there was a recognisable Liberal opposition in parliament to Lloyd George's coalition government and that Holt was part of it. But the protests of dissident Liberals have been largely concealed by the timidity of the front bench.[35]

Holt's line on the War, including his opposition to conscription, his support for the Lansdowne Letter of November 1917 and his rejection of the idea of the 'knock-out blow', alienated him from his constituency party in Hexham. From the summer of 1916 he had begun to think seriously about the possibility of a negotiated peace. An acrimonious exchange of letters with the local party chairman helped him to the decision that he could not contest the constituency when the return of peace in November 1918 permitted the resumption of

---

31 *Manchester Guardian* 4 May 1918.
32 Robert Holt diary 1 Dec. 1907, 920 DUR 1/9.
33 P. Clarke, *Liberals and Social Democrats* (Cambridge, 1978), p. 198.
34 Holt to Asquith 5 April 1918, Holt Papers 920 DUR 14/27/14.
35 B. McGill, 'Asquith's Predicament 1914–18', *Journal of Modern History* 39 (1967); E. David, 'The Liberal Party Divided 1916–18', *Historical Journal* 13 (1970).

domestic party politics.[36] Chosen instead as Liberal candidate in Eccles, but understandably without the 'coupon' of endorsement from Lloyd George and Bonar Law, Holt had no answer to the tide of nationalism which characterised the first weeks of peace, including the election campaign. His equivocal attitude towards the War and his less than enthusiastic espousal of a peace that would 'squeeze the German lemon till the pips squeaked' left him out of tune with the overwhelming mood of the British electorate. Holt argued that the government was composed of 'untrustworthy people', whose appeal to the country was 'a dirty trick', but his message won few converts.[37] Though he could not have realised it at the time, Holt's parliamentary career was at an end.

The 1920s saw Holt make several attempts to recover a seat at Westminster and he was unlucky not to succeed in more than one of these. He also took steps to reconstruct his business career. With Asquith's star clearly waning and with no one of appropriate stature emerging to replace him, it was inevitable that sooner or later the party would fall under the control of Lloyd George. This was a development which Holt bitterly resisted. His undying animosity towards Lloyd George emerges from almost every page of the diary. Throughout the twenties Holt fought his corner within the Liberal ranks. 'It is much too serious', he noted 'to find a lot of rascals in charge of everything for honest men to stand down no matter how hopeless a chance they seem to have.'[38] But Holt was swimming against the tide. Liberalism needed Lloyd George if for no other reason than his money. The Lloyd George political fund was an essential prerequisite of an effective Liberal electoral campaign and most erstwhile critics were prepared to trim when Lloyd George's financial carrot was dangled before them. Holt's position was honourable but unrealistic. 'We ought not to touch the money – it is the price of dishonour and will bring a curse to whoever handles it.'[39] The Welshman's patronage of the party's summer schools helped to restore his credentials with many Liberals (if not with Holt), even before he became party leader in 1926.

By 1929 Holt's political career appeared to have reached a complete impasse. Likewise Liberalism as a political force seemed doomed unless Proportional Representation – for which Holt had worked since before 1914[40] – could be secured. What remained of the parliamentary party seemed firmly in hands which Holt deemed to be unworthy. In the aftermath of his last electoral defeat he wrote:

> Everything possible was done in Cumberland but I am afraid we just can't carry the seat in a three cornered contest . . . It will be a very anxious time for you [Walter Runciman], especially with Ll.G. who can't be trusted. I don't

36 Holt to H. Lees 7 Jan. 1918 and H. Lees to Holt 16 Jan. 1918, Holt Papers 920 DUR 14/27/218–219A.
37 Holt to W. Runciman 1 Dec. 1918, University of Newcastle-upon-Tyne, Runciman Papers 169.
38 Ibid., 17 Dec. 1918.
39 Ibid., 23 Nov. 1928, Runciman Papers 204.
40 M. Pugh, *Electoral Reform in War and Peace 1906–18* (London, 1978), p. 12.

think any party can carry him and yet he has fanatical admirers who are first class Liberals.[41]

After 1929 Holt concentrated on his business career, watching the political scene from the sidelines with an interested but increasingly remote eye. He was by any criteria a wealthy man, although his writings suggest that times were less comfortable after the War than they had been before. He had for some years been senior partner in the Blue Funnel Line and in 1927 he became chairman of the Mersey Docks and Harbour Board in succession to the long-serving Thomas Rome. At the end of 1929 Holt decided to undertake a world tour in the interests of Alfred Holt and Company and this led to his temporary retirement from the Dock Board chair, though he retained his membership of it. In 1935 Holt was made a baronet for his public services, an honour which Beatrice Webb had predicted for him as early as 1913.[42] His father – perhaps a stauncher radical – had been one of very few men who have actually been gazetted as a baronet against their will. (The elder Holt's witty letter of refusal had been misinterpreted by Lord Rosebery as an acceptance.)[43] In his last years Holt extended his business interests, becoming chairman of the Elder Dempster Shipping Lines and also chairman of Martins Bank.

The years of the second Labour government (1929–31) saw increasing disarray within the Liberal ranks, a process of disintegration which culminated in the breakaway of the Liberal National wing under Sir John Simon in June 1931. These developments filled Holt with despair. When a by-election became due in the East Toxteth division of Liverpool in 1931 he wrote:

> In my opinion it is a mere waste of money to fight elections as a Liberal unless the candidate is in a position to stand as a virtual independent on the strength of his personal position in the constituency. The Liberals in Parliament must stand for a coherent policy and be in general agreement on important questions before we can make any effective fight in the constituencies.[44]

Had Holt wished to make another attempt to return to Westminster, offers from local constituency parties were not lacking. Approached by Penryn and Falmouth in July 1931, he pleaded that his commitments in business and public works prevented him giving the necessary time to fight the campaign properly and to do justice to the Liberals of the area.[45] Even when it became clear that the next General Election would be fought largely on the issue of Protection, Holt, whatever his feelings about the sanctity of Free Trade, declined to stand for North Cumberland, partly on the grounds of the expense involved and partly because he was convinced he could not win.[46]

41 Holt to W. Runciman 4 June 1929, Runciman Papers 224.
42 Beatrice Webb diary 8 Dec. 1913.
43 B. Webb, *My Apprenticeship* (London, 1926), p. 218.
44 Holt to R. Muir 19 Jan. 1931, Holt Papers 920 DUR 14/27/264.
45 Holt to Col. T. Tweed 5 July 1931, 920 DUR 14/27/359.
46 C. Roberts to Holt 23 Aug. 1931, 920 DUR 14/27/314.

xxii *Introduction*

The election of a National Government with an enormous parliamentary majority caused Holt no rejoicing, but thereafter his political interventions became increasingly rare. In the famous Wavertree by-election of 1935 he merely confused Liberal voters with his assertion that the government had embarked on a 'policy of extravagance, protection and thinly-disguised Socialism.'[47] To the end of his life he still remained faithful to those principles of reduced government spending and low taxation which seemed now more appropriate to the days of Gladstonian finance than the middle of the twentieth century. In 1936 he accepted the presidency of the Free Trade Union; meanwhile the world at large increasingly saw its salvation in tariffs and Protection. As the British economy struggled to emerge from the Depression he confidently wrote:

> What would do this country good would be a 30% fall in prices including wages and 50% in taxes.[48]

Saddened by the sight of his beloved port of Liverpool ravaged by Nazi air power, Holt died at the age of seventy-two on 22 March 1941.

* * * * *

Few if any problems of modern British political history have occasioned such a scholarly output as the eclipse of the Liberal party as a party of government in the twentieth century. Since George Dangerfield fashioned his brilliant, if fatally flawed, gem, *The Strange Death of Liberal England* in 1936, historians have tumbled over one another in an historical debate which has become particularly acute over the last two decades and in which genuine consensus still seems a long way off. The Liberal party's demise has been variously ascribed, with historians drawing attention to the mutilation of its principles and philosophy, particularly during the First World War, to a successful outflanking movement on the part of the nascent Labour party, to the suicidal feuds between the rival followers of Asquith and Lloyd George and to subtly differing combinations of these factors.

With such a range of interpretations on offer the chronological focus of historical attention has ranged with corresponding freedom. There are those for whom the fatal mistakes of Liberalism were made during Gladstone's declining years when a blinkered leadership succeeded in diverting the party from the 'natural' paths of social reforming radicalism charted by Joseph Chamberlain and others. In such an interpretation the 'New Liberalism' of the 1890s Progressives never threatened to capture the party at large and the stunning electoral triumph of 1906 is but a misleading aberration in an otherwise fateful decline. Others have asserted that the Liberal party which entered the First World War was an essentially healthy organism and that in the years immedi-

---

47 P. Waller, *Democracy and Sectarianism*, p. 337.
48 Holt to W. Runciman 28 July 1938, Runciman Papers 292.

ately before 1914 the party was not, *pace* Mr Dangerfield, 'dying strangely,' but launching a successful counter-attack on the Labour movement. In this scenario the years of war and, in particular, the events of 1915 and 1916 take on critical significance. Then again, recent historiography has seen renewed interest in the history of Liberalism after 1918, a development which contains the implied suggestion that not until the 1920s did the party's electoral chances become fatally compromised.

Much of the range of this debate is explained by the failure to define precisely what it is whose decline is being analysed and explored. A political party is a multi-dimensional entity. If it is Liberalism as a political philosophy which is under scrutiny, then there is something to be said for focusing on the problems of an individualistic and non-interventionist intellectual framework confronting the requirements of a state whose government by the turn of the century, and particularly after 1914, self-evidently demanded an increasingly collectivist approach. Yet Liberalism was always a broad church and some Liberals clearly did adapt their thinking to suit changing circumstances. Indeed, it is a striking feature of inter-war history that the Liberal party still managed to attract impressive intellectual support for its policies long after there was any realistic possibility of the return of a Liberal government. 'If the Liberals met their death during the war,' writes Dr Bentley, 'they did not do so at the hands of their thinkers.'[49]

If it is the high politics of the Liberal party – Liberalism at Westminster – which holds the key, then historians must inevitably turn their gaze to the war years and the Asquith-Lloyd George split of December 1916. This breach – as Holt's diary clearly shows – was never healed despite an uncomfortable reunion for a few weeks in 1923 to fight the General Election of that year as a 'united' party. Alternatively, if attention is drawn to the party in the country, British Liberalism may be viewed as the largely innocent victim of an electoral and political structure to which it was fundamentally unsuited. Even at a time when the Liberals considered themselves the natural party of government, their support was dangerously concentrated in the 'Celtic Fringe.' Few English constituencies consistently returned Liberal M.P.s at all eight General Elections between 1885 and 1910.[50] After Labour had come on to the scene, though before 1918 its challenge was theoretical rather than actual, Liberalism slowly became the loser in a political game designed for no more than two participants. After the Great War Liberal support was simply too thinly spread for the party ever to secure a national majority. In large numbers of constituencies it could poll relatively well. But in only a few could it confidently expect success.[51] These realities hit home in the General Election of 1922. By 1929 the position had come to appear hopeless. The Liberals secured support from 23% of the

---

49 M. Bentley, *The Climax of Liberal Politics* (London, 1987), p. 123.
50 Ibid., pp. 30–31.
51 P. Clarke, *Liberals and Social Democrats*, p. 235.

electorate, but won only 59 seats. In the twenties Liberalism thus lost credibility in the electorate's eyes as a possible governing party.

Whichever focus is chosen, Holt's diary and the years which it covers (1900–1929) offer a convenient framework of study. Though historians would disagree passionately about the precise meaning of these years in the history of the Liberal party, all would concur that they are central to Liberalism's fate. 1900 saw the formal establishment of the Labour Representation Committee, the body which, transformed into the Labour party, was to replace Liberalism as the principal left of centre alternative to Conservatism in twentieth-century British politics. 1929 was the last occasion on which Liberals themselves believed that they had a realistic prospect of at least being able to influence the formation of the government. The party faced the General Election of that year in better spirit than at any time since the War. Its Election Manifesto had a more impressive intellectual content than that offered by Labour and the Conservatives combined. The anti-climax of the result – in seats if not in votes – forced those, including Holt, who remained within the Liberal party to consider whether the future held out any effective political future for them.

Thematically as well as chronologically Holt's diary charts the party's problems. In the realm of political philosophy Holt, though not a particularly cerebral politician, represented that strand of pure and unadulterated nineteenth-century Liberalism – the free trade, non-interventionist ethos of Cobden and Bright – which came to an intellectual impasse when confronted by the realities of the twentieth-century state. The 1920s saw Holt bewildered and disheartened, encumbered by pre-war doctrines which seemed to have little relevance to post-war problems. Quite simply there was nowhere for him to progress. As Holt himself put it in 1926:

> difficult and even hopeless as the position is, there is no place for some of us except in a Liberal party. The Tories and the Labour are equally impossible.[52]

The diary also provides insights into the Lloyd George-Asquith split, emphasising that this represented not merely a clash of personalities but a fundamental divergence between two versions of British Liberalism, two distinct habits of mind and outlook which could never be properly reconciled. Again, Holt's failure to secure re-election to parliament after 1918, despite frequent respectable performances at the polls, epitomised the experience of countless Liberal candidates in this decade, struggling to free themselves from the electoral *cul-de-sac* of third party status.

* * * * *

Throughout its history the Liberal party represented a broad coalition of interests and Holt's position within this spectrum is not easy to define. The

---

52 Richard Holt diary 24 Oct. 1926.

parliamentary party contained almost as many shades of philosophical stance as it did members. As one writer put it in the 1920s:

> The public still asserts that if Asquith, Lloyd George and John Simon are all Liberals, there must be three Liberalisms, not one Liberalism. And the public are right. Liberalism, like the Church of England, covers a multitude of beliefs. As long as you profess Gladstone in one and God in the other, you can remain within the fold.[53]

The complexities of the situation render such simplistic divisions of Liberalism as 'left' and 'right' almost meaningless.[54] Holt may have thought of himself as 'of the left', but many of his ideas now appear little short of reactionary. His views on unemployment are illustrative:

> Nobody suggested that the unemployed should be allowed to starve, but he suggested that if they got enough money to keep alive they should do something for it. Why should not the unemployed be required to reinstate the Sunday morning delivery of letters?[55]

Holt's socio-economic vision, often revealed with great clarity in his diary entries, had virtually disappeared by the coming of the Second World War. Swamped by the Keynesian consensus, aspects of it have only recently resurfaced in the thinking of the New Right of the 1970s and 80s.

To describe Holt as an 'advanced Radical' misleads as much as it enlightens.[56] It is true that Holt's political companions tended to be located on the radical wing of the Liberal party and Holt had done much to establish the authenticity of his radical credentials by his attitude during the Boer War – 'the test issue for this generation.'[57] But radicalism at this time implied a readiness to use the power and authority of the state as a vehicle for social improvement, a 'socialistic' tendency which was anathema to Holt's most basic beliefs. As Beatrice Webb noted Holt 'would be a good party Liberal . . . if the Liberal party were more economical in armaments and less given to taxation of the rich man on behalf of the poor.'[58] Holt himself defined his attitude towards the economy in an article in the *Daily Telegraph* in November 1918:

> The habit of looking to the State for help instead of trusting to its own hard

---

53 Hesketh Pearson writing in *John Bull* 7 Feb. 1925.
54 The pre-war Liberal Imperialist, Asquith, found himself, especially after December 1916, the nominal champion of those who sought to uphold traditional Liberal doctrines. Lloyd George, on the 'radical left' before 1914, emerged by 1916 as the ally of right-wing Tories. On a lower plane Josiah Wedgwood opposed British entry into the War in August 1914, fought in Flanders and Gallipoli, becoming a convert to conscription in the process, emerged as one of the earliest advocates of a Lloyd George premiership, yet ended his days in the Labour party.
55 *Birkenhead Advertiser* 11 Feb. 1931, reporting speech by Holt at a meeting of the Birkenhead Chamber of Commerce.
56 B. McGill, 'Asquith's Predicament 1914–18', p. 290.
57 L.T. Hobhouse in *Nation* 30 March 1907.
58 Beatrice Webb diary 8 Dec. 1913.

xxvi *Introduction*

work and ability saps the vitality of any industry and produces inefficiency. Exposure to competition is the best security that an industry will be thoroughly efficient.[59]

Indeed, in the years before the First World War, Holt achieved his greatest claim to fame as the organiser of the 'Cave' which opposed Lloyd George's last peace-time budget on the grounds that the Treasury should aim to scrutinise and limit spending rather than raise taxes simply to enable the government to spend at will. *Punch* displayed Holt and his followers as the backwoodsmen of the Liberal party, intent to preserve the vested interests and privileges of plutocrats against the reforming zeal of the Chancellor of the Exchequer.[60] As Holt himself put it, the Cave represented

> a combined remonstrance by businessmen and some survivors of the Cobden-Bright school of thought against the ill-considered and socialistic tendencies of the Government finance.[61]

It is also revealing that many of Holt's wartime associates within the Union of Democratic Control and allied organisations – men such as Hobson and Morel – drifted steadily away from the Liberal party and towards Labour. After the War several formally transferred their allegiance, whereas it never occurred to Holt that he could serve out his political days as other than a Liberal. That leftward hurdle was one which his intellectual make-up could not surmount. He was after all the same man who had written critically of Sidney and Beatrice Webb and their 'great idea of spending money so as to please the working classes. Not to my idea a very high minded type of political opinion. . . .'[62]

* * * * *

Holt's diary was neatly and compactly hand-written in two hard-backed exercise books. His habit varied between weekly or more frequent entries and longer, retrospective pieces covering several weeks or even months. In the latter case the individual entry dates given by Holt in the original can be misleading. Holt's use of punctuation was idiosyncratic and inconsistent. His tendency was to employ a dash where either a comma or full-stop would be more appropriate. I could see no advantage in preserving the punctuation of the original and have reverted to more normal usage. Otherwise the diary is reproduced as it was written, save for the exclusion of the majority of the non-political entries. Additional editorial material is indicated by the presence of square brackets.

---

59 *Daily Telegraph* 6 Nov. 1928.
60 *Punch* 15 July 1914.
61 Richard Holt diary 19 July 1914.
62 Ibid., 12 March 1903.

THE DIARY OF RICHARD DURNING HOLT

1900

[When Holt began his diary the self-confidence of Victorian England was being severely shaken by the experiences of the Boer War. Outwitted and outmanoeuvred by the enemy, British forces under Sir Redvers Buller had ended 1899 humiliated and in retreat. The Unionist government of Lord Salisbury was obliged to send out Lord Roberts, the leading soldier of the Empire, to wage a full-scale military campaign. In 1900 the war took a dramatic turn for the better. One by one the besieged towns were relieved and by the end of the year Roberts was able to return in triumph, leaving Kitchener to finish off the war.

For the Liberal party, however, the war was little short of a disaster. Still torn by the dissensions which characterised the post-Gladstonian party, Liberals were bitterly divided in their attitudes to the war. Liberal Imperialists led by Rosebery, Grey and Asquith gave the government whole-hearted support. At the other extreme were men such as Harcourt, Morley and Lloyd George whose opposition to the British line rapidly earned them the label 'pro-Boer'. Somewhere in between these two factions lay a majority central grouping under Campbell-Bannerman who, while detesting the war, believed that the government had had little alternative but to begin military operations.

In such circumstances the Unionist cabinet decided in September to go to the country. The 'Khaki Election' offered the government every advantage to play the card of patriotism against a disunited opposition. In the circumstances the Liberals did surprisingly well and the balance of forces in the House of Commons remained essentially unchanged.

If the South African crisis were not enough, 1900 saw also a potentially dangerous situation emerge in China. The anti-foreigner Boxer Rebellion threatened the complicated web of commercial relations by which the European powers sought to control the trade of China. For Holt this was a particularly pressing issue in view of the interests of the Ocean Steam Ship Company.]

[February 17] I have decided to keep a diary or short historical record of the doings of my particular family.

I intended to begin this book on January 1st but being neglectful the book was not purchased till February and I make this first entry on 17th February.

Our domestic circumstances are as follows. We live at 11 Devonshire Road, Princes Park, Liverpool, with a household consisting of, in addition to our two selves, our daughters Grace, aged nearly two years, and Anne, just over three months, two nurses, four maid servants and a gardener who comes twice a week.

February 27 General Cronje and 4000 Boers surrendered to Lord Roberts at Paardeberg.

March 1 Sir R[edvers] Buller relieves Ladysmith. The town [Liverpool] was wild with joy: flags, assemblies, processions, cheering, almost cessation of business – to my mind very un-English. The defence of Sir G. White has been most gallant and the privations of besieged severe. The resistance made to Buller by the Boers most able and determined and our soldiers magnificently brave.

Voted for elective auditors and of course gave my vote to the Liberal nominee Edward Mounsey, who was returned by a majority of fifty over the Socialist, the Tory being 60 above Mr. Mounsey.

The whole poll only came to 1000 votes out of 100,000 and is a disgraceful farce.

March 18 Attended morning service at the Cathedral – this to please Eliza. It lasted two hours and was dull. The sermon . . . was commonplace and I thought rather vulgar.

March 27 . . . In the afternoon attended the meeting [of the National Liberal Federation] at which the principal event was a very fine speech by Dr. Spence Watson. The war, of course, was uppermost in the thoughts of all, the delegates being I think fairly equally divided as to its merits, though because the best speakers were against the justice of our conduct those of us who condemn the war appeared to be in a large majority.

March 28 . . . In the evening a big public meeting at which Sir Edward Grey was the speaker, taking the place of Sir Henry Campbell-Bannerman, prevented at the last moment by illness. A capital speech in every way, though Sir E. Grey seemed to speak too tenderly of Rhodes and of course he firmly asserted his conviction that we are justly at war.

April 15 . . . In the afternoon took a walk through Minchinhampton and Avening with Sidney Webb. Much interested and largely converted to a scheme for improving the labouring classes by a minimum wage.

May 18 About 9 pm arrived news of the Relief of Mafeking after a siege of about 213 days. Great blowing of horns and sirens and I understand a huge crowd in town.

May 19 Further great demonstration, coupled with a good deal of intoxication.

June 20 . . . Perhaps it is not unsuitable to make some reference to the general state of affairs in this country. We are enjoying great industrial prosperity and have done for 2 or 3 years past. Wages and prices are both high, except in the common articles of daily life. Coals 20/- a ton where 12/- or 13/- was the price a year ago.

We are still at war in South Africa and appear to make small progress in the capture or destruction of the Boer military forces tho' the principal places in their territory are in our occupation. . . .

There is now an anti-foreign outbreak in China of a serious character and the legations and other Europeans in Pekin are besieged and possibly even massacred.

A large force of marines etc. from the European fleets commanded by the British Vice-Admiral, Sir E.H. Seymour, has gone to their assistance but all telegraph wires in that part of China are cut and whether these troops have reached Pekin, or have retired to Tientsin, or are isolated mid-way is unknown at present. . . .

Altogether the state of foreign affairs is not very pleasant, the more so as considerable jealousy exists amongst the powers with regard to their interests in China and there is always a fear that they may fly at one another instead of working for the common end.

August 21 . . . China trade is naturally rather disturbed but now that the Ambassadors have been rescued things are improving a little. Pekin has been occupied by the allies – but what will happen next no one knows.

Affairs in South Africa don't seem to progress much and I am afraid the ultimate settlement is a long way off.

October 4 . . . This day was the polling in Liverpool for the General Election: the Liberals only contested the Kirkdale and Exchange Divisions, in both of which we were badly beaten, by 2500 and 1200 respectively . . . The principal cause of our defeat here as in most large towns was the Irish Catholic vote which was either cast against us or abstained in the hopes of getting an Irish Catholic University from the Tories. Generally speaking the election resulted in an 'as you were': the Liberals losing 3 seats net. Ground was lost in Scotland partly thro' the Irish in Glasgow and partly through the war, very many Scotch families having members engaged in it. This General Election will be for ever remembered owing to the baseness and blackguardliness of the Tories who did not hesitate to represent their opponents as traitors, even attacking one candidate (Mr. Rose in Cambridgeshire) who had lost two sons in the War on this score.

The only success in which we were intimately interested was that of Richard Rigg jr. in North Westmorland which he carried by 579 – the first Liberal returned for the county since 1832.

November 1 . . . My uncle Leonard Courtney retired from Parliament. My time mainly occupied with the municipal elections which terminated in the Liberals winning four seats and losing two. These elections broadly speaking were very satisfactory, the Liberals winning wherever they put forward a really good candidate and only losing seats in Sandhills and Gt. George where the candidates were very inferior.

November 15 The polling for School Board took place, remarkable for the success of Mr. George Wise, the Protestant lecturer who headed the poll with more than double the number of votes given to Florence Melly, the next on the list . . . Mr. Wise's success was not very creditable to the electorate as he had no qualifications for the work and a large part of his supporters were merely the public house Tories who have a domestic feud with the more respectable section of their party and use professions of extreme Protestantism as a cloak.

December 2 Politically we are all much agitated about the war which drags on without in any way seeming to draw to an end and there are new elements creeping into British military methods which are very distasteful to many: burning of farm houses and turning out women and children. Lord Roberts returns home now and transfers the command to Lord Kitchener.

1901

[British military victories at the end of 1900 merely intensified Liberal hostility. With the government insisting on unconditional surrender by the republics, the Boer soldiers turned to guerilla warfare and the British army retaliated by burning Boer farms. Women and children were crowded into hurriedly constructed and insanitary concentration camps in which death rates were intolerably high. Campbell-Bannerman now launched a campaign against the conduct of the war and in June 1901 denounced the conditions in the camps as 'methods of barbarism'. A vote by the general committee of the National Liberal Federation in early December – attended by Holt – confirmed Campbell-Bannerman's position. When Rosebery made his first political speech for five years at Chesterfield on 16 December, he appeared to accept Campbell-Bannerman's position on the war by demanding a negotiated settlement. But he also called upon the Liberal party to 'wipe its slate clean' and adopt fresh domestic policies. Like most Liberals, however, Holt seized only upon Rosebery's pronouncements on the war as a basis for reuniting the party.]

January 20 Went to church where Dr. K[lein] preached an excellent sermon on the necessity for making Christian principles a rule for practical conduct in life. He also in the prayers referred to the Queen who is very ill.

January 22 The Queen died this afternoon after a reign of nearly 64 years. The nation much affected for the Queen had undoubtedly been an ideal constitutional sovereign and she has greatly endeared herself to the multitude by her excellent private life.

January 25 Went to the Town Hall at 12 noon to hear the new King proclaimed, calling himself Edward VII, a distinctly English name. The proclamation was read on the balcony by the Lord Mayor (Mr. Crosthwaite) to an enormous crowd on the flags. Many were also on the galleries and even on the roof of Brown's Buildings . . . Everybody in mourning, but private dinner engagements not cancelled.

January 27 Church decorated with purple and black mourning: looked dismal, especially as almost everyone was in black. Dr Klein preached very well, taking his text from Ecclesiastes, Chap. 2 v 9. 'So I was great and increased more than all that were before me in Jerusalem: also my wisdom remained with me'.

February 4 Read the accounts of the Queen's funeral: evidently a most impressive ceremony. Indeed the only contretemps – the jibbing of the artillery horses at Windsor – seemed almost appropriate as the blue jackets had to take their place with the traces.

March 18 Dined at Reform Club. New Century Society . . . discussion opened by Herbert Rathbone with a paper on municipal politics. Most members of the society want a programme but to my mind the real need is a body of honest administrators who are under no tie to any trade or interest. The Salvidge party are playing a very astute Tammany game – liberal measures in everything that does not affect the pockets of the public house. Councillor Burke gave an instance or two of cases where this section of the Tory party offered to carry motions set down by Liberals if they were allowed to move them and get the kudos. Otherwise they would throw them out.

July 1 Mr. Albert Crompton retired from business leaving us younger men, Maurice Davies, George and self as virtually managers of Ocean S[team] S[hip] Co. . . . Mr Crompton has always been a very kind and agreeable friend to me in business and I can only regret that his peculiar views (Positivist) on religion have prevented him from extending that friendship to social life.

September 21 The war in S. Africa continues to drag on its weary length without any immediate hopes of cessation. Every day we hear of a few Boers killed or captured and there is a steady loss of British troops. It is hard to see what satisfactory end can be hoped for.

Recently the most startling event has been the murder of President McKinley by an anarchist named Czolgosz – a senseless crime with no real object.

The President was a man of good private character and some public dignity but will not I think figure in history as a great man.

October 14 It is very disgusting to find no candidates for municipal elections and to witness the general apathy as to political affairs which are undoubtedly serious. Martial law has been proclaimed throughout Cape Colony which virtually means that all law is suspended and it is certainly a hideous irony that England who went to war ostensibly (and with a vast number of people really) to obtain equal rights for all white men south of the Zambesi should now be taking away old established rights from her own Colonists.

The execution of many rebels seems to me a grave blunder as each death must leave scars behind which will not readily heal and after all if Great Britain is to keep S. Africa in her empire it can only be done in the long run by satisfying the majority. Surely the most generous course is the only true statesmanship.

November 30 Went to see a League match (Association football). Liverpool v. Aston Villa at Anfield. A most extraordinary sight – galleries for spectators all round the ground and these quite crowded. On the whole not a good development of modern city life, reminding one of a Roman circus, but free from brutality.

December 4 Attended meeting of general committee of National Liberal Federation at Derby. Rather a rowdy and ill behaved but very unanimous meeting. Passed a resolution in favour of an effort at peace to be obtained through a Special Commissioner.

December 19 . . . Dined at annual meeting of New Century Society . . . held at the Exchange Hotel, mainly on account of the bitter feelings of the Liberal Unionists in the Reform Club.

Subject of the moment is of course Lord Rosebery's speech at Chesterfield which while it condemns all men and all parties has the merit of declaring definitely for a settlement by consent in S. Africa. The war drags on its weary length but tho' we seem to be gradually crushing down armed resistance there are as yet no signs of a return to civil life and government. I own the ultimate prospects of a happy settlement of the political difficulties seem to me most remote and unfavourable.

December 30 . . . Dined in town and stayed to monthly meeting of Federal Council: a very good and unanimous meeting. It seems as though people were at last getting alive to the dangerous state of our affairs and there is a more real and earnest wish for peace than at any previous time, to which I think Lord Rosebery's speech has much contributed.

December 31 . . . in public affairs a year of little note and mean ideas but I believe this period of retrogression is only a temporary backset.

Probably the sacerdotal ideas of religion fostered by the Oxford movement have culminated, and are the cause of the apathy and littleness of present day politics. I trust and believe that the future will show an increase in and a strengthening of our own views of simple Christianity which I believe to be the true basis on which to establish the community.

I know I have expressed my meaning badly: I don't want any established church – Unitarian or otherwise. What I mean is that in the main it is the belief that what God wants of man is that he do right, i.e. love his neighbour, and not that he profess particular theological opinions or requires a consecrated place or an ordained priest, which will bring with it a great improvement in our social and political conditions.

1902

[The end of the South African war in May allowed some semblance of unity to return to the Liberal party. Equally important in this respect was the introduction of Balfour's Education Bill, which heralded the end of the local school boards, set up under the Education Act of 1870 and much cherished by non-conformists. Instead the bill proposed to establish a system of state schools, administered by local authorities, and the extension of rate aid to the voluntary schools, which were largely Anglican establishments. The Unitarian Holt reacted with predictable hostility.

At a personal level 1902 was not a happy year for Holt. An apparently trivial incident in the summer led to a serious family rift which was never fully repaired. Holt's diary makes only a brief and oblique reference to the episode and his father's diary is equally discreet. But it is possible to piece together what happened. A dispute over a family dog ended with Holt's youngest brother Lawrence attacking and severely injuring his sister Molly. The various members of the family took sides in the quarrel. Relations between Holt's parents were permanently strained and an extraordinary agreement was reached whereby Molly and her sister Betty left Liverpool to settle not less than twenty-five miles away. Holt acquiesced reluctantly in this arrangement: 'Though I don't in the least believe the policy of living away from home permanently is either right or desirable for the girls, I can only hope that if they adopt it, it will turn out all they hope.']

January 8 . . . Then went on to Hope Hall to attend the annual meeting of the South Africa Conciliation League. . . . Threats of and incitements to violence caused fears of a riot but the police were in very great force and taking most admirable precautions enabled the meeting to be held in perfect order. One mob made a faint hearted attack from Brownlow Hill but were dispersed without batons.

January 16 . . . Most of my time is occupied – very happily – in 'the daily round, the common task' – a life which does not lend itself much to diaries but is exceedingly pleasant to live.

February 5 Annual meeting of Ocean S[team] S[hip] Co[mpany]. Nothing of moment. The year has been fair rather than brilliant and the managers get nothing above the minimum of £5000 for their work. My share of this is about £1320.

February 14 Lord Rosebery's visit – first to a demonstration in the Philharmonic Hall and then to a dinner-supper at the Reform Club. Personally I was much disappointed with his speeches, particularly with the clean slate metaphor which strikes me as capable of very little sensible interpretation except as a wholesale abandonment of principle. His pronouncement against Home Rule was even more objectionable for his reasons and ungenerous mode of expression towards the Irish than for his actual practical conclusions.

The only really good point in his speeches was the advocacy of a peace based on consent in South Africa.

February 15 Heard him again at the Junior Reform Club, a hotbed of Imperialism which I fear turned his head. Actually this club counts for nothing in Liverpool, being almost less politically than they are socially.

February 19 Went to Leicester to annual meeting of General Committee of National Liberal Federation. The meeting was very unanimous on the Executive Committee's resolutions and made all amendments be withdrawn. This was satisfactory as we carried unanimously a resolution demanding peace by consent in S. Africa. Returned home the same evening without waiting to hear Sir H. C-Bannerman's speech which by all accounts was excellent.

February 21 . . . Lord Rosebery sends a letter to the Times announcing definite separation from C[ampbell] B[annerman]. A great pity, but I hope and believe this will lead to no split for C.B. has led the party in the House of Commons with great devotion in a most difficult position and deserves, what he wont get, the loyal gratitude of every Liberal.

February 25 . . . attended meeting of New Century Society where I had a breeze with Liberal Imperialists who walked out in the tantrums.

It is curious how people who use most offensive language and epithets towards others dislike hard hitting back.

April 5 . . . Cecil Rhodes' will published: an extraordinary document emphasizing what I should take to be the message of his life – a desire to obtain good and noble ends solely through the expenditure of money.

May 19 . . . Rather a busy time in politics with a reactionary Education bill, designed to put education under the control of the denominationalists, and a re-enactment of the Corn duties. A tax on corn is a most iniquitous measure, pressing most hardly on those nearest the line of absolute pauperism.

I have been chosen treasurer instead of Secretary of the Liberal Federal Council.

June 2 Particulars of peace published which show we have acted with generosity and make it more than ever regrettable that similar terms were not offered 14 months ago when a peace would have saved much life and misery. A little 'mafficking' took place but not much and we must hope the public in this country will now finally turn back on what I can only consider a very disgraceful page in the nation's history. The credit for peace is universally assigned to Lord Kitchener.

June 24 . . . The news of the King's severe illness and the consequent postponement of the coronation became public this afternoon. This is a great upset for all the arrangements for festivities and rejoicings, but the public seem to me to have taken the news very coolly. The truth is that the King is not respected on personal grounds and the coronation ceremonies and rejoicings have been arranged for the gratification of the idle and thoughtless rather than for the more serious minded. The proclamation of two Bank Holidays on Thursday and Friday causes much annoyance to the busy business people.

July 27–August 6 Serious trouble at 54 Ullet Road – row between L[awrence] and M[olly] . . . I have acted as peacemaker, but it is all very sad.

November 1 Municipal elections resulted in the Liberals winning three seats all at the South End of the town. There were only 5 bona fide contests.

The municipal contests were immediately followed by a parliamentary contest for East Toxteth where Herbert Rathbone made an excellent fight reducing the

Tory majority to about 370. The education bill was the main bone of contention. Polling on Nov. 6th Thursday.

[end 1902] I find keeping a diary rather impossible to do properly, probably because I don't give steady application to it, but amuse myself one way or the other and let time slip by without making entries as the events occur. And most of the events which do occur in such lives as ours, regular, fairly busy with matters of no great interest to those not immediately concerned in them, are hardly worth chronicling.

A shooting party, or a dance, or a dinner and the record of the company thereat can be of little interest except to oneself in later years as showing who one's friends and associates were.

From the middle of November till Christmas of 1902 was just an uneventful period, full of ordinary business, our affairs requiring a good deal of attention, one or two visits to London in connection with the [China] Mutual [Company] purchase as the old directors could not manage the distribution of the compensation for disturbance fund. On one of these visits Uncle Leonard took me as his guest to the Political Economy Club where Lord Brassey, Sir C. Dilke and others discussed the new agreement between the Govt. and the Cunard Co. for subsidising two fast steamers and in this discussion I was allowed to join. . . .

It is delightful to see our children gradually growing both physically and mentally, casting off foolish habits and becoming more sensible and well behaved. To see them learning to be useful, to do little bits of work and to play with intelligence.

1903

[The process of Liberal reunion was confirmed following Joseph Chamberlain's famous speech in Birmingham in May, in which he advocated a policy of Tariff Reform and Imperial Preference. All Liberals felt able to unite in defence of the sacred doctrine of Free Trade. By this stage Holt's first attempt to enter parliament in the West Derby by-election had fallen foul of the Unionists' continuing domination of Liverpool politics. Holt had no answer to the Tory Democracy cultivated by Alderman Salvidge and his party machine.]

January 7 . . . On getting home we found ourselves in the thick of the work of finding a candidate for the West Derby Parliamentary Division vacant by the death of Mr. Higginbottom.

This not an easy job with so big a majority – 2900 – against us. Our first effort was to get Mr. Richard Molyneux, Lord Sefton's brother, to stand and for this purpose my father and I called on Lord Sefton on Sunday. However he would not and Mr. A.A. Paton would not, so on Thursday January 8th I was selected as Liberal candidate, the Lord Mayor, Mr. W.W. Rutherford, being the Conservative candidate. . . .

The next week was entirely given up to electioneering – we had meetings on Tuesday, Thursday and Friday at which Messrs. R. Cameron, Broadhurst, R. Rea and J.H. Lewis spoke and very good meetings they were too. Records are kept in a separate book. All our party worked splendidly including the ladies. Eliza worked heart and soul and the two girls came from Church Stretton and stayed with Uncle Alfred. But alas! our work and hopes proved vain. We were beaten by 2200 votes.

At any rate it was a pure election as far as we were concerned.

Of course the constituency had been debauched by the late member's treating and Mr. Rutherford's very open hospitality at the Town Hall has produced a great impression on the electors. The poll was on Tuesday January 20th.

After this we returned to the monotony of private life and the working off of the arrears engendered by the election.

February 3 Went up to London having some little business in the City and took Eliza too. Next evening dined at the Courtneys who asked some young Liberals to meet us. Mr. and Mrs. Massingham, Mr. Masterman, journalists, Mr. and Mrs. Ramsay MacDonald, Labour organiser and London County Council, Mr. Hirst, journalist. Mr. Hugh Law, Irish M.P. came in after dinner. Altogether a very pleasant evening.

February 18 . . . It is really impossible to say how kind everyone has been over the election. One could not have received more appreciation if one had been successful. The Liberals of Liverpool have ever been most kind and generous to me and I owe much to them.

Eliza was a jewel [at a Reform Club reception] and a perfect wife for a candidate and would be politician. She is so helpful and encouraging.

March 12 Spent next day in City, E[liza] visiting amongst friends. Had another party at the Webbs, two M.P.s Herbert Samuel and [Reginald] McKenna, the latter a particularly pleasant and amusing and, I should judge, able man.

The Webbs of course are very Imperialistic, with a great idea of spending money so as to please the working classes. Not to my idea a very high minded type of political opinion though accompanied by most devoted work in the public interest.

March 23 Rather startled to receive Dr. Klein's resignation of his pulpit. It is difficult at present to see exactly what his reason for taking this step is, health being the foremost stated reason and tho' apparently he is not in the most vigorous health this does not appear in itself sufficient especially as I don't think he is much amiss. The other reasons as alleged are mainly dissatisfaction with our system of Church Government in which he does not think the Minister plays a sufficiently conspicuous part. This in his case, I think, is due to his own laziness.

April 20–25 This week we have held in Liverpool the National Triennial

Conference of Unitarians etc. The Conference was most successful, many excellent papers being read particularly by Dr. Hunter, the Congregational Minister of London, and some of our own divines, Mr. Jacks, Mr. Wood and Mr. Jupp. Professor Carpenter was the president and preached a most admirable sermon in the Philharmonic Hall on the evening of Tuesday 21st when a great service was held there. The ground floor was nearly full – the boxes well filled and the gallery sparsely occupied.

On the Wednesday at 4 pm I proposed a resolution condemning the Education Act – my only contribution to the Conference proper. In the evening we had a full, almost crowded, reception in the Walker Art Gallery and on the Thursday a public meeting in St. George's Hall.

May 3 Dr. Klein conducted the services at Ullet Rd. Church for the last time. We have all been much puzzled to understand the motives for his conduct. Whether it is merely piqued vanity – thinking himself insufficiently appreciated – or whether he contemplates some change of religious communion. The administration of the Communion this day was most extraordinary and can never be forgotten. It was extremely painful. I am sorry he leaves us thus for he had many great gifts, probably outweighed by his faults, tho' I used not to think so.

July 2 Spent most of day hanging about Parliament Committee rooms where Board's bill was before House of Commons Committee – a very dull Committee. In the afternoon I gave evidence.

The worst of writing up a diary some days after the events is a tendency to omit important things and I find I have quite omitted to say that on the Wednesday afternoon [July 1] I attended a special meeting of the National Liberal Federation (General Committee) at the Caxton Hall, Westminster, where Asquith moved a resolution condemning Chamberlain's proposal to abandon our Free Trade policy. This resolution was supported by representatives of different districts and different trades, and I was invited to speak briefly as a Liverpool shipowner. The meeting was enthusiastic and unanimous and Asquith's speech excellent.

August 21 . . . town [Liverpool] is expanding everywhere, amidst all the outward signs of great prosperity.

October 7 I was back in Liverpool to be elected Chairman of the Docks and Quays Committee of the Dock Board in place of good Mr. Fernie, unhappily recently deceased. This elevation was unexpected, but as for some reason the Committee would not have Mr. Chadwick, who had acted as deputy during Mr. Fernie's illness and Mr. Rome could not serve, they were forced to take me . . . It is undoubtedly a great honour for one so young – 15 years I should say the youngest of the Committee – and I value the honour as my dearest Uncle George was chairman of this Committee when he died.

October 23 . . . Some work at municipal elections during the following week. I spoke 3 times but no ward in which I am particularly interested was contested.

The result left the Liberals as they were but the Conservatives lost 3 seats to the Protestants, headed by George Wise – a curious development. Hampson, Lord Mayor elect, was heavily defeated.

December 16 Spoke at public meeting in Wavertree West Ward for Free Trade. A. Emmott, M.P. for Oldham, principal speaker. Good meeting.

December 31 . . . I fancy in business and trade generally it has been bad, tho' our own business has not suffered very heavily. Things have never been nearly as bad as in the autumn of 1902. Of course the expectation of war between Russia and Japan is rather damping to one's spirits, but I can't help thinking this may still be postponed.

In our own family not an unfortunate year. A general tendency for the feelings excited by the misfortune of the summer of 1902 to subside, tho' things are far from being what they ought to be.

1904

[By 1904 it was the turn of the Unionists to experience internal dissension as no consensus emerged within the party over Chamberlain's tariff proposals. Balfour's government found its position becoming increasingly uncomfortable. The outbreak of war in the Far East between Russia and Japan was a cause of concern to Holt in view of the potential threat to the interests of the Ocean Steam Ship Company.]

January 4 . . . Had a good talk with Mr. C[harles] B[ooth] on his joining J. Chamberlain's 'Commission' – I think a most unfortunate step. He seems more taken with the preferential idea than anything else, which seems to me wholly illusory as a means of binding the Empire together.

January 19 Duke of Devonshire's meeting at Philharmonic Hall to which we went in C's box: audience consisted mainly of Liberals. Sir W. Forwood in chair, with poor local assistance except the two M.P.s, A. Taylor and McArthur, the latter of whom is very weak on Free Trade. Lord G. Hamilton and W. Churchill also spoke. Latter flippant and not very attractive to me.

The Duke's speech was long and very firm. Not an interesting or particularly attractive speaker, but clear and certain and carrying great weight from his position.

The protectionists had just suffered a heavy reverse at Norwich, losing a Tory seat by 1800 votes, tho' a Socialist or Independent Labour man also stood and polled 2400 votes.

January 25 Federal Council, mainly occupied in defending Edward Evans' leadership against abominable aspersions of Daily Post. I think Joseph C's fiscal reform (?) is on the wane. Ald. Salvidge now says Protestantism must come first.

February 9 . . . Otherwise I spent most of my day time in the City, our business being naturally a little anxious in consequence of the Russo-Japanese war which broke out 2 or 3 days earlier.

February 26 . . . Politics are getting warm, the Government doing every foolish thing and making themselves detested. Balfour's own conduct towards the Free trade members of his Cabinet in the last autumn and the proposed introduction of Chinese labourers into South Africa on conditions not distinguishable from slavery being especially unpopular occurrences.

March 7 I went to London this evening to give evidence next day before Committee of the House of Lords in favour of Dock Board Bill for establishing a minimum tonnage of 50% of the gross register.

March 12 . . . Lords amendment consists in fixing uniform tonnage of 50% of Gross Register instead of a minimum of 50% and is of course much more severe on our opponents than our original bill and as we found we could safely accept it, we, after consulting our counsel . . . decided to do so.

April 22 Went down to Church Stretton . . . to speak at a public meeting in Church Stretton on behalf of Mr. Horne, Liberal candidate for the Ludlow Division of Shropshire. The position in this county tickles my fancy, for a band of Liberals from diverse parts of the country . . . have swooped down on it and are making the old security of tenure of the Tory squire very precarious – to his great annoyance.

May 4 Spoke against Licensing Bill at the Rotunda.

July 13 Up to London again over our wretched Dock Board Bill. Travelled up with Hughes and Glynn. Spent that afternoon and Thursday lobbying and had the 'satisfaction' of the bill being thrown out by an immense majority. Board of Trade behaved disgracefully.

July 16 Earl Spencer unveiled memorial statue of W.E. Gladstone in St. John's Gardens and did it very well . . . Lord S made a capital little speech also at luncheon at the Reform Club. The Tories came and behaved very well.

July 19 King's visit to Liverpool to lay foundation stone of Cathedral . . . Eliza and I went to Landing Stage and saw King and Queen embark on Royal yacht. Got a very good view.

October 14 Freedom of the City of Liverpool presented to my father and to Earl of Derby in the Town Hall for their services to the municipality. My father has been a City Councillor for 27 years and was first Lord Mayor.

Dear Dad did his part admirably and was obviously greatly affected.

October 16 A day begun in happiness and joyful hopes ended in deepest sorrow.

In the first place we knew something like a reconciliation at my old home had begun. Then came Eliza's confinement as a culmination of our hopes for nine long months. Everything seemed well, the doctor, Campbell, satisfied. But it dragged on in a puzzling way and finally artificial delivery had to be resorted to and the child was born dead, suffocated through the cord being round its neck.

Such a dear little child – quite perfect – and the long hoped for boy. Indeed a tragic ending for us.

Fortunately my dear brave Eliza was none the worse.

October 18 . . . The days following have fortunately been pretty busy, as there is a big spurt in the China trade and the municipal elections which on Nov. 1st resulted in the Liberals winning 4 seats and the 'Protestants' one. In Edge Hill ward where I had taken considerable interest we were only beaten by 13 on a poll of over 2400 and this was a forlorn hope.

[end 1904] Somehow or other I have got out of the way of making regular entries in this book, largely I fear through laziness and want of system and at the end of the year I find myself without an entry since that of Nov. 7th. . . .

Just before Christmas I was approached with a view to standing for Parliament for the Abercromby division of Liverpool, offering now fair but not certain prospect of success. I gave a definite no as I understood my business friends would not agree but subsequent discussion made it seem probable they would consent. However the seat is now offered to another so I may never have the chance.

E[liza] and I would dearly like it, but it is difficult to make up one's mind. Clearly the office has claims, which it is difficult to put aside. Then my family have so much money invested in the steamers which really ought to be looked after. I myself have work here, eg. the Dock Board, which it would be hard to give up. On the other hand there is some ambition, some wish to move on a larger stage and an honest wish to help in crushing the miserable Jingo and protectionist movement. I don't know what the final decision will be.

1905

[A General Election was in the air throughout 1905, but Balfour did not resign until December, leaving Sir Henry Campbell-Bannerman to form a minority Liberal administration. Nationally the tide had turned against Unionism, giving Holt good reason to expect that he would be successful at the forthcoming General Election.]

January 19 Officially announced that Major J.B. Seely, one of the seceding Tories, will stand as Liberal candidate for the Abercromby Division. This is rather a blow to my hopes, but a good thing for the Liberal party.

February 22 Was again adopted as Liberal candidate for the West Derby division.

March 6 Started electioneering in the quiet way – organising Committees and getting names and men. Virtually I have to manage my own election, which should really not be the candidate's work.

March 14   Opened our campaign with a very fair meeting at Earle Road schools, following this up on the 16th by another at Albany Road. Principal topic being the fiscal question. I find it takes one full evening to prepare a speech for about 40/50 minutes which is what the candidate should give.

[? April]   Somehow or other, partly from business and partly from idleness I have let my records get hopelessly in arrear, but there has been, as usual, little to record except work at office, Dock Board and politics and a small amount of social gaiety.

April 13   We had a great demonstration at the Philharmonic Hall at which Winston Churchill was the principal speaker and made a very good speech. All the Liberal candidates for Liverpool . . . said something. Mine was to second a vote of thanks to Edward Evans in the chair which I did in a few minutes. But the audience gave me a most splendid reception, as long or longer than to a leading speaker, which was quite marked and very kind of them.

   . . . The probable reason for this was that on April 17th – Monday – I was to and did debate the fiscal question publicly with Mr. W.W. Rutherford, M.P. for the West Derby Division. The debate aroused extraordinary interest in the town. It took place in the Sun Hall, Kensington, and as each side gave away 2500 tickets besides 1000 free places there must have been nearly 6000 present, and a great many more were turned away at the doors. Sir Thomas Hughes very kindly took the chair. Rutherford spoke for thirty minutes, then I for 30, then he had a second turn of 15 and I the like. This last was shockingly interrupted by persons walking out and I could scarcely get a hearing as I was barely able to speak on account of a bad cold. The impression was that we had the best of the argument and certainly the meeting was quite as favourable to us as to him. My friends were unquestionably pleased and encouraged.

July 27   I am a bad diary keeper. My conscience often reproaches me but when once circumstances have made me get behind I find it very difficult to take things up again.

October 18   Another long spell of inactivity in diary writing and probably this entry is only a flash in the pan . . . As usual we worked away through the latter part of the month at the municipal elections, when the Liberals had the satisfaction of gaining 5 seats and what was most gratifying to me personally we carried both Edge Hill and Low Hill wards. No Liberal had been successful in West Derby division since about 1876 when my uncle, W.D. Holt, was defeated and as I have worked hard there for 10 years it was very pleasing to be at last successful. The third ward, Kensington, was captured by a Socialist, Mr. Morrissey, who had made himself prominent as elective auditor and was probably elected on personal grounds.

... Later on, the week beginning the 20th [November] we had political work, a meeting at the Rotunda on Monday 20th at which Walter Runciman, M.P., was the principal speaker and made an excellent speech – as also next day to an afternoon meeting of businessmen in the Exchange Hotel.

Then on Wednesday C.P. Trevelyan, M.P., came down and addressed an inadequate meeting in the Liverpool Institute at which Seely and I also spoke.

I enjoyed meeting these men very much and they attract me strongly towards Parliamentary work, in which direction I receive every encouragement from my dear wife.

1906

[Despite the overwhelming Liberal victory in the General Election of 1906, the political pendulum swung much less violently in Liverpool and Holt was unable to secure his seat at Westminster. A few months after the election Holt's mother died. She had been a semi-invalid for some time and suffered a heart attack at the beginning of April from which she never recovered. Her last years had been marred by the domestic sadness of a divided family and, depressed, she had taken to cocaine. Beatrice Webb recorded her feelings with startling frankness shortly after her sister's death. 'In Lallie there was executive ability of uncommon degree, a vivid force and picturesqueness of speech, but ugliness of body and uncouthness of manner. But . . . real genuine generosity towards individuals and towards causes shone out as the dominant note in feeling and conduct.']

[April] No entries during a long period for when the mumps were over we found ourselves right in the thick of the general election. Mr. Balfour resigned and left Sir Henry Campbell-Bannerman to form a government early in December and dissolve Parliament in January.

Now in April it is impossible to write with any real interest of these events. I, as arranged, again stood for West Derby and was again beaten by disagreeably large figure of some 1850 votes. Fortunately Cherry and Seely were both returned and as Austin Taylor who got in unopposed shortly after became an avowed Liberal we virtually obtained three Liberal seats in Liverpool: not very good at a time when the whole country was so overwhelmingly Radical. One of the curious things in the election was the failure of all the family connection, L.H. Courtney, C.A. Cripps, A.S. Cripps, E. Lawrence and myself.

. . . So what with the necessity of clearing up the arrears left by the General Election and of finishing off all sorts of work before going abroad, I managed to get very busy, and to make no entries in the diary. But I suppose an ardent, or even conscientious, diarist would not let such considerations injure his diary, and as one of my grievances is now remedied – I have at last got a writing desk of my own where I am comfortable – I must really make an effort at continuous entries.

[**March 1906**] [In Paris Holt visited the *Comédie Française*] The piece was not

A modern photograph of 54 Ullet Road.

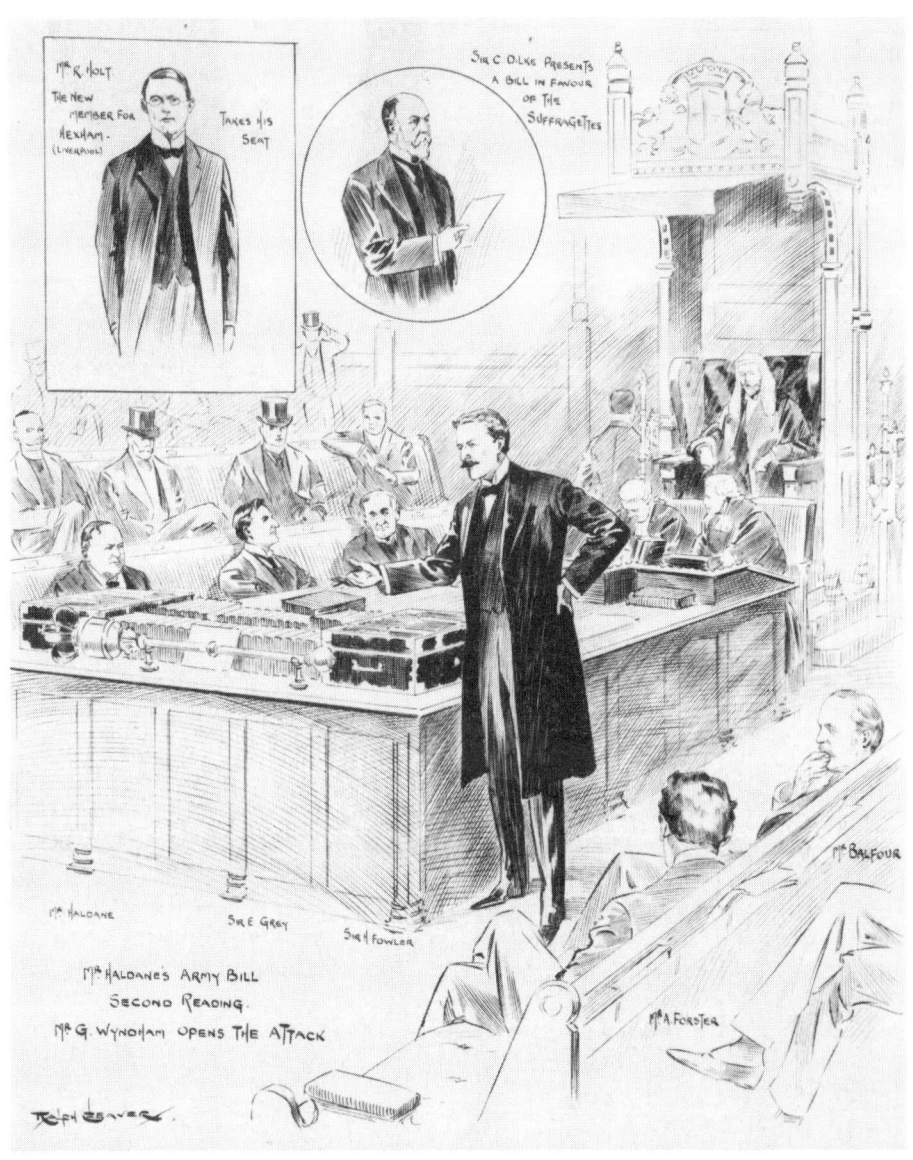

A debate in the Commons in 1907, when R.D. Holt first took his seat as member for Hexham.

very interesting turning on the relative claims of an effort to seduce a married woman and of an attempt to seize the throne of some small state. Two jobs dear to a Frenchman but with neither of which an Englishman has much sympathy.

May 24 About 2 pm my dearest mother passed away. At breakfast we heard she was very ill and on arrival at 54 Ullet Road found all hope had gone . . . There never was so good a mother – always sacrificing herself for others, no matter how they treated her. Never did I know anyone so brave and courageous, so helpful in difficulties.

November 1 Municipal elections – very uninteresting and manqué, the Liberals losing 2 seats net though badly beaten in nearly every contest. Luckily most of our men were returned unopposed before our opponents, or we either, realised the situation, for the Catholics, against the advice of the Irish leaders, elected to vote against our men all along the line, even tho' 2 of our candidates were themselves Catholics: the motive being to vent their spite on all Liberals for the Education Bill of the Government which aims at establishing public control of all schools maintained out of public funds.

It really seems extraordinary that any body of men can be found to deny the right of the public to exclusively control education for which they exclusively pay. But I suppose no one brought up in the freedom of Unitarian principles can in the least understand the Catholic (Anglican and Roman) point of view that children must have the right? (as they think) theological opinions drummed into them when unable to really understand, for fear that in their more mature age they will not accept these opinions.

November 11 Eliza and I had a letter from Betty announcing her engagement to marry Niven McCrie, a solicitor in Edinburgh . . . Of course none of us knows anything of McCrie, except what Betty tells us – that he is hard working and self made, from the farming class and of course not what is known in the world as a good match.

[end 1906] The business continues satisfactory. Not as good as in 1905, still 1906 has been a very successful year for us. We have had 9 new steamers during the year and count fourth amongst British ship-owners and what is more we have our ships fully employed.

1907

[Perhaps realising that his political ambitions would be hard to fulfil inside Liverpool, Holt finally secured election to parliament in March following a by-election in the Hexham division of Northumberland. As one of four hundred Liberal M.P.s on the crowded government benches, the new member no doubt found it difficult to make his mark. In any case the diary is at its thinnest during these early years of his parliamentary career.]

July 28 Just over six months since the last entry and perhaps the most important six months of my life except those leading up to my most happy marriage.

The day before Good Friday, March 28th, I was declared elected member of Parliament for the Hexham division of Northumberland by 5401 votes against 4244 polled by Colonel C.L. Bates, the Conservative candidate.

In the middle of February Lord Allendale died and was succeeded by his son, Hon. W.C.B. Beaumont who since 1895 had represented the Hexham division in Parliament and 2 or 3 days later I received a telegram, quite unexpectedly, asking if I would allow my name to go before the delegates for consideration. I at once replied 'Yes', (this was on a Friday afternoon), and on Saturday at dinnertime I received another telegram saying I was chosen.

So up I went on Monday evening to submit myself to the delegates on the following day. I arrived late at night and was put up at the Hydropathic kept by Mr. Grant, a most enthusiastic Liberal and canny Scotchman.

Never did I spend such a miserable night. Excitement stopped me from sleeping and next morning I felt fit for nothing.

However in spite of this the delegates did choose me although they ought to have chosen Gerald France, a good local man, who afterwards behaved very generously towards me.

Next day the campaign began, Eliza coming up to join me, and for five solid weeks we kept pegging away. E. was splendid and after the election was over it was said that she and Mitchell, the agent, had won it for me.

1908

[Despite its overwhelming parliamentary majority, the Liberal government soon ran into trouble as many of its measures fell foul of the Unionist dominated House of Lords. In the wake of their party's crushing electoral defeat in 1906, Balfour and Lord Lansdowne, the Unionist leader in the upper house, had determined to use the veto power of the hereditary peerage to block the government's reforming zeal. Holt came at an early stage to believe that the nettle of the Lords' power would have to be grasped. After the mauling of the government's Education Bill he wrote to Walter Runciman: 'I should say concentrate on the House of Lords – pass the next Budget (which must not on any account fall into the hands of the Tariff Reformers) and the bill for dealing with the H. of Lords and then let us try our chance with the country. As things are we are simply being made fools of and if we let existing things go on the whole party comes to a contemptible end'.

Holt's father died in December. Robert Holt had never been a favourite of his sister-in-law, Beatrice Webb. In 1899 the latter recorded: 'Our brother-in-law is not improving with age: his small-mindedness and secretiveness has degenerated into a restless kind of vanity, an undignified love of social esteem. It is pathetic to see his little mind always reverting to the glory of having refused a baronetcy.']

August 31 This Diary has practically come to an end, the work of Parliament coupled with the office taking up my time and energy. I don't know if any more entries will be made – they certainly wont be systematically. This book has not been opened for over a year and would not be now if Eliza and the children had not been in America since June 30 (day of leaving Liverpool).

I don't know why I write now. They are due back on Saty. September 5th, I expect well and strong. Political things really ought to command attention, but I am idly on a holiday now and think only of steamers – at the office – and what I am to shoot at Windermere where I go tomorrow.

My father has been very ailing this last year or so – a gradual loss of bodily and mental health. Not pleasant to watch.

December 10 My father died this morning as the result of gradual enfeeblement. He had gone down hill very rapidly since August and for about five weeks had been confined to his bed, during all which time he had been very drowsy, tho' when awake cheerful and happy and as loving as ever . . . Mine was the very best of fathers – always kind and generous and the most unselfish of men.

The newspapers are full of the most laudatory comments.

1909

[Holt's diary records none of the parliamentary drama which followed the Lords' rejection of Lloyd George's famous People's Budget in November. Holt himself did much to establish his radical credentials by joining the self-styled Reduction of Armaments Committee, which attempted to oppose the Naval Estimates for 1909–10. Naval expenditure increasingly emerged as a crucial dividing issue between Imperialists and Radicals on the government side.]

February 15 . . . We here have decided to move, once more, to 54 Ullet Rd., a house too big for our requirements, but from its excellence and size, nearly unsaleable. And I should hate to part with the house my father built and loved – perhaps to a Tory.

March 8 . . . Parliament is very attractive to me and Eliza likes the social life and the agreeable acquaintances.

April 14 I am more and more ashamed of the raggedness of this diary. There never seems time for regular entries. Parliament and business, together with the necessity of looking after one's seat and the correspondence entailed thereby, filling up one's time very fully . . . E. and I are both in the final convalescent stages of an attack of influenza. I believe mine was caught through going up to London to vote for the Government against the ridiculous naval scare vote of censure when I had a very heavy cold. . . .

1910

[The rejection of the budget by the House of Lords necessitated a General Election in January. The Liberal government was returned to power, but its massive majority of 1906 was now wiped out and it was left dependent on Labour and Irish Nationalist support for its parliamentary survival. The failure to resolve the constitutional crisis by negotiation in the course of 1910 necessitated a further General Election in December, fought this time specifically to give the government a mandate to deal with the House of Lords. This produced scarcely any change from the verdict of January. Holt was successful in Hexham in both contests. Parliamentary arithmetic now ensured that Irish Home Rule would occupy the centre stage in the government's legislative plans.]

May 20 Worse and worse. When I look at the volumes of old family diaries – my grandfather's, Auntie's, my father's – so carefully and regularly written up, I really do feel ashamed of myself.

Today is a brilliant warm day – a public day of mourning (alias holiday) for the funeral of King Edward VII who died just a fortnight ago. Therefore I am at home for one day with nothing to do.

The last year has been a big one for England and we are now in the middle of the Constitutional Struggle arising out of the rejection of the 1909 Budget by the House of Lords. That session of Parliament lasted from February to December after which we had a general election in which the Liberal party lost in the South and Midlands some 100 seats but thanks to the very strong anti-Lords feeling in the North and Scotland still retained with the Irish and Labour parties a majority of 120 votes against the Lords and protectionist parties.

I was again elected for Hexham by a majority of 1061, on an awful snowy day at the end of January: a winter campaign in the North is no fun. Eliza is always a splendid helper and of my relatives Arthur Hobhouse, Lawrence (who stayed a week), Phil, Betty and Molly turned up to help. Everybody was most enthusiastic and good.

This year we have a house in London, 30 Sloane Court, the best we have yet had, but owing to the horrible device of a spring recess for the whole month of May we have not got fair use out of it. And our efforts at entertainment were stopped by my stupid little attack of German measles in the middle of April.

[end 1910] After the King's death Parliament did not reassemble till the early middle of June and political fight was very absent. Indeed we had little contentious business.

Personally I had rather an interesting time being on two Committees, one a joint special with the Lords to discuss the Water Supplies Protection Bill – really to consider the whole question of water supply especially that derived from underground sources. This was a very interesting enquiry. Then I was and am engaged on the Departmental Committee for considering the amalgamation of the Customs and Excise.

Another general election. The Constitutional Question not being settled by agreement Parliament was dissolved at the end of November really to decide whether the King should create enough peers to carry the Parliament Bill.

The general result in the country showed no change and was therefore a victory for the Liberal party.

We had a very pleasant election. My opponent was A.H. Chaytor, a barrister who had just inherited money. My majority 790, the falling off being mainly due to the old register.

The whole a bold and successful stroke.

1911

[1911 saw the successful passing of the Parliament Act, without the necessity of a mass creation of peers to ensure its passage through the upper house. There was, however, no slackening in the intensity of political tension thereafter. The introduction of Lloyd George's National Insurance Bill served to reveal that Holt's radicalism did not extend to interventionist measures of social reform. In August Holt faced serious industrial unrest in Liverpool. All his inclinations were to take a strong line against concessions to the strikers. 'The shipowners here,' he wrote to Walter Runciman, 'have got their backs up over this monstrous job and are not going to let Tom Mann manage labour whatever it costs. I am horribly afraid the Corporation may give way about reinstating the tramwaymen who have struck – but if they stand firm we are all right.']

April 16 This session of Parliament I have been placed on the Local Legislation Committee to which all the private bills promoted by Corporations and Urban District Councils are referred. Generally this means 3 mornings every week from 11.30 to 4, listening to evidence and discussing clauses – really a pleasant and interesting work and useful too, but it does take a good deal of time.

The constitutional question is making progress and we are steadily pushing on with the Parliament bill. Last week we practically finished the first clause removing for ever from the H. of Lords all control over finance and what is more obtained something like general consent as to the definition of a 'Money Bill'.

April 23 Went up to London the previous Tuesday. E.L.H. with me. Arrived at H. of C. about 6.45 and stayed there till 5 a.m. in Committee on Parliament bill. Very wearisome, mainly with obstruction. The Government supporters kept absolutely dumb as every speech justifies three or four in reply and time can't be eternally wasted.

April 30 I went up to London the previous Monday and spent a busy week there – but a lonely one as all my family was in Liverpool. We are getting on steadily with the Parliament bill and I think are well up to time. Committees in the morning and one morning in the city at a China Conference meeting filled up all my time.

June 5 . . . In London I have been very busy especially lately with the Customs and Excise Committee considering our report. That and the Local Legislation Committee do walk into one's time.

One of the disappointing things about the House of Commons is one's utter inability to speak on important questions when one wants to do so. In a 3 days debate on the Insurance bill I could not get in and I have always had the same experience on similar occasions. And yet furious as one feels, it is really impossible to suggest a remedy for everybody has an equal right and if everybody had a chance and used it nothing would ever be done.

All London is disfigured with scaffolding in preparation for the immense crowd which is to see the Coronation procession. Royalty is a horrible nuisance on its ceremonial side tho' probably the best institution for this country – especially as binding together the self governing Colonies, or dominions as the new style is.

But to spend £950,000 on the Coronation Durbar in India really rises in my gorge. It is monstrous in so poor a country to spend such a sum on display. I am afraid George and Mary (Rex not Holt!!) like being stars in a show.

Last week Parliament Bill was read a second time in House of Lords. The general opinion is they will end by swallowing it whole.

On Sunday May 28 I met General Botha at tea at Uncle Leonard's. A very fine man, not bitter but cool and level headed, perhaps not very clever, which is often a great merit when wounds have to be healed.

I don't like the clever Home Secretary, Winston Churchill. He has a bad face and is needlessly provocative to the Tories, which lengthens debate.

June 8 E.L.H. returned from London. Why dont we live here always. Is Parliament a huge mistake and would it not be better if we lived in this almost sumptuous home and minded the business and local affairs. That was always my father's view and that no-one but those of first rate political abilities and opportunities ought to go to London. I don't know but doubt.

June 9 To Hexham where we spent the weekend visiting our constituents. Surely it is a great privilege to have been drawn into acquaintance with so many good people in a wholly different sphere of life whom I should never have got to know but for politics.

June 22 Coronation of King George V and Queen Mary. E.L.H. and I had tickets for the Abbey and of course availed ourselves of them. We went about 7.30 a.m. (quite unnecessarily early) by motor to the H. of C. . . .

Our seats were in the South Transept and fortunately we were able to see the actual crowning of the King seated in St. Edward's chair. We saw the homage done and the Queen's procession but not the King's. The most glorious sight of all was the dresses of the Ladies of the Bedchamber: gold brocade quite plain shot with different colours.

The service lasted about $2\frac{1}{2}$ hours and was fine but not religious. The voice of the Archbishop of Canterbury carried wonderfully through the building.

June 23 E.L.H., Nancy and I went to see the second procession from H. of C. We had excellent seats. The Queen looked very pleased, the King bored.

June 24 Grace and I went to Naval Review: not very well done or interesting, but an enormous number of warships.

July 23 . . . Parliament has been mainly occupied with the national Insurance Bill. Very few really like it and it is a wonderful testimony to Lloyd George's powers of management and persuasion that it should even have a chance of going through against so much silent hostility.

No other minister could have made any show with it. I must say I dont like it: there is too much interference. I spoke on the Naval Prize Bill – that is for the ratification of the declaration of London and it was considered a success.

July 24 Went to London staying at National Liberal Club. This afternoon Prime Minister was to have made his statement with regard to the Creation of Peers to carry the Parliament Bill but a small section of Tories led by Lord H. Cecil and F.E. Smith made such a disturbance that the P.M. was unable to make himself heard. Then Balfour tried to answer a speech he had not heard – an impossible task – and we listened in silence, though there was great difficulty in suppressing some of our men. Sir E. Grey moved the adjournment. F.E. Smith tried to speak but was shouted down by our people under instructions from the Whips and the Speaker adjourned the sitting.

I did not approve of stopping Smith, who would almost certainly have made a fool of himself. He is clever – too clever – and unprincipled: a nice pair with his friend Churchill.

Altogether a very disgraceful scene which has done the Tories much harm.

August 6 . . . I was prevented [from going to Scotland] to my very great disappointment, because I must go to London tomorrow to vote against Balfour's censure resolution and on Tuesday for the rejection of the Lords' amendments to the Parliament Bill.

Last week on the Naval Prize Bill in Grand Committee I carried an amendment against the Govt. striking Prize Salvage out of the bill. I shall be curious to see whether this decision of the Committee is accepted or whether the Govt. will restore this wrong system on report. Prize money altogether got badly handled in the discussion and the Govt. agreed to introduce words to allow of pooling prize money so that the evil of rewarding naval officers for capturing non-combatant property at a high rate while they get very little for service in action may be done away with.

August 7 Vote of censure on Govt. for advising creation of peers to carry veto bill. Asquith's justification magnificent and completely crushing. Good majority. Tremendous heat.

August 8 Lords Amendments considered and rejected as regards all of real importance. Fled to Scotland after pairing with Alfred Cripps at 11 pm. Heat fearful.

August 22 . . . Liverpool in throes of great strike and much disturbance brought about by 'peaceful' picketing which led to serious riots, the use of the military and finally the shooting of two or three people in a riot at the North End.

Public opinion has been very much shocked at the violence of the strikers and the recklessness of the Strike Committee who brought about an almost total cessation of transport, famine for the poorest, a substantial rise in the death rate as the result of starvation, in order to remedy comparatively trifling grievances.

As far as I can observe nothing has been obtained by the Strike, all the concessions having been made before. Indeed thanks to the very firm attitude of the shipowners led by Alfred Allen Booth with Lawrence as his right hand man, I consider the position of the employers was stronger after the strike than before.

The sympathetic strike is an abomination and utterly destructive of friendly relations between master and man in any trade.

August 25 . . . Strike ended. Ted who has been working as an amateur stoker at the Lister Drive power station released from duty. Very many young men in Liverpool have done the same work and saved the town from darkness and pillage.

[November] Parliament reassembled on Oct. 24th since when I have spent a backwards and forwards life in the railway. The autumn session is the most intolerable of evils for a country member – no home in any way and this autumn taken for a measure I dont like, the Insurance Bill.

The pleasantest part I have had was the work in Grand Committee on the unemployment part.

November 24 Went to Hexham by evening train for half yearly meeting of Northern Liberal Federation on the Saturday.

November 25 Very successful afternoon gathering at which Stephen Gwynne – M.P. for Galway City – expounded Home Rule. E.L.H. arrived at tea time after which we went to evening meeting – about 1500 in the Corn Exchange – when Seely was principal speaker. Lord Allendale in the chair. I proposed resolution to which Master of Elibank, chief whip, responded. M of E and Seely very flattering to R.D.H.

November 26 Returned to Hydro at Hexham. Went to Haydon Bridge in the afternoon to discuss dispute at Settlingstones mines with the miners' representatives and afterwards with Watson, the manager. Not much chance of an accommodation I fear as so much unnecessary bad blood has been made.

Last summer the manual labourers, misnamed the working classes, got quite beyond themselves and seemed to think they might rule the universe by threatening to do no work if others did not give way to them.

December 24 Parliament was prorogued on the 16th after a long session which should be memorable as we cut the claws of the House of Lords. The Tories have been very quiet on this subject and will, I think, accept the position. What the Insurance Act will do I cant guess. Opinions are very varied and not on party lines. Let us hope the sanguine views will prove right.

Now for 2 months quietly at home with the best wife and three little girls in the wide world. We really love one another.

December 31   The last day of a very remarkable year. The Coronation of George V, the passing into law of the Parliament Act, the extraordinary long spell of dry, fine, warm weather throughout the summer should leave this a memorable year for a very long time.

Trade, probably for everybody, has been very good and certainly our firm has done quite extraordinarily well. So too my domestic and private affairs have been most satisfactory.

1912

[By 1912 parliamentary attention was fixed upon the government's Home Rule Bill (although Holt wrongly predicted that the Welsh Disestablishment Bill, which was working its way through parliament at the same time as the Irish measure, would cause more problems.) Under the terms of the Parliament Act there was an inevitability about the ultimate success of both bills which only added to the tensions in the political atmosphere and the vehemence of the Unionist opposition. Most of Holt's time, however, was taken up with his chairmanship of a select committee on the conditions of employment in the Post Office.]

January 14   Had a letter from Mr. Lewis Harcourt asking me to help in the Anti Woman Suffrage Agitation to which I replied that I was already an adult suffragist. This is a very curious political situation and it will be most interesting to see how it develops. The most powerful ministers and also the leaders of the opposition divided on the subject.

[February 5]   On Tuesday the 30th I went up to London by the midnight train to help the Chancellor of Exchequer receive a deputation from the Customs and Excise services with regard to the report of the Committee.

He invited McKinnon Wood and myself to lunch and was very pleasant and chatty. Had a good talk about Ulster and Home Rule, all agreeing that Home Rule was neither popular nor unpopular in Great Britain and that it could not be imposed upon Ulster by force and that if possible the Protestant counties in Ulster should be exempted.

February 7   Annual meeting of Ocean S[team] S[hip] Co[mpany]. Profit over £500,000 – an immense record.

February 25   . . . The general effect of the debate on the address has been highly favourable to our party and we are in great good spirits.

Prophecy for the session: Welsh Disestablishment will give more trouble and cause more bad feeling than Home Rule.

March 3   . . . Parliament very dull with supplementary estimates, everybody's mind being occupied with the coal strike. . . .

Coal strike in full swing. Men asking a minimum wage without guarantee of work. Great deal of excitement, partly newspaper fed and talk of nationalisation of coal mines.

March 11   Last week I went up to London on Tuesday morning returning by the midnight train on Wednesday. On arrival found a letter from the P.M. asking me to be a member of the Royal Commission on the Civil Service, which I accepted and then almost directly a message came that Herbert Samuel (P[ost] M[aster] G[eneral]) wished to see me, so I went to his room when he invited me to be Chairman of a H. of C. Select Committee on Postal Servants' grievances, which I also accepted.

This will be a very stiff job. Two flattering invitations. We are getting on.

Coal strike still rampant. Prices rising, so I gave the outdoor men 5/- each to cover extra cost. At present we have enough to take the steamers out up till the end of next week, but cargo will, I think, soon cease to come down for them. There is much curtailment of railway services and many works are being closed, but at present there has been little or no ill effect in Liverpool beyond the rise in price.

April 8   Since I last wrote we have had the coal strike in full swing, but today it is supposed to be over and the men will return to work during the week.

All through the struggle the Government and especially the Prime Minister have been unwearying in their efforts to get the parties to come to terms and finally settled the matter by an Act of Parlt. giving the miners a minimum wage to be settled by District Boards chosen equally from masters and men with an independent chairman. The men made great efforts to have their schedule of rates inserted in the Act, but the Govt. stood firm, thanks to pressure from some of the independent supporters behind including R.D.H. and the men have therefore regarded the Act as a defeat, though it really is a victory for their original contention.

The country has held out better than anyone could have expected. Our cargo has continued to turn up in spite of the curtailment of the railway service and thanks largely to 3000 tons of Belgian coal . . . we have despatched all our steamers except the Deucalion from Glasgow.

[June]   Almost directly after this H. of Commons appointed a Select Committee to consider the grievances of the Post Office servants. I was chosen chairman, an appointment nominally made by the Committee but really by the Postmaster General. The other members, Liberal: Dawes, France, McCallum. Tory: Gilmour, Orde Powlett, Boyton. Nationalist: Brady. Labour: Tyson Wilson.

A chairman's job is anything but easy and the amount of preparation involved is enormous. This has kept me very busy and much concentrated in London. This diary therefore has fared badly as it is now June 22nd and I am making casual entries during a short visit to Liverpool.

August 5   . . . The work of the session has been very dull except for the Committee, which indeed has taken up most of my time and prevented me from doing much else.

Work of this sort makes it impossible to prepare any other subject and the number of subjects on which one dare speak without preparation is very limited.

Early in July E. and I went to a Court Ball at Buckingham Palace and thoroughly enjoyed ourselves. The show was magnificent – ladies in their best frocks and jewels and gentlemen in gorgeous uniforms. Probably not more than 20 were like myself in simple velvet court dress.

The King is not much to look at, nor a very pleasant looking person. Conscientious, serious and dyspeptic is his reputation and he looks it. The Queen a fine body of a woman. . . .

Business successful, but for incessant strikes, brilliantly so. There has been a very bad dock strike in London, stupidly conceived for inadequate reasons and rather cruelly repressed by the employers against A[lfred] H[olt] and Co. and others' advice. Now we have a strike at Birkenhead because the labourers there will not adopt the system successfully enforced in Liverpool.

Trade throughout the country is very brisk.

November 15 In the midst of the horrible autumn session, a real spoiling of my life. It makes things altogether too strenuous and breaks up home life . . .

Public affairs are unusually interesting owing to the war in the Balkans and altogether unexpectedly complete success of the Balkan powers. It is to be hoped that the frightful loss of life and misery which must result for the survivors will end in widening the area of good government and orderly civilisation as it probably will do and thus a blessing to mankind may result.

Let us hope too – as now seems fairly certain – that the Great Powers will not so assert themselves as to make the war extend beyond its present limits.

On Monday last the Government for the first time since they took office in 1905 were beaten in the House of Commons by 21 votes – a snap division cleverly engineered at a time when their North Country supporters had not returned from their week end visits home. The inevitable result of prolonged sessions, for business men like myself must attend to their businesses.

On Wednesday the 13th (my 44th birthday) the Tories made a disgraceful scene – the second of the Parliament – because the Government proposed to reverse the vote in a straightforward manner and the House had to be twice (the second time finally) suspended in confusion.

The open adoption of physical violence as a means of getting their own way by the Tory party appears to me a very serious and dangerous circumstance.

December 25 . . . The autumn has passed off very well in Parliament, the Tories having done very badly since the above mentioned row and being now engaged in a violent quarrel in the press on the merits of food taxes.

I have been busy at my committee and have had no time to take any active part in general politics but I have had some interesting experiences partly as a member of a sub-committee of the Committee of Imperial Defence to advise on the importation of food in wartime and partly as an adviser to the Secretary for War (J. Seely) on the transport of the 'striking force.' In this capacity I met General French.

1913

[Home Rule continued to dominate the political landscape throughout 1913. With the Unionists going through a renewed crisis over tariffs at the beginning of the year, the government's prospects still seemed favourable. With some uncertainty on the international horizon Holt placed himself firmly in the anti-conscription camp and viewed with displeasure the apparent determination of the First Lord of the Admiralty, Winston Churchill, to preserve the peace by preparing for war. To the like-minded C.P. Trevelyan Holt wrote in November: 'We have got to take our Admiralty and War Office severely in hand and when Home Rule is out of the way some of us ought to put anti-militarism first. Winston's speech at the Guildhall was disgraceful. Twice as powerful in submarines as any other power! What a waste of good money!'

Towards the end of the year the report on Holt's committee on the Post Office was published – 'at once disingenuous and hostile to the postmen', noted Beatrice Webb. It was, she continued, 'a poor shambling document which got the Government into hot water and thereby injured Dick's chance of becoming an Under Secretary'.]

February 16 . . . Parliament has just risen after passing Home Rule and Welsh Disestablishment through the H. of Commons only to see both rejected by enormous majorities in the Lords.

However things are different now and we have only to wait patiently and loyally for another 12 or 15 months to secure our objects.

It has been very trying for the ordinary member and certainly the last month with no London residence and constantly going backwards and forwards has tired me a good deal.

February 23 . . . I am much amused at finding myself involved in these warlike matters. A few months ago I was most confidentially consulted by Seely about the conveyance of the Army to Armageddon and met Sir John French and General Cowans on the subject. It is all funny for a civilian and peace man.

March 9 Got back yesterday from a week's visit to Hexham. Went up on Friday Feb. 28, speaking at Haltwhistle that evening. The annual meeting was at Hexham next day when Lord Allendale took the chair . . . .

Afterwards spent 5 evenings speaking twice a night. As there was not much to talk about I had to make much the same speech every night, which was easy but dull.

March 16 Spent most of the week in London. Debate on the address. Things very quiet there.

My Post Office Committee has been reappointed so my time is fully engaged for the session.

Everything looks well for the Liberal party. The Tariff Reformers are in furious ill temper as the South Westmorland Tories have adopted an avowed Free Trader, Col. Weston, as candidate at a bye-election.

May 21 . . . One hates to leave Liverpool which at this time of year looks its very best.

But if one gave up London the interesting work and the interesting people with whom one is brought in contact would be a considerable loss.

June 29 . . . There is really nothing to chronicle beyond my usual round of Parliamentary duties and engagements in which there is no change. My whole time has been taken up by the Post Office Committee and I have not been able to spare any for the more general political interests.

I am just back from a flying visit to Northumberland where I addressed a meeting at Greenhead on Friday evening and then on Saturday attended the annual meeting of the Northern Liberal Federation at Newcastle when I was elected President for the ensuing year.

July 12/13 . . . Tomorrow E. and I return to London for ten days or so. My P.O. Committee is getting to the final stages with its report. Home Rule and Welsh Disestablishment have both passed the H. of C. for the second time and in all probability will both be rejected by the Lords, but next year they must pass, we hope. They certainly have not lost favour with the public.

November 16 . . . On Saturday November 8 E.L.H. and I journeyed to Middlesbrough where as President of Northern Liberal Federation I took the chair for Lloyd George's third Land Campaign speech.

Not a very impressive performance as his Economics are hopelessly bad. He is quite capable of supporting any proposals which he believes may help the people for whom his sympathies are enlisted. . . .

Then on Wednesday November 12 E.L.H. and I went to London as I had to see Lloyd George about the P.O. Committee report. The P.O. servants are affecting much fury at not getting more but in reality they are very well treated.

[December] It has been a most prosperous year for Alfred Holt and Co. and I fancy for most shipowners and many other businesses. But at the moment there are signs that this unexampled wave of prosperity which we have enjoyed for 2 or 3 years is passing away: not rapidly.

In the world at large there has been much turmoil and a horrible war but fortunately the Great Powers have kept the peace amongst themselves and there are now signs everywhere that the financial strain is causing a reaction against militarism.

1914

[Throughout the first half of 1914 the Home Rule Bill moved inexorably towards the statute book with only the possibility of unconstitutional action by the Protestant Ulstermen abetted by the Unionist opposition in parliament capable of holding it up. Holt's diary reflects contemporary preoccupations and it is not until the beginning of August that his attention turns to threatening developments on the continent. Before then, however, Holt had made perhaps his most significant single contribution to national politics in opposing Lloyd George's Finance Bill. Holt headed about forty

Liberal M.P.s who rebelled against the Budget on the grounds that parliament was being asked to raise money for grants which would not go into effect until 1915. Asquith thought the manifesto of the Holt Cave to be 'a very able document and to most of its arguments there is no real answer'. The government's majority on second reading fell to 38 and on 8 July to 23 when Holt's group abstained on an opposition amendment. The cabinet was forced to abandon rating reform for a year and to reduce income tax by one penny.

From August onwards all attention turned to the War. Holt found it incredible that Britain should have been drawn into a continental power struggle, but rallied behind the government once war was declared. As yet, however, the full horrors of the conflict were not apparent.]

February 8 . . . On Wednesday we held the annual meeting of the Ocean S[team] S[hip] Co. – as usual poorly attended – and announced a splendid result, the best yet recorded. A most gratifying year for all of us.

Tomorrow we leave for London to start the Parliamentary session with a good [deal] of regret after a most happy and comfortable winter. . . .

Now comes the tug of war and awkward it may be with the Tory party disorganized and threatening civil war.

March 22 . . . My time has been mainly spent on the Royal Commission on the Civil Service over which I have taken a good deal of interest since returning to London, particularly as I should otherwise have been short of something to do. The Chairman – Lord McDonnell – a very decent old boy, but peppery and commonly nick-named the Bengal tiger, has quarrelled with a good many Commissioners and in particular Sir H. Primrose, an old and very able civil servant who, out of mere spite, is determined on a minority report. This I have been trying to avoid and have persuaded the majority to amend their report by incorporating all that is best in that of Sir H. Primrose. It is rather pitiful to see grown men quarrelling in disregard of public interest.

The Political Situation is most interesting and difficult. The Tories' threats of civil war over Ulster have clearly carried them further than they want to go and the more moderate and sensible appear to realise the danger.

April 10 . . . During the last three weeks we have had most exciting times in politics beginning on March 22nd or thereabouts when certain officers mainly in the cavalry stationed at the Curragh announced in reply to some stupid enquiries made by Sir Arthur Paget, the General Commanding in Ireland, that they would rather resign their commissions than suppress civil war in Ulster. The row appears to have begun in connection with some quite necessary strengthening of the garrisons at the depots in Ulster which was supposed – Heaven knows why – to be going to lead to an outbreak by the Orangemen. As a matter of fact it passed off quietly.

The officers in the Army are Tories almost to a man and no doubt the Tory party have calculated that if Ulster resists Home Rule by force the Army will refuse to support the Government, but on facing the position and having it pressed upon them that private soldiers might do likewise in case of strikes they have felt the grave danger resulting from a refusal of military obedience. This has made them more willing to attempt a settlement of the Irish question by consent which nearly everybody now wants, except perhaps some of the party leaders particularly A.J. Balfour and the old Tories who speak of Ireland as though it were 20 years ago.

Meanwhile owing to an extraordinary jumble at a Cabinet meeting – the story of which is scarcely credible and if believed indicates grotesque slackness of management – Seely has resigned his position and Asquith has taken the War Office in addition to the P. Mship. Sir John French and Sir J.S. Ewart have also resigned. The whole story is curious and I strongly suspect the origin of the trouble to be Winston who has great influence over Seely, a much weaker character.

Poor Mrs. Seely hated this association.

April 19 Spent this past week at home, things being very quiet in Parliament and my presence unnecessary to the Whips.

May 10 . . . Since I was last in Liverpool we have had a good deal of interest in Parliament including the more conciliatory speeches of Carson and Balfour in the Vote of Censure debate. The settlement of the Ulster question still seems to hang in the balance with conciliators and diehards on both sides.

During this time we have had a debate on Post Office servants (Holt Committee) when I made much the longest speech I have ever delivered in Parliament (1 hr. 20 mins) and with considerable success.

Nothing of note otherwise.

July 19 . . . In Parliament I have been active in what has been called the 'Holt Cave': really a combined remonstrance by business men and some survivors of the Cobden-Bright school of thought against the ill-considered and socialistic tendencies of the Government finance.

The financial proposals of the year were such as could not possibly be carried out on the score of time and the protest made by the group with which I acted and which compelled me to be spokesman and joint organizer was successful and ended by knocking a penny off the income tax.

We have certainly travelled a long way from the old Liberal principle of 'retrenchment' and I deeply regret it.

The more I see of socialistic developments the less I like them, the stronger I feel in favour of leaving individuals the maximum of personal freedom including the right to make a thorough mess of their own affairs.

The principals in the 'Cave' besides myself were Sir C. Nicholson, P.A. Molteno, A.G.C. Harvey and Sir G. Agnew. We may congratulate ouselves on having avoided bitterness. Indeed a great many of the Cabinet secretly agreed with us, inter alia McKenna and John Burns.

July 26 . . . Parliament quiet on account of the Buckingham Palace Conference, as to the Constitutionality of which there has been much misgiving.

THE LIBERAL CAVE-MEN;
OR, A HOLT FROM THE BLUE.

HARASSED CHANCELLOR. "IT'S NOT SO MUCH FOR MY FEET THAT I MIND—THEY'RE HARDENED AGAINST THIS KIND OF THING; BUT I DO HATE ROCKS ON MY HEAD."

Punch's view of the 'Holt Cave', 15 July 1914.

My own feeling is that under the circumstances the Government could not neglect any step which might produce an agreement, in which they failed, as we understand at present on account of Tyrone and Fermanagh as to which I never thought an agreement could be made.

On Thursday the Dock Board Bill was rejected on second reading on account of their refusal to recognise Trade Unions. I spoke and told in their favour but I am told that the fact that I explained that I had opposed at the Board their labour policy and advocated recognition was very prejudicial. But this could not be helped.

August 2   We are all in the midst of the most miserable alarm.

When I wrote last Sunday Austria had just started warlike proceedings against Servia by reason of the latter having given an only partially satisfactory reply to Austria's communication on the subject of the Pan-Servian agitation and the murders of the Archduke Franz Ferdinand and his wife. The reply of Servia was sufficiently humble and ought to have been the basis for a satisfactory settlement but Austria at once proceeded to arms.

Even a week ago we thought not much of it but now Russia is supporting Servia, Germany Austria and presumably France Russia. What England will do seems uncertain tho' it is almost impossible to believe that a Liberal Government can be guilty of the crime of dragging us into this conflict in which we are in no way interested.

The fear of war has produced a paralysis of business, the Bank Rate being advanced from 3 to 4% on Thursday, to 8% on Friday and 10% on Saturday, the Stock Exchanges in London and all the big towns being closed as also many of the produce exchanges.

Today an 'Echo' has been published (how these horrors benefit the press!) and we are told that Russia and Germany are actually at war.

The Admiralty here are taking up merchant vessels as fleet auxiliaries, the Alcinous for one.

The Home Rule controversy has been temporarily closed owing to the national peril in spite of the horrid business in Dublin last Sunday when the troops fired on a mob without orders killing 3 people.

August 9   Great European War. During the week all Europe has been involved in war or nearly so. Austria is at war with Servia and Russia, Germany with Russia, France, Belgium and Great Britain. This is certainly a most peculiar result of a quarrel between Austria and Servia and it seems incredible that Austria, Gt. Britain and France can remain long at peace while Austria's ally Germany, who is ostensibly fighting only in Austria's quarrel, is at war with the rest.

Italy has remained neutral judging Austria and Germany to be the aggressors.

I had thought we might and should have kept out of the war but when Germany decided on an unprovoked attack upon Belgium, whose neutrality Germany equally with ourselves had guaranteed, it seemed impossible for us to stand by. Germany has acted with great brutality and haste and is, in my judgement, the party mainly responsible for this war.

So far there is not much news. We have only had war for five days, but Germany has suffered a severe check from the Belgians in an unsuccessful attempt to take the fortified town of Liège.

August 12 . . . Parliamentary session adjourned for a fortnight on Monday on which day I was called back on account of a possible difficulty over Home Rule.

Lunched that day with Uncle Leonard and Aunt Kate who are both, as might be expected, much distressed about the war for which they blame Edward Grey – unreasonably in my opinion.

Business is going on fairly well and confidence seems to be gradually recovering.

August 28 . . . Nothing much doing in Parliament except emergency bills for dealing with various situations arising out of the war. Most of them would be better, I believe, if they had never seen the light of day, but at the moment there is a passion for doing something.

It is extraordinary to notice the change which has come over Parliament. The feeling almost unanimous and several bills passed through all stages by 6 o'clock which at any other time would take a couple of full days to get second reading alone.

The war progresses. Germany progresses on her western frontiers apparently by mere force of numbers suffering immense losses but gradually pushing the allies back. British troops have been engaged throughout the week at Mons and at Le Cateau on the left wing of the Allied line and have suffered severe loss – 2/3000 at the first and perhaps 10000 at the latter place, but they have held their ground. The whole thing is awful in its destruction of human life and happiness and due to nothing but the German desire to rule over everything by force.

August 30 On Saturday we had the cheering news that the British fleet had got in behind Heligoland and sunk 3 German cruisers and two destroyers, without losing a ship or indeed much loss of life to us.

This is good, showing great courage and skill on the part of our sailors and good gunnery, the essentials of success in naval warfare or indeed in anything else.

Then today we have an official statement from Lord Kitchener, now secretary of state for War as a non-politician – quite a constitutional innovation but in the present temper of the nation thoroughly sound – that the military position is not unsound and that though our losses are heavy those of the enemy are far heavier and their attack has for the present been discontinued.

September 4 Went to London on Monday morning for Parliament returning on Tuesday after a long, tiring day. Nearly had a row in H. of C. over a speech by A.J. Balfour on the Irish question which seemed quite needlessly provocative to the Home Rulers. Let us hope that this difficulty will be settled before we meet on September 9th.

No real news from the war except that the Anglo-French army after steady fighting has been forced back almost to Paris. The Russians appear to have been badly beaten by the Germans in East Prussia and to have won a great victory over the Austrians at Lemberg. As the latter have already been badly beaten by the Servians they have not made much out of their war, so far. In ordinary life things are going uneventfully and extraordinarily much as usual. A good many especially of the younger clerks have volunteered and are training. The labouring classes have not come forward so well partly on account of the not very liberal provision for their women kind.

There is too much talk of charity, a great encouragement to many not to help themselves.

September 26 Since I last wrote in this book I went first to London for Parliament, thence on September 9 to Abernethy, back on the night of Monday 14th to London and then on Thursday 17th to Liverpool. Parliament was prorogued on the 18th, the Home Rule and Welsh Disestablishment Bills becoming law under the Parliament Act but the operation of both being postponed by a short Act until after the war is over.

No great events have happened. The German advance in France is on the whole being pushed back, I am afraid with great slaughter on both sides.

Russia is defeating Austria who is apparently suffering considerable disasters in every direction, even at the hands of Servia.

Stanley Russell has enlisted in the Liverpool regiment (of comrades or 'pals') and seems likely to get a commission as there is a great shortage of officers.

September 29 Nothing further to chronicle except a spell of very fine weather. The war news comes to this, that the Germans are being very slowly pushed back in France, which as their project was to overwhelm France at once must be counted a defeat.

October 25 . . . Whether it is through the desire to encourage brought about by the war or for any other reason all the friends to whom I have sent venison have written unusually grateful letters.

During this week the German cruiser 'Emden' sunk our Troilus not far outside Colombo along with several other ships. This cruiser has done a great deal of damage and I must say the failure of the British Navy to bring any of the German marauding cruisers to action is not very creditable.

The war goes on as savagely as ever, without much prospect of an early end. Nothing of special note since my last entry.

November 1 Nothing fresh as to the war. Things drag on without coming to any very definite point.

On Monday I went up to Hexham to confer with the executive committee as to a very unfair attack made upon me by the Tory party at a time when there is supposed to be a political truce, returning the following day. The result is that I am to spend the present week addressing meetings in the constituency – a horrible waste of time.

November 2 ... Went to Hexham this afternoon and addressed meetings at Haltwhistle, Corbridge, Rothbury, Prudhoe and Haydon Bridge in the order named, one a night, returning late on Friday night and sleeping at Preston. Dull work, apparently to some extent successful as about 30 people were known to have enlisted immediately after the meetings.

Eliza stayed in Liverpool converting the house into a hospital which operation was complete when I returned on Saturday: very well done.

[November] ... During the time intervening between the two preceding entries I have been largely in London attending Parliament and the Royal Commission on the Civil Service, which is now completing its report on the Foreign Office and Diplomatic Service. ...

This house (54 Ullet Road) is now a hospital and contains 16 soldiers. 20 have been here but 4 are discharged. Very nice men mostly with arm and shoulder wounds and all able to walk.

The war is progressing slowly but favourably. Indeed the feeling in official circles in London is most optimistic.

But oh! What a horrible waste of good life, the best of the peoples, and also of the power of making life itself desirable.

December 12 ... On Thursday morning we all heard of the action off the Falkland Islands with the almost complete destruction of the German squadron. There are now only 3 small cruisers and about the same number of converted merchantmen left to worry us.

About 30 soldiers now in this hospital, the 3rd instalment of 15 being mostly invalids – frostbite and rheumatism.

December 31 ... 1914 has ended – a year which for us has been fair and happy in spite of the hideous catastrophe of the war in which so far none of ours has been lost or seriously injured. When the new troops get into the fighting line as they will do in the spring we can scarcely hope for an equal immunity.

1915

[In the course of 1915 it became increasingly clear that Britain would not be able to fight the War on the sort of limited scale which had been her traditional approach to landbased European conflicts. The diary contains increasingly regular and disillusioned references to the country's mounting casualty lists. For Holt the formation of a Coalition government in May was a turning point. By the end of the year the campaign for conscription was becoming irresistible. For purist Liberals such as Holt the two developments were inextricably linked – compulsion was the direct result of coalition and epitomised the dire consequences which inevitably followed from the prostitution of Liberal principles.]

January 3 ... We have decided to move into No. 52 till the hospital here is discontinued.

January 26 Since I wrote last we have had rather a broken time. From the fifth to the twelfth I was at Hexham addressing 'recruiting' meetings, the Tories having at last fallen into line with us.

On the whole it was a successful campaign, but very dull. Eliza stayed in Liverpool looking after the children and the move into Croxteth Gate.

Sunday the tenth I went over to Walter Runciman's nice place Doxford at Chathill and had a very pleasant visit.

Afterwards I had a visit to London on business and another trip to Hexham on January 23rd for the annual meeting of the Association.

January 31 . . . News today that a German submarine has sunk 3 merchant ships outside Liverpool – very disagreeable.

February 28 No very great news since my last entry. I have been attending Parliament during the short sittings of this month, staying at a flat in Whitehall Court (No. 150) which we have rented and where we are most comfortable.

The war has made but little progress, the most interesting event to us at any rate being the unsuccessful attempt of a submarine to destroy Laertes on her way to Holland. Capt. Propert stood on the bridge for 45 minutes under rifle and machine gun fire while dodging the submarine which finally missed its shot with a torpedo. This has attracted much attention and Capt. P. has been given the Distinguished Service Cross.

Today we are all interested in the attempt to force the Dardanelles to which may every success result.

I have been appointed on a committee of three with Tom Royden and Mr. Ernest Glover of London to advise the Admiralty on transports.

March 14 Another fortnight in London during which I have spent a good deal of time at the Admiralty on my advisory duties. So far we hardly appear to have done work worthy of the expenditure of time and nothing of great value can be done without a discussion of the naval and military requirements. . . .

War going fairly well without much great change.

March 21 Went to London on Monday evening returning on Thursday evening, so as to spend three days assisting the Admiralty. Nothing of importance during the week.

Today took Phil's children and Dorothy to see the troops march past Lord Kitchener in front of St. George's Hall . . . Terrible to think of so many fine young men going to get killed.

March 28 . . . Spent 3 days in London at the Admiralty. Nothing of interest in public or private life.

Made the hospital up to 40 beds, all filled last night.

April 4 Spent the middle of the week in London as is now necessary . . . .

The principal event of the week has been the torpedoing of the Elder Dempster boat, Falaba, by a German submarine with the loss of about 100 lives –

civilians, including women. This is sheer brutal murder intended to terrorise the people of this country in which it will fail.

Some idea that Holland may join us, but I doubt it.

April 11 . . . Our Theseus had a marvellous and very spirited escape from a submarine and was hit 5 times by shells.

May 16 . . . My time mainly spent at Admiralty with moderate satisfaction. Not really impressed with management of this great department.

On Friday 7th a German submarine torpedoed the Lusitania causing the loss of about 1500 lives – all civilians – amongst whom about 120 Americans . . . The result of this crime appears likely to go far and the American President has sent a very strong note to Germany. Unfortunately there has been an outbreak against Germans throughout the Empire: natural but not creditable, ending in mere pillage by ruffians.

General Botha appears to be scoring a big success in German S.W. Africa and has occupied its capital, Windhoek. What a testimony to Liberal principles and the good sense and statesmanship of old C.-B. Few men have done more for the Empire than Sir Henry Campbell-Bannerman. Without him South Africa must have been lost at this crisis.

Heard yesterday that my friend Harry Timmis had lost his only son in the war. . . . Too horrible and tens of thousands more must go the same way.

Played cricket yesterday – scored 3.

May 30 Since I last wrote . . . the Government has come to an end and a 'Coalition' Government is installed in its place.

Why this has happened is not clear to anyone. There has been a campaign in Lord Northcliffe's press, but that could not have produced the result, and a quarrel between Winston Churchill and Lord Fisher at the Admiralty. Liberal opinion is dissatisfied and many Liberal members including R.D.H. are vexed and suspicious. The P.M. attended an impromptu meeting of Liberal members on Wednesday 19th and alleged foreign affairs of an unrevealable character as his reason in a speech impressive but not ultimately convincing.

I do not believe the new government has more administrative capacity than the old – if anything the reverse – and it is real administrative capacity not any appearance of strength which matters now.

June 6 I should have mentioned that before going up to Abernethy I sold our carriage horse and during the past week I sold – practically gave away – the brougham and harness. This step was taken as a means of economising during war but it marks the end of horse traction in ordinary town life.

Last week in London does not augur well for the Coalition government. Suspicion that it is the result of a dirty intrigue is strong and the Liberal vexation and anxiety as to its future policy is most serious.

I return to London tomorrow when there will be some consultations between independent Liberal members.

June 20 Spent the last fortnight in London at the usual work: nothing very interesting to record. The Government and the House are settling down, the latter to watch the former rather in an anxious and puzzled frame of mind.

The unpleasant suspicions remain and it is obvious that the public has not been told the whole truth. Moreover the progress (or want thereof) in Flanders and the Dardanelles is not satisfactory. The expense is enormous and we cannot last at this pace for an indefinite time.

Have been associated for some time with a little group in the H. of C. organised by Sir C. Nicholson which he playfully calls the seven wise men: himself, J.W. Wilson, Russell Rea, Sir T. Whittaker, L. Jones, Murray McDonald, Falconer and myself to whom Sir F. Cawley and Middlebrook have now been added. We are meeting regularly and discussing the situation with a view to giving the Government a Liberal pull whenever possible.

Conscription has been talked of, but I am glad to think is at present abandoned.

Went up to Hexham on Friday 18th to see my committee and discuss position. Found all well.

July 4 . . . Nothing very fresh in politics. Still a great feeling of disquiet as to the capacity of the government. Russia is doing badly and the Allies generally not well, yet the issues are so vital that we cannot afford to lose.

July 11 Went up to London last Monday early to take part in debate on National Register Bill. Did not get called by the Speaker, which was rather a surprise as I quite understood I was to second Sir T. Whittaker's motion for the rejection of the bill.

The Bill was carried by a large majority after definitely anti-conscriptionist declarations by the P.M. (at question time) and McKenna who closed the debate.

Have taken a room at Nat. Liberal Club till end of July. How I hate being in London alone.

General war news rather better. German S.W. Africa completely conquered by General Botha and forces of Union of S. Africa. What a tribute to the statesmanship of C.B. and to the Liberal as opposed to the Prussian spirit.

July 18 Spent this week as last. Nothing of interest in Parliament or in public affairs.

August 1 In London from Monday to Thursday, during which time Parliament adjourned till the middle of September.

Nothing of special interest except that the Germans are evidently on the point of obtaining possession of Warsaw.

August 5 I have just come back from a couple of days in London spent on the Admiralty business . . . Tomorrow I go to Scotland – hurrah!

One feels just a little ashamed of going off to enjoy oneself when there is so much misery and sorrow in the world, but clearly there is no use in increasing the sum of wretchedness by making myself and others uncomfortable for no good purpose.

We had all better keep fit and ready for whatever may turn up.

September 5 . . . Nothing of interest has happened except that Alfred Holt and Co. have bought seven steamers from Royden and their interest in the China–New York trade for a prodigious sum of £750,000. This deal I negotiated with Tom Royden at the Admiralty on his overture and trust it may be successful for us . . . Nothing fresh from the war. Russian reverses the regular thing.

September 9 Returned from London by the dining train having gone there by the corresponding train on Monday. The object of the visit was of course attendance at the Transport Department of the Admiralty.

During my stay in London there were two so-called raids by the Zeppelins, or air ships, the first about midnight on the Tuesday when damage was done along the south of the Thames up to the Old Kent Road and the second about 10.30 on Wednesday. I was dining with the Courtneys, the only other guest being Fischer Williams. When in the drawing room after dinner our conversation was interrupted by the noise of guns, but we really saw nothing though we quite understood what was happening and took the prudent course of sitting tight in the drawing room till the event was over. Going outside only incurred the risk of injury from the falling missiles of the anti-aircraft guns without the most remote prospect of advantage. The Zeppelin passed over Waterloo station where, I am told, a little damage was done to Liverpool Street Station where a good deal was done, incidentally starting a substantial fire in a warehouse near St. Pauls which was clearly visible from the Embankment after I had returned to the National Liberal Club. Several people were killed – eight I understand – in an omnibus which was struck by a bomb. The sum of these two air raids is that about 20 people were killed and 180 in all killed or injured of whom 5 were soldiers. It is murder not warfare.

My sensation during the firing was exactly what I feel in a thunderstorm – a dread of sudden death which one knows it is absurd to permit to interfere with any important action and I believe I act accordingly. The advantage was with the firing for it is not accompanied by any electrical disturbance in the atmosphere.

September 19 London in the middle of last week as usual, but nothing of fresh interest there.

In politics the conscriptionists are supposed to be intriguing behind the scenes and are openly trying to push their most objectionable policy to which the whole Labour movement appears likely to offer violent opposition.

During the week our Antilochus fought a German submarine off the coast of Algeria and we believe sank her. Capt. Flynn is very confident on that score.

September 25 . . . I was in London from Monday to Friday attending Parliament and my other duties. McKenna introduced his Budget in a very clear and able speech.

October 24 Went up to London on Tuesday morning returning on Thursday evening. Spent most of the time in discussing Clauses of Finance Bill which impose customs duties without corresponding excise. A curious suggestion from a Free Trade Ch. of Exchequer against which I voted steadily.

We are getting into a great mess financially and I fear we are spending money much too fast as compared with the military result.

November 7 I was in London as usual during the middle of the week. On Tuesday Asquith made a statement as to the War, in particular with regard to the Gallipoli expedition which must now be regarded as a failure. Generalship there has probably been bad and I cannot believe that the original attack without any military force, thereby warning the Turks to fortify the whole peninsula, was justifiable. Carson spoke explaining his resignation and did not raise himself in public opinion. His idea of compelling Greece to join us was felt to be monstrous. The Government's position is very strong as tho' no one thinks them really competent no alternative appears tolerable, least of all Carson or Lloyd George.

[November 15] . . . E.L.H. returned to Liverpool on the Tuesday, myself on Thursday on which day the Royal Commission on the Civil Service signed its final report and came to an end. Whether any result will happen from its labours, having regard to the war, is, I think, very doubtful.

November 28 I spent last week in London going up on Monday and returning on Friday night. Nothing much doing, except the usual routine of small matters at the Transport Dept. where I really spend most of my time when in London.

December 26 I went up to London again on Monday and on Tuesday took part in the debate on the motion to raise the Army from 3 to 4 million men, speaking against the proposal and warning the Government and the House against the financial and commercial disaster likely to ensue from the further abstraction of labour from industry. Several others spoke in the same sense and I think we made a stir, but of course the vote was carried.

December 31 . . . 'Give peace in our time, Oh Lord!' is the lesson of the year. Yet I feel no certainty of peace by the end of 1916.

1916

[At the beginning of 1916 Holt was prominent among those Liberals who tried vainly to oppose the government's conscription bill, looking for a lead to Sir John Simon, who had resigned as Home Secretary over the issue – 'there are all the elements of a first rate Liberal party and for months we have only wanted a leader.' With increasing intensity Holt came to feel that the War was demanding unacceptable measures of encroachment by the state. One area of particular concern to him was the merchant navy. To Walter Runciman he complained that 'the mercantile marine will step by step become controlled entirely by the Government . . . whereas, as you know, I regard with intense dislike the interference with the freedom of individuals.' Not surprisingly, while the popular mood remained dominated by patriotic support for the government, Holt's increasingly critical attitude began to cause concern in his constituency. The disaffection which had first arisen over Holt's attitude to the budget of 1914 naturally increased. As early as January 1916 the Chairman of the Hexham Liberal Association warned Holt of the dangers he was running. 'I have no doubt you will give good reasons for your attitude towards the [Conscription] Bill which is perfectly consistent with the principles you have always advocated. It is impossible, however, to get the public to give a full, fair and calm consideration to such principles just now. Personally I have a good deal of sympathy with your point of view but I am bound to say that the general tendency appears to be in the opposite direction.'

Holt shed no tears at the fall of Asquith's government in December. In his view it freed true Liberals from the tainting constraints of association with an alien political philosophy. He was now completely disillusioned with Lloyd George, whose views seemed to have turned full circle from pre-war days when he had been a standard bearer of Liberal Radicalism.]

January 2 The year opens with a gale and every prospect of political disturbance for the Prime Minister has let it be known that he has adopted the policy of conscription towards which the Tories have been pressing him for the past twelve months.

January 9 I went up to London on Monday. My energies have been transferred from the Transport Dept. to a special Committee on Admiralty expenditure of which Herbert Samuel is chairman and of which the only other member is Sir G. Franklin of Sheffield, late of the National Telephone Co.

On Wednesday and Thursday we debated the Conscription bill, Sir J. Simon, who resigned the Home Secretaryship on the question, leading the opposition. There was a good deal of excitement and I thought the opponents made out a case (I was one of them) but sentimentality and fear of defeating the Government carried the day and we were defeated by 403 to 105. I told for the minority and also spoke. I had hoped for a better show but several of our friends failed us at the last moment including dear J.W. Wilson. Chas. Hobhouse who was very strong against conscription most unaccountably went back on us, made an inconclusive speech and abstained.

January 16 Came home on Thursday. We debated the Conscription bill on Tuesday and Wednesday when the Irish deserted us and some others and the division was 431 to 39. I did not speak but voted of course.

February 4 I have got behind with my chronicle mainly because instead of coming home for the week end of January 23rd E.L.H. came up to London and we stayed there.

During this visit we took a house – 39 Cadogan Place – for next season. It seems a very nice house but I wonder what the season will be like and whether we shan't find we have wasted our money.

The little group who had opposed conscription formed themselves into a permanent organisation – Sir J. Simon, chairman, Whitehouse, secretary, J.H. Thomas, the railway men's representative, Leif Jones and R.D.H. committee.

Last Monday night the Zeppelins made a raid over England which is supposed to have been aimed at Liverpool tho' they got no nearer than Crewe. As usual a considerable number of civilians (some 60) were killed including many women and children and no object of importance achieved.

It is simply murder.

February 13 A whole week in Liverpool undisturbed. Such a relaxation. Friday was O.S.S. Co. annual meeting when we announced a bonus of 10% in addition to the dividend already paid of 25%. The shareholders were so pleased. Steamers' earnings £1,250,000.

February 20 Went up to London on Tuesday morning, dining that night at Sir J. Simon's. The other guests L. Jones, J.H. Thomas, J.H. Whitehouse (M.P.s). Afterwards a reception of anti-conscriptionists – altogether very pleasant. . . .

Thursday afternoon deputation of Dock owners to P.M.: very large, but not very successful. The speaking poor and diffuse and Lord Devonport, a persona ingratissima, getting to loggerheads with P.M.

March 12 For the week end of February 27th E.L.H. and I went to Hexham to see our political friends, staying at the Hydro. We had quite a satisfactory visit and I think allayed the anxiety which my independence in Parliament had caused. . . .

On Thursday the 9th I made a Free Trade speech in H. of C. on which I have been much congratulated. It followed on one by J.M. Robertson and to both the P.M. gave a friendly and fairly satisfactory reply.

April 27 . . . Grace and I returned [from the Lake District] on Monday as I had to go up to the 'secret' session of Parliament on Tuesday.

Before the Low Wood visit she and I had been to Dundee where she christened the Troilus: a most successful launch. A[lfred] H[olt] and Co. have taken an interest in the Caledon yard and provided money for an extension and improvements.

The 'secret' session of Parliament was really very absurd as no 'secret' was revealed which any intelligent man did not know before. The only thing which the government could not have said openly was that France was insolvent and relying upon us for finance. This has long been obvious but could scarcely be stated publicly by Government.

The proposal to raise more soldiers in this country appears to me extraordinarily foolish. What we ought to do is to husband our resources and make sure that we can last the course.

At the end of March our Achilles homeward bound from Australia was torpedoed and sunk in the Bay of Biscay. Four men killed – a brutal murder –

but I am afraid Capt. Edmondson was not very alert.

April 30 At church this morning heard that General Townshend had been obliged to surrender with 10,000 men at Kut-el-Amara on the Tigris after a siege of over 140 days. I wonder if this will give the Government the quietus they deserve.

It seems hardly possible that public opinion will not be moved.

May 7 Went to London on Monday returning on Friday. Rather a hard week over the second reading of the second or wider Conscription bill.

On Thursday I moved the rejection of the bill on second reading, Lees Smith seconding. We had a good debate – so we thought – and made a good show. L. George made a very wild speech, throwing all considerations of financial prudence to the winds. The Liberal wobblers were much alarmed but of course they voted for the Coalition.

I see I have made no record of the revolt in Dublin: a very foolish and wicked affair. Birrell felt himself bound to resign and I suppose he was. A most attractive man and a real Liberal but I have thought for some time past that he was becoming too cynical and careless.

May 29 Have been in London since my last entry. Nothing fresh to record. We worked away steadily against the conscription bill without producing any appreciable result upon it. On the other hand I do think we helped to make it less popular.

June 7 The day following my last entry E.L.H. and I went to London. That evening Stephen Hobhouse, whose wife is in Northampton gaol for distributing anti-conscription leaflets, came to dinner . . . S.H. quite a fanatic but his wife has been abominably treated.

On Thursday June 1st I made a speech in H. of C. on the treatment of anti-conscriptionists. The best thing I have yet managed. . . .

On Saturday heard of North Sea battle which at first was made to appear a defeat for us but appears to have been a victory.

Then on yesterday afternoon heard of Lord Kitchener's death in the Hampshire. It is curious how much the public estimation of that man exceeds that of the circles most nearly connected with Government which for months past have been talking of how to get rid of him.

It was supposed that when he went to the Mediterranean it was an excuse to get him out of office but that he frustrated it by taking the seals with him.

June 19 . . . Nothing to record here. The Russians are apparently making real progress against the Austrians on their S.W. front and we are all expecting a big attack by the British on the West. Pray God if it comes my brother Philip may get through safely. I fear terrible loss of life.

August 6 Since my last entry we have been almost entirely in London and are now looking forward to our summer holiday at Abernethy.

There has been fierce fighting at the front. Just before it began my brother Philip was slightly wounded and sent home so that he was out of the worst fighting. George Herdman, a curious but talented lad, was killed as also Pete Melly and many other Liverpool boys. It is all too horrible and one doubts if any military success can repay us for the loss of life.

Work in Parliament has been interesting but severe. All the old principles of the Liberal party have been virtually abandoned by its leaders – even Free Trade – and the Home Rule settlement of Ireland to which the Nationalists and Ulstermen had agreed was torn up at the last moment by the English Tories.

The betrayal has been cruel. War seems to arouse so many bad passions that Liberalism cannot live in its atmosphere. Let us have peace as soon as possible.

September 5 . . . The war has been dragging on a rather weary course but during the last fortnight Rumania has entered on our side which probably puts both Austria and Bulgaria in a precarious position. This evening I go to London to look after my work at the Admiralty.

Affairs at India Buildings are flourishing marvellously. No wonder those who are suffering severe loss through the war are casting envious eyes on the shipowners and other small classes who are making great profits.

September 24 . . . The fighting on the Somme goes on with steady Allied gains, but no dramatic coup.

I have spent mid-weeks in London on Admiralty business.

November 12 The last fortnight has been spent mainly in London, E.L.H. coming up for a long week end to consider taking a permanent residence there and to inspect houses for the purpose. Nothing has been arranged tho' we much liked a house in Lowndes Square, No. 63. . . .

Politically there is nothing to record. The war drags on its weary course. Nothing much happens on the western front except slaughter, largely I understand because the wet weather has made operations impossible and also from an insufficiency of guns for an attack at a second point.

There is some anxiety as to our food position. Poor crops in England and France due to the taking of agriculturalists for fighting, failure in N. America and scarcity of shipping to bring everything from Australia.

November 26 . . . During the last fortnight I have been mostly in London . . . .

I have been doing curious work at the Admiralty, investigating ship builders' claims for accelerating the delivery of war ships and, with Mr. Baddeley, the assistant secretary, actually settling them. The ship-building dept. of the Admiralty appears to be in great confusion.

Fancy any ordinary institution allowing an absolute stranger, such as I am, to settle what payments they are to make to their contractors.

December 10 . . . Again I have spent a fortnight in London and such a fortnight. The coalition government destroyed from within by an infamous conspiracy between Lloyd George, Bonar Law and the Northcliffe press.

The newspapers will give the facts. I am overjoyed at finding the Liberal leaders almost to a man free from the Coalition and its degrading compromises and I believe the mass of the Liberal party in the H. of C. are not really sorry.

L.G. has behaved scandalously and the section of Liberals he takes with him are certainly not men conspicuous for their character. The new administration is essentially Tory: the Labour element – got in by heavy bribery – will in all probability prove a negligible factor.

Think of the Marconi business. L.G. is now surrounded by men who slandered him, having betrayed those who strained their consciences to protect him. Think of 'Limehouse' and the Budget.

I wonder how it will turn out. My prophecy is Peace followed by Tariff Reform.

Things are not going well over the war.

Have bought a house in London – No. 63 Lowndes Square.

Today Colonel Bullock, Unitarian Minister at Ottawa, Col. of Canadian infantry, preached in our church as he did last Sunday when I was absent: another unexpected event – in Khaki. A good sermon, of practical religion.

[end 1916] . . . The year 1916 will be regretted by few if any. There has been much private sorrow through the heavy fighting of the war and the general results of the fighting have been less satisfactory to the Allies than had been hoped and particularly the collapse of Rumania during the late autumn. But the prospects for next year are in every way better and we ought to win thro'.

Moreover the Germans etc. are evidently feeling the pressure of the blockade, whence their desire for peace which I venture to think will be concluded before mid-summer.

1917

[In 1917, with prospects of outright victory apparently receding, war weariness became a characteristic feature of a much wider spectrum of opinion than hitherto. Since late 1916 Holt had been giving serious thought to the idea of a negotiated peace and he bitterly resented Lloyd George's continuing pursuit of a 'knock-out blow'. But Holt and like-minded M.P.s looked in vain to Asquith to take the lead in opposing the government in parliament. The apparent apathy of Liberal ex-ministers on the vital questions of the day caused him as much anguish as did the attitude of the government itself. Much of Holt's energy was therefore directed towards such journals as the weekly *Common Sense*.

Not surprisingly Holt was very enthusiastic about the famous Lansdowne Letter published at the end of the year, which gave a great boost to the 'peace by negotiation' movement. He was among those who signed an Address of Thanks to Lansdowne in recognition of his lead in the cause of peace. As Holt proclaimed, 'By this great act of leadership he has immensely lightened the burden of others who feel they ought no longer to be silent on the most urgent question of our national life.' F.W. Hirst even drew up the details of a prospective alternative cabinet to be headed by Lansdowne with Holt at the Exchequer.

By December Holt was involved in moves to organise an effective parliamentary opposition despite Asquith's reluctance to lead it. In doing so, he was fully aware that this might have fatal consequences for his position at Hexham. 'You, in the constituencies, will have to decide whether you will support that opposition or a Conservative with dabs of Socialism Government.' Deprived of the opportunity to explain himself to a public meeting of his constituents, Holt set out his views in a letter to a local newspaper. His statement that Britain should have no desire to deny Germany her place among the great commercial communities of the world was bound to cause serious offence. As the local party chairman warned: 'It may seem quite harmless to you, but in the event of an early election I can conceive of a great deal being made of it and that it could be used not fairly perhaps but very successfully against your candidature.'

Another of Holt's concerns at this time was the question of electoral reform. He had worked for the Proportional Representation Society since before the War and now took a prominent role in parliament in discussions on the Representation Bill. Not all Liberals, however, yet recognised how crucial the absence of proportional representation would be to the party's future prospects.]

January 14   . . . In public affairs the principal interest has been the exchange of notes and manifestoes on the subject of peace. The statement of their terms made by the Allies to President Wilson has met with general approval and seems to me distinctly reasonable and good.

January 21   . . . Heard this week that I had been chosen Treasurer of the Free Trade Union in place of Sir A. Mond, retired on joining the L.G. Government and now a protectionist more or less.

February 4   On Saturday went with E.L.H. and G.D.H. to Hexham and interviewed the Executive Committee, I think satisfactorily, and we are now to take steps to secure the seat. . . .

Friday was O.S.S.Co.'s annual meeting – satisfactory with remarkable results. No wonder those who suffer in money as well as personal sacrifice feel grudgingly towards those to whom war has brought a fortune.

February 11   . . . On Friday . . . E.L.H. and I dined with Courtneys. Present Mr and Mrs. C.P. Trevelyan, Hirst and Ramsay MacDonald. Pleasant but our fellow guests (and indeed our hosts) if not pro-German are too anti-English for my taste. . . .

On Saturday went to an adult suffrage meeting at Kingsway Hall and heard an excellent speech from Simon . . . Nothing of interest in Parliament this week.

February 18   . . . Nothing very important in Parliament. Generally speaking the Government has not come well out of the debates and their Parliamentary ability is manifestly inferior to that of their opponents, or rather of those who are not included in the Government. . . .

On Friday E.L.H. and I dined with Sir J. Simon at 36 Eccleston Square, meeting C.P. Trevelyans and R.C. Lamberts and all had a very pleasant evening. Simon propounded the excellent idea that Asquith should move resolutions in H. of C. adopting the recommendations of the Speakers Conference on electoral etc. reform. I hope it may come off. If Asquith would attend the H. of C. with half the assiduity of Pringle, encourage his friends and intervene when a favourable opportunity offered, in a fortnight he would be master of the place and put an end to the L.G. villainy.

March 11 I am afraid I shall never be a diarist, as last weekend I quite forgot my diary and the week before E. and I were in Liverpool. . . .

On Wednesday 7th I gave a Free Trade dinner at H. of C. Earl Beauchamp, Lord Ashton of Hyde, Sir C. Hobhouse, McKinnon Wood, Sir J. Simon, Sir W. Runciman, Sir J. Barlow, Sir Swire Smith, Sir C. Nicholson, Sir G. Toulmin, J.W. Wilson, J. Brunner, E.T. John, T.C. Taylor, Wiles, R.C. Lambert, Shortt, Pringle, Chas. Roberts, Arnold, J.M. Robertson, N. Buxton, Leif Jones, all MPs, were the guests. A successful evening.

Nothing of very great interest in Parliament except perhaps the Irish debate and row on Wednesday. L.G. has quarrelled with them and he certainly made a miserable speech equally defective in matter and manner.

April 1 Somehow or other my entries are always being left to a time of leisure which never arrives. I have been in London fairly hard at work during these last 3 weeks except that last weekend was spent in Liverpool.

There have been one or two interesting things in Parliament particularly the debate on the electoral reform Conference when Asquith did move a resolution adopting the compromise and pronounced himself in favour of women's suffrage. This ought to make us sure of a good and comprehensive Reform Bill especially as the large vote in favour of the resolution makes it impossible to attach any authority to a Parliament elected on the present franchise and registration laws.

The advance of the British and French armies in France and the capture of Baghdad are good features which should help to a satisfactory peace, but I am not sure that the revolution in Russia is not better. A liberal Russia should make an autocratic and militarist Germany impossible. The bad feature of these times is the success of the submarines against merchant shipping and the consequent danger to our food supplies, much aggravated by the poor potato crop of last year and the bad winter which has kept back all farming operations, still further impeded by shortage of men.

April 15 On Thursday 5th E.L.H. and I went down to Hexham and spent Easter there travelling on to Liverpool on the Tuesday . . . Our friends appeared to be in good humour and were certainly very kind and affable.

April 22 . . . During the week heard that Frank Seely, our friend General Seely's eldest son, had died of wounds at the front. It is cruel to have all these lads killed.

On the resumption of the H. of C. we had an excellent debate on the suppression of the foreign circulation of the 'Nation' newspaper. I believe the vast majority of the House condemned this absurd interference with the free expression of opinion but a division was staved off by the loquacity of those who are afraid of beating the Govt. and having to face a general election.

The scarcity of food is getting serious. Potatoes are very scarce, the crop having been unusually bad, and people like ourselves are pressed to leave them to the less well to do. Wheat flour is short and we are urged to use substitutes which do not exist and we are threatened with the destruction of live stock because there is no food for them.

April 29 . . . The German submarine attacks are getting worse. We are losing more merchant ships week by week and our Navy does not appear to be getting any grip of the submarine.

May 13 . . . The secret session did not advance us very much: the Government gave a sanguine view of the submarine and food supply questions but admitted complete uncertainty as to how the Russian position will develop. This is a grave question. At present it looks as if the Russians are unable to fight this year and probably unwilling to continue the war. If so, our military position is very difficult as the Germans become free to concentrate all their troops in the West.

During the past fortnight we have lost two ships at the hands of the submarines: the Troilus, the new steamer launched by Grace at Dundee a year ago sunk a day after leaving Glasgow on her first voyage going out by the N. of Ireland and the Calchas homeward bound from America. Very vexing.

May 28 . . . Nothing very much in politics. The Reform Bill was read a second time on Wednesday last by a huge majority. Nothing much in the way of speaking.

June 4 . . . A temporary lull in the war except for heavy fighting on the Austro-Italian front. I gather we are shortly to have another great British attack on the north of the line but perhaps rumour is a lying jade.

June 16 . . . I have been here since Sunday, to take part in Parliament where the Reform Bill has been under discussion and many other interesting things. . . .

The prophecy of a British attack in the north proved true and we have apparently won a great victory at Messines with some chance of a further advance there.

On Wednesday last there was an air raid on London in which much damage was done in the city and East end. I was at the Temple station at the time and saw one of the aeroplanes very high up. My fears were greatly assuaged by finding myself next to Rawlinson, the member for Cambridge University, as I realised that death would almost surely make a pair. Swire's office narrowly escaped, a building at the corner of Fenchurch Street being wrecked.

July 8 Yesterday morning there was another air raid with fortunately much less loss of life though I hear more damage to property. I was at Hyde Park Corner at the time (about 10.30) and promptly took refuge in the Tube – the safest place I could think of. The aeroplanes were visible across Hyde Park flying low and our guns were firing shrapnel at them but I gather made no hits tho' some (4?) were destroyed off the Coast. . . .

Parliament has had much of interest before it. The Reform Bill has got a long way through committee with most of its important provisions safe except Proportional Representation which was rejected last Wednesday by 32 votes.

July 22 Hurried out of bed by false alarm of air raid. All took shelter in basement. Much noise convinced us that some bombs were falling close to but now, 4 p.m., we believe there were none nearer than Essex. . . .

E.L.H. and I spent last week end in Liverpool. We have settled to close the hospital at the end of September and transfer Croxteth Gate to L.D.H.

Government is going badly. On all sides they have few friends but everyone is still afraid to turn them out when they cannot see who will replace them. The regular Liberal opposition are getting rather bolder, which is a good sign. There has been little fresh in the fighting. Russia made a successful attack but it came to an early end and apparently the Russians will not now fight except for the section under Brousiloff's personal leadership.

The political crisis in Germany and change of Chancellors does not tell any very clear tale, but apparently the militarists remain in possession subject to accepting a Pacifist formula.

July 29 Nothing very particular during the week. I have been chosen one of the members of the House of Commons Committee on expenditure of which Herbert Samuel is to be Chairman.

On Wednesday E.L.H. and Grace dined at the House where we made up a pleasant party with Shortt, Leif Jones and C. Trevelyan. Shortt was very full of his Committee on Medical re-examination which has exposed a great scandal and led to a complete surrender by War Office on the subject of recruiting.

October 29 There has been nothing of much interest since we came to London but tonight (11 p.m.) we are warned of an Air raid which means that as it is a moonlight night a squadron of German aeroplanes is on the way to scatter death right and left at haphazard amongst the peaceful citizens of London. So far their raids have done very little damage – indeed where people have kept under cover almost none.

A week ago I had a small party at H. of C. to say goodbye to Simon who has joined the Army as Intelligence Officer in the Air Corps. I think a great mistake when independent and able men are so much wanted both in Parliament and the Law Courts.

November 1 2 a.m. Just as we were getting into bed about 11.30 last night came the warning of an air raid since when we have been sitting up in the lower rooms more or less dressed and more or less courageous. Some played patience, some read.

Guns made a great noise and our own shells seemed to be bursting right above the house. We thought we heard an aeroplane but did not distinguish any bombs exploding. Now (2.15 a.m.) it seems to have stopped.

November 22 This raid did very little damage – a few bombs dropped about Streatham where some half dozen people were killed, but all the disturbance was our own guns. . . .

In public affairs we must note a growing spirit of oppression by the Tory-jingo knock out blow lot. Yesterday they decided to deprive conscientious objectors of their votes. A day or two before that no pamphlets were to be published about war or peace without the Censor's permit. It is a black outlook.

Affairs in Russia and Italy are very bad. The bright side is the failure of the submarine menace and the recent victory in France leading us almost to Cambrai.

December 3 Had a hard week in H. of C. with Reform bill which we finished except for Irish redistribution. Had several pretty straight party divisions principally on Alternative vote. Tories with assistance of a few bad Liberals disfranchised conscientious objectors – an abominable piece of persecution and intolerance. Very fine speech by Lord Hugh Cecil on this subject. Asquith failed to turn up and our front bench did nothing causing scandal and offence to many earnest Liberals.

On Tuesday I had a small party at House to discuss situation. Leif Jones, Sir C. Seely, Sir W. Collins, G. Collins, Bliss, Nuttall, Arnold, Brunner, Haydn Jones, Molteno and one or two others. All very dissatisfied, decided to welcome 'intelligent, patriotic and active opposition'. Thursday had a confabulation with Walter Runciman, McK. Wood, L. Jones and Pringle as to starting something like opposition. All very anxious to land Reform Bill safely before having a big row.

This day came out Lord Lansdowne's letter in Daily Telegraph and of course it is the subject of conversation. I hope it will lead to reason in our Government. It will certainly let loose a lot of tongues.

[On 29 November the *Daily Telegraph* published a letter from the Conservative elder statesman, Lord Lansdowne, in which the former Foreign Secretary, articulating a growing mood of war weariness in the country, called for a compromise peace before the belligerent powers destroyed their own societies in the illusory quest for outright victory: '. . . its prolongation will spell ruin for the civilised world, and an infinite addition to the load of human suffering which already weighs upon it.']

December 17 . . . The Lansdowne letter of course made a hubbub. The Northcliffe and Knock out press and individuals furious, but the moderate men have plucked up a lot of courage and are stating their opinions. Some amongst us – Leif Jones, Sir W. Collins, J.W.W. Brunner, C.E. Price, Shaw, Bliss, Rendall and self went to Asquith and I think impressed him. At any rate his Birmingham speech went a long way in the Lansdowne direction. Have done something myself towards organizing an H. of C. debate in support of the L[ansdowne] policy in which the Runciman coterie mentioned above – now joined by G. Lambert – are also movers.

Several good debates in H. of C. We are picking up our courage.

December 24 ... The last few days in London were quite interesting. On Tuesday there was an air raid about 7 p.m. which caused an adjournment of the H. of C. for about 3 hours, effectually stopping discussion on the non-ferrous metals bill. I don't think much damage was done. A bomb was dropped in Hemmerde's chambers in the Temple at the time (or nearly so) when he was making a speech in H. of C. in favour of fair treatment for Germans. On Wednesday we had a War Aims debate opened by Sir W. Collins at the instigation of the Runciman group above referred to and it was very successful in the way of expressing reason and moderation. Unluckily, through a misunderstanding – partly my fault – Ponsonby spoke second, as usual expressing extreme ideas and Balfour, who was seedy, at once replied to him only. After that the moderates spoke, ending up with Runciman, and Robert Cecil gave a satisfactory wind up, disclaiming Carson's extravagances. More courage is wanted, but I hope the small party we have pulling together may be the nucleus of better things.

On Thursday Ll. George was very 'piano' – got a bad reception, quite icy. Asquith also moderate.

December 26 We really did have a very pleasant Xmas under the circumstances, but what with war, family disputes and dispersions it was a mere shadow. There is not a young man in the place and only quite little boys.

December 30 ... The important news of the last few days lies in the Russo-German peace negotiations. Germany appears for the first time to have really offered the evacuation of Belgium etc. Peace ought not to be impossible for clever negotiators.

December 31 End of 1917, a year of sorrow and disappointment. When will it all be over? And what sort of a country will it be to live in? Things look bad for the class we belong to. We are likely to see all sorts of queer economic experiments by the poorer classes in the name of social equality.

1918

[Despite deriving momentary encouragement from Lloyd George's famous speech to the T.U.C. on 5 January, in which the Prime Minister appeared to accept the goal of a Wilsonian-type peace, Holt continued to find himself estranged from majority opinion over the conduct of the War. By the end of January he had agreed with the local Liberal party in Hexham that he would seek a new constituency at the next election, although no formal announcement was made until later in the year. From the pages of *Common Sense* Holt called for a coalition of all who wished to explore the possibility of a peace by negotiation, and an important meeting of Lansdowne's supporters was held at the Essex Hall in February. But in the atmosphere of the time it was only too easy for extreme Nationalists such as Lord Northcliffe to dub Holt and those who thought like him as 'pro-German.' Holt's other great problem was that his group lacked the leadership of a nationally respected figure. Asquith continued to maintain an equivocal attitude towards Lloyd George's government, even though Holt made a personal appeal to him to take the lead especially over the question of the further extension of conscription. 'What ought to be done now', wrote Holt to John Simon, 'is to organise the overthrow of the present Government.' But this was a step which Asquith seemed reluctant even to contemplate. For Holt on the other hand opposition at this time was a question of principle, irrespective of the consequences: 'L.G. is ruining the country and, whether we can stop him or not, do let us try.']

January 2 Went to Hexham in the afternoon staying at the Hydropathic . . . Quite pleasant and people reasonable enough and not disagreeing materially from my views about peace, but I found a certain dissatisfaction with my conduct as their representative which I felt unreasonable and based mainly on incorrect reports of what I have said.

No personal unfriendliness. Also a general conviction that I cannot get returned. No doubt many Liberals are drifting to the Labour party, bitten with the idea of state interference and as a consequence of the destruction of political interest due to the so-called party truce and the infernal coalition.

January 13 . . . In public affairs during the week we have the report of Lloyd George's speech to the Trades Union delegates on Saturday, Jan. 5th when he abandoned the Knock-out blow policy against which I spoke in Oct. 1916 and indicated reasonable terms of peace. A great step forward, to which I think the debate of Dec. 19th in H. of C. (which I organized principally) was a great contributing cause.

There is also a growing scarcity of food due to the foolish attempts to regulate prices in order to please the wage earning classes. Butter etc. has become almost non-existent, at least so they say. The main cause of trouble is the over swollen army. There are not enough left to do the work at home.

January 20 I went up to London on Monday morning . . . Tuesday and Wednesday were strenuous days in the Committee stage of the non-ferrous metals bill and I got tired, but it was great fun. Leif Jones, Hemmerde and I did most of the fighting. C. Hobhouse, Runciman and J.M. Robertson helping. Came to Liverpool on Friday morning and right glad to be at home again.

January 28 Rather a tiring week in London as I was a little under the weather with a narrow escape from influenza. I returned on Thursday. No great news. Spent week end trying to fix up local leadership of Liberal party for which Wilfred Stoddart appears the most likely.

Today E.L.H. goes to Hexham for a Women's Liberal meeting and I to London. E.L.H. now head of American Red Cross here and correspondingly engrossed and busy.

February 7   When I got up to London on Jan. 28th I found an air raid and a bad one in progress and starting to walk home was in Shaftesbury Avenue as the second attack began and entering Leicester Square station as bombs were dropped in Covent Garden. However we did not suffer. Found a very empressé invitation to lunch from Mrs. Asquith, so accepted for Feb. 1st. Had the option of previous and subsequent Wednesdays and really it was very pleasant. Guests besides ourselves, Sir Algernon West, Bishop of Southwark, Mr and Mrs. Paget Hedges and a Mrs. Bridges, wife of a General.

February 21   . . . Parliament opened next day [February 12] and we spent the week on the Address. On Wednesday I moved an amendment censuring the political conclusions of the Versailles Council which produced many good speeches entirely against the Government. Balfour who spoke in defence was extraordinarily bad – did not know what Count Czernin had said or what the Versailles Council had decided. Division poor, spoilt by folly of Charles Trevelyan who eulogised rantingly Trotsky and the Bolsheviks. . . .

Sir W. Robertson dismissed [as Chief of the Imperial General Staff]. The Prime Minister again wriggles out of a tight place because no one is ready with a satisfactory successor. Austen Chamberlain made a powerful intervention with a strong condemnation of the connection between the Government and the press.

I stick to my view that we cannot prosper with a Prime Minister who is universally recognized as a liar and a treacherous fellow.

March 17   . . . I to London, meeting – by hazard – Lord Beauchamp at Worcester with whom I travelled. We both attended a meeting that (Monday, February 25) afternoon at Essex Hall to support Lansdowne's policy.

There has been a curious interlude since then. On Friday March 1st Graeme Thomson sent for me to the Ministry of Shipping and invited me to go to Malta to organize the system of convoys in the Mediterranean in conjunction with the British Admiral there. I consulted Walter Runciman next day and reluctantly – under his advice – agreed to go. I saw the people concerned in the M. of Shipping and collected information and after an exchange of letters with Maclay arranged to see Sir E. Geddes, First Lord of the Admiralty, on Wednesday March 6th at 3 p.m. When I called he was unable to see me and no further appointment was made tho' applied for by the M. of Shipping. On Saturday I was told by G. Thomson that the political ministers had vetoed the appointment on political grounds. This decision was a great relief to me as I did not wish to go and much prefer minding politics in London.

On March 13th Sir Walter Runciman entertained Asquith at dinner at H. of C. I suppose nearly 100 Liberal members were present and no Front Bench (or rather ex Cabinet men). A. made an excellent speech and had a most cordial reception. Some members also spoke to him urging less magnanimity and more action. To my surprise and horror I found myself told off to sit next to Asquith and give him a proper atmosphere. It was pleasant, but I thought myself insufficiently important. However it shows there are people who think well of me.

March 24 . . . Nothing much in London. On Wednesday morning a deputation of Dock Owners to President of B[oard] of Trade to protest against increases of wages. This I have been trying to secure since early in December but people are very timid and unenterprising. In the afternoon two important debates in H. of C. – first on ship-building as to which the Govt. statement was not satisfactory and then on a private Gas Bill which drew a very serious statement from President B. of T. as to the coal and inland transport position. I offered a few remarks on both discussions.

On Friday I went to Derby to hear Asquith at a special meeting of N[ational] L[iberal] Federation. Was pleased that he greeted me on platform with marked cordiality. He delivered a good address on the future – after war that is – but I suspect we shall yet have to fight on the conduct of the war and the making of peace. . . .

Bad news from the front in France.

March 26 News from France rather better. Must wait and see. Things rather in balance.

March 31 Quietly at home. Nothing much during the week except continued very severe fighting in France during which the Germans have made progress at, apparently, very heavy cost in men. This great assault on their part seems to be prompted by a bad state of domestic affairs as they must lose utterly if they fail, while they do not win against England and America if they succeed.

April 7 . . . Position in France remains much as it was – terrible slaughter. It is now certain that a British army, the fifth, failed badly for which General Gough is blamed. Reports of violent action contemplated by our Govt. in the way of legislation with regard to military service – probably true, but we shall see on Tuesday when Parliament reassembles. Railway travelling getting very difficult – slow and lavatory carriages being taken off etc.

May 5 Since my last entry I have spent a busy time with headquarters in London. The first ten days were occupied with the debates on the Military Service Bill which raises the age to 51 (and potentially to 56) and includes Ireland. Of course I opposed it and indeed took a prominent part, especially behind the scenes. The Irish were very furious and thanks to them we had some fairly good divisions, but tho' the bill was certainly shorn of some objectionable features it passed, as was inevitable when Asquith refused responsibility for turning the Government out. In this I think he did wrong, tho' after his past experiences and in view of the certainty of a perpetual press attack on any ministry of his it is no wonder he is not anxious to seize the reins.

But I think he ought to be pushed into it. L.G. is a public danger and A., tho' he has many faults, is far preferable particularly if he can be kept in good company.

On April 18th I went to Bristol as one of the Committee on Public Expenditure to examine the National Shipyards now being constructed on the

Wye and at Portbury by Avonmouth. The only other member of the committee able to go was J.F. Mason, M.P. for Windsor, the chairman of the sub-committee . . . None of the sites are really good for shipbuilding. The rise and fall is excessive and the water cramped for launching. The expenditure is great and I judge unnecessary unless the war is to last indefinitely.

The next week end I went to Newcastle to address the League of Young Liberals on the State and Individual Liberty and I understand made a good impression on a not very large audience. . . .

The war continues with much heavy fighting but no great change of position. Johnny Edwards was killed some ten days ago by a stray shell or bomb after distinguishing himself in the fighting and emerging unhurt with the Military Cross conferred on him the day he was killed. Paul Hobhouse has been missing since the first day – March 21st – and I fear there is no real hope of hearing of him again. Two good lads – alas a drop in the ocean of lost lives and bright hopes.

May 19 . . . Yesterday H[enry] B[ell] W[ortley] and I went over Iris and Daffodil, the two Wallasey ferry boats which took part in the extraordinary and brilliant attack on Zeebrugge. Not nearly so much knocked about as one would have expected and yet a shell passed through Iris making two not very large holes and killed about fifty men. . . .

An interesting time in Parliament. Asquith seems to be moving towards a regular opposition, badly needed. The reports from Ireland are most unsatisfactory.

June 2 . . . The second stage of the German attack has been in progress all week and certainly there has been very little comfort for us in it, unless it be that this time the heaviest part of the attack and the main responsibility for failure has fallen upon the French. It is almost impossible for plain people to understand the situation, but it is impossible to find any explanation creditable to the brains of the rulers of England and France.

On Wednesday we met at Walter Runciman's house – L. Jones, Pringle and myself, as we have done nearly once a week – except when W.R. was ill – since January. The organisation of Liberal party was discussed, particularly Whips Office which I have long said was inadequately manned.

Gulland, an excellent fellow, very well liked by us all, ought to retire as his health is undermined by diabetes.

Sir Donald Maclean would be the best successor and we urged W.R. to consult H. Samuel and McKenna and get Asquith to act. Asquith as leader is most unsatisfactory. Heard that he was not in intimate communication with Grey – no ill will but no common interest. Pitiable.

June 11 . . . Today we defeated Govt. in Grand Committee on the Emigration Bill – quite a joke. The news from the front is not good and I gather the position is worse than appears.

Just after Whitsuntide I was elected President of the British and Foreign Unitarian Asscn., an office I always coveted for the childish reason that I was the first whose great-grandfather (Richard Potter, M.P. for Wigan) had held it.

June 16 Nothing very fresh. Politically a quiet week. On Wednesday some of us – L. Jones, P.A. Harris, Pringle, Hogge, G. Baring, T. Walters, Roch and self waited on Asquith and urged him to greater efforts, in particular to press for greater information as to the position of the military operations. Quite pleasantly received and we spoke plainly but civilly.

In the morning I had been at a Conference at Hirst's office on the possibility of pushing the Lansdowne programme. It is all very unsatisfactory.

June 23 Things have been going on much as usual. Perhaps as a result of the interview recorded above Mr. A. did, on Tuesday, support an interrogatory of the Govt. on the military situation which was excellently opened by Roch. No reply was forthcoming but it is promised for tomorrow – a funny system of Government, with 80 Ministers a reply to the Leader of the Opposition takes from Tuesday to Monday to produce.

The Irish position is shocking: conscription insisted upon in April, when Home Rule was promised as the 'price for emerging successfully from the war': both abandoned in June. How long, O Lord, how long?

June 27 A disappointing week. Neither on Monday nor on Tuesday did Asquith play up as he should have done. I fear he 'funks' Lloyd George and feels that the venomous, incompetent, clever, plucky little Welshman is his master in debate.

Wednesday, being devoted to Scotch education, had a dinner party here – Mr. and Mrs. Herbert Samuel . . . Samuel has some great merits, inter alia he talks quite simply and unaffectedly of his Jewish interests.

July 7 . . . Parliamentary business not exciting. All waiting for the next move on the western front which has been unaccountably delayed. Meanwhile the Americans are coming across in large numbers – one million now over and about 250,000 per month coming.

Much dissatisfaction with management of Liberal party.

My relations with my constituents at Hexham are and have been very unsatisfactory – the uncomfortable armed neutrality type – and I shall be glad when they end. The Whips are looking for a new seat for me and there is some prospect of Rochdale, which would be interesting.

July 15 . . . On Friday I went with J.F. Mason to inspect Chatham Dockyard, Sir T. Bell and Admiral Power escorting us. This was an interesting visit and luckily the weather kept fine in spite of its generally showery nature. The yard is a curious place, ramshackle and badly planned. No money ever spent systematically. Fancy walnut trees with fruit on them between the buildings of a shipyard. . . .

Another German attack has begun, after some curious events in Germany where the political situation is very confused.

August 7 Off to Scotland, hurrah! The session ends tomorrow and I have been very busy and had much of interest to do, but I am afraid without much good result, except that really good work is never thrown away.

November 3 . . . Much has happened. I have definitely resigned my connection with Hexham and have been chosen Liberal candidate for the Eccles Division of Lancashire. This may prove a blessing for Eccles is much nearer Liverpool than Hexham and the constituency is easier to work and the interests of the place are much more akin to my own. I resigned from Hexham in July and in September E. and I paid a farewell visit which took the form of a tea party at the Club. Wentworth Beaumont has been chosen as my successor as Liberal candidate and I hope and think he will retain a seat which I should almost certainly have lost. Though the constituency has been difficult with its large area and the unattractive character of the accommodation there which no doubt kept us away when it would have been wiser to go there, it has until the last few years been a pleasant connection and I liked many of my supporters very much. The attitude I have taken up over the war and some war questions has been unpopular with some, and those who agreed with me had not the backbone to fight matters out. They would not let me hold meetings and try to enlist the support of my constituents and without this nothing could be done.

I was introduced to Eccles by the Whips with whom I have always been on good terms and curiously enough through the friendship of Gordon Harvey was invited by the Royton division at almost the same time. I chose Eccles on advice from headquarters, largely because the industries were more varied and the place more convenient for Liverpool.

On Oct. 26th I went to Eccles with E.L.H., addressed the Liberal Council and was unanimously chosen.

Meanwhile we – i.e. Great Britain and her allies – have greatly prospered in the war. Bulgaria and Turkey are out – have capitulated, Austria is finished and in revolution. All there seems in chaos. Germany is asking an armistice and the question is, can this be arranged before there is a revolution in Germany too and without more loss of life and property. What a misfortune that at this time our country should be dominated by little men. Never since Lord North's time has our Government been so poor in character nor the suspicions of corruption so widespread and, I fear, so well founded.

And we understand we are to have a general election in a few weeks with no clear political issue but a request for a blank cheque in favour of a gang of men united by no common principle of public policy. . . .

Both [Grace] and Dorothy have recently had attacks of influenza of which there has been a serious epidemic with many deaths, and I have had a mild touch perhaps due to my exertions last week end when in addition to Eccles on Saturday I spent Monday at Gorton in a long succession of British and Foreign Unitarian Assocn. meetings.

November 12 Yesterday we heard the glad news that an armistice with Germany had been concluded and that fighting was at an end. The country appears to have taken it very quietly and the rejoicings which were and are very real did not become rowdy or unseemly. The H. of C. adjourned after hearing

L.G's statement and went to a thanksgiving service at St. Margaret's. Now we come to the difficulties of returning to peace conditions which wont be helped by the misery and disorganization to which Germany has reduced herself. The Kaiser is supposed to be in Holland and most of the German princes have abdicated or been expelled. What a nemesis! However no one will be sorry for them.

King George seems to be secure and was enthusiastically cheered at Buckingham Palace yesterday, but one hears unpleasant reports of Bolshevism underground in this country. Pray heaven we escape any social convulsion.

Last week end I was in Liverpool with E.L.H. visiting Eccles and getting ready for the campaign.

November 17 . . . Parliament is to be prorogued on Wednesday and the general election to start at once, the poll being held on December 14th.

This ends my connection with Hexham begun in February 1907. Until the second year of the war it was pleasant and successful, but since the formation of the first coalition in May 1915 things have been very unpleasant. I could not support that Government in any unquestioning manner and my old friends would not allow me to hold meetings and put my views before our supporters as I wished.

Now we shall see what happens at Eccles. L.G. has made his deal with the Tories and has squared or intimidated a great number of Liberals. I will not go to Parliament pledged to a man or a coalition which I do not trust and I believe our present P.M. and his entourage to be thoroughly corrupt and self seeking, utterly devoid of knowledge and very anxious for popularity.

The great danger we have to face is the disappointment of the wage earning classes when they find the promises made to them cannot be fulfilled. . . .

Last night we had a small dance here for the children. What a comfort not to have bombs dropped as was the case less than a year ago.

December 1 Back at 54 Ullet Road, my real home. Perhaps I am the only person left who feels like that, but whatever happens this is my home and all other places are temporary abodes. I could live in New York or, I suppose, Madrid or Timbuctoo with my dear loving and beloved wife and my children and be quite happy and yet never be really at home. I suppose the difference lies in the association with the things which once belonged to those I loved as a child – the old diaries telling of bygone Holts and Durnings and such like – and the good old simple Unitarian faith which is just as true as if whole worlds had been induced to profess it.

Since I last wrote I have been almost entirely occupied with the election. E. and I have taken rooms at the Midland Hotel Manchester from which Eccles is distant 40 to 60 minutes by tram-car. The campaign, on a clearly anti-L.G's coalition ticket, seems to be going well. Of course we miss the young men and our meetings are not so full as they might be, but everyone else has the same complaint. On Wednesday last Earl Beauchamp came to speak for me and spent the Tuesday night as well at the hotel – a most pleasant companion, I might almost write friend.

On Friday dear Sir Charles Nicholson died suddenly after a few hours illness from influenza at the hotel in Doncaster where he was conducting his election as an L.G. candidate. I have seldom met a man who had more kindliness and good will – a really true friend. Not a strong character politically, easily 'squared' by quite trumpery employment and being given the appearance of importance when the reality was wholly non-existent. No one could have failed to love him. He was a sort of godfather to our children and from 1912 till 1917 a regular summer visitor to Abernethy, but this year I did not ask him as I knew his health was failing. I dont think he was ever the same man since his son was killed flying $2\frac{1}{2}$ years ago.

December 8 . . . Grace joined us in Manchester on Monday and has been with us ever since, helping with the election and generally behaving very nicely. The week has been full of the usual election activities and so far as we can judge all is going well.

One of the worst features about this election is the steady pandering to anti-German feeling which can only add to the difficulty of making a good peace which will avoid the seeds of fresh trouble.

December 15 It seems pretty clear that the poll yesterday was disastrous. So far as we could judge in Eccles the men were sulky and did not vote. The women came up much better and apparently voted Tory, probably on the anti-German cry. The same story seems true of Manchester where a complete Liberal debacle is expected. It is tragic and also horrible to know that at a great crisis in the world's history the people of this country should have been rushed by an appeal to every low and unchristian motive made by a gang of politicians (not statesmen) of the worst character. . . .

One thing is satisfactory. We carried the thinking men and women enthusiastically with us.

December 23 E. and I went to London on the Monday. I returned on Thursday and the rest of the family including Anne on Friday. My principal business in London was steamers and I am glad to think it is probable that we shall soon be free of the Shipping Controller who has really done his work very well. I saw some politicians and find the same impression everywhere – complete defeat of the Liberal party. Indeed Sydney Arnold was the only man I met who thought he was in, but one hears good accounts of McKenna and J.W. Wilson. Cecil Whetham stood for Cambridge University and made a very good fight. The University polls have been very obscurantist.

December 28 Went to Eccles for the declaration of the poll. It was awful – worse than I had expected. Marshall Stevens got 15,821 and I 3,408. A real wash out. Our good friends were horribly disappointed, only Hughes had realised how bad things were.

The election is a complete disaster to the Liberal party. Only some 25/30 independent men returned and all the leaders rejected. Asquith, Runciman, Samuel, Simon, J.M. Robertson, McKenna, McK. Wood, C. Hobhouse and the four whips. Dear Jack Wilson scored a personal triumph at Oldbury for which I am grateful indeed. It is a proper homage by his own people to a good, honourable man. The only Liberal at all of my kidney returned is Sydney Arnold. Scarcely a man in Lancashire and none of the coalition men when opposed by Tories. Labour has won some seats, largely from Tories, and lost others including those of their anti-Coalition leaders MacDonald, Anderson, Snowden, Henderson.

Tom Royden returned for Bootle. He will be a minister soon and hates L.G. as much as I do – so he says – lucky dog.

December 29 Quiet day, everybody rather knocked out and inclined to be tearful – except the victim who plans a useful career in Liverpool to start tomorrow.

December 31 . . . And so 1918 ended, a year of varied fortunes. First the German success in March which caused great suffering and loss of life but never could have won them the war. Then our successful attacks all through the summer, the dramatic defeat of the whole Turkish Army in Palestine, the collapse of Bulgaria and of Austria, and finally of Germany. And at the end of the year the wiping out of the Liberal party at the general election. What will come of this remains to be seen, but I dont like the French and Italian attitude towards peace questions. The latter are merely greedy, the former having suffered horribly at German hands not unnaturally wish to get something back, but will there be a generous peace likely to secure the future?

President Wilson is visiting Europe and has only just left England where he has had a splendid reception, but it is doubtful how far he got on with M. Clemenceau.

1919

[Though Holt now began to resume his business career, he remained optimistic about an early return to parliament, especially in view of evidence in the course of the year that the popularity of the Lloyd George Coalition was beginning to wane. P.A. Molteno wrote to Holt that 'Liberal principles are as necessary as ever and likely to reassert themselves,' but the question was whether in the post-war world there was any place for the sort of Liberalism in which Holt and those like him believed. With Asquith very much a fallen idol in his eyes, and in any case himself without a parliamentary seat, Holt increasingly placed his faith in Donald Maclean to lead a Liberal revival. By the end of July Holt had been adopted as prospective Liberal candidate for the promising constituency of Louth in Lincolnshire.]

January 19   I have been hard at work at office and Dock Board, recovering my position.

Last night Dr. Carpenter arrived in order to speak at a meeting held at the Royal Institution by the Liverpool District Missionary Assocn. in support of League of Nations idea. I took the chair and Sir A. Booth was the other speaker. A well attended meeting and a great success.

February 9   . . . On Wednesday we had a dinner at Lowndes Square. Sir J. and Lady Simon, Mr. and Mrs. Runciman, Mr. and Mrs. Walter Rea, Leif Jones, J.W.W. and ourselves. I thought very pleasant and some useful political talk after dinner. All rather opposed to Asquith's return to H. of C. and generally wishing another leader.

There is a grand chance for Donald Maclean – can he do it? Why did Sir J.S. marry Lady S.? She appears to be quite inferior with nothing but energy and good humour and, I suspect, a Roman Catholic.

February 16   . . . On Saturday went to Eccles to a farewell tea party, a most successful entertainment with particularly good amateur music in the evening. Really our supporters there have been a first rate lot, unluckily not numerous enough.

March 30   . . . Then on Wednesday I travelled down to Liverpool to propose T. Rome as chairman of the Dock Board at the meeting on Thursday, April 3rd. Rome is not an ideal man, deficient in culture and social standing and not, I gather, a really successful business man. A good many people outside expected that I – the next in seniority – would be invited to take the chair but I am glad that has not been done. I could not have refused and the position would have been embarrassing from the point of view of a return to Parliament. . . .

On Wednesday E.L.H. was elected on the executive committee of the Women's National Liberal Federation. Mrs. L. George being at the bottom of the poll with Mrs. Guest next above her. In fact the L.G. party were utterly routed. On Friday I was chosen chairman of Works Committee of M.D.H.B., a place held for many years by my uncle Alfred and before that I was chairman of the Docks and Quays Committee, where my uncle George had also been chairman.

April 13   . . . On Friday Grace and I were guests at Sir W. Runciman's great dinner for Asquith. About 570 guests in the Connaught rooms, all the elite of the Liberal party were present, i.e. society elite. Mr. A. made a good but not inspiring speech. Kenworthy, the victor of Hull, turned up and in five minutes satisfied the audience that he was a bounder. Next morning Mr. A. entertained the defeated Liberal candidates to breakfast at the N[ational] L[iberal] Club, the five ladies were present. The best speech was by D. Maclean who spoke firmly and showed the determination wanted in a leader. The spirit of the meeting was good.

I believe the best thing that can happen to the Liberal party now is that A. should gradually drop out and let Maclean step into his place. Runciman, Samuel and Simon have all made mistakes and exhibited weaknesses which unfit them for leadership, while Maclean, having been deputy chairman in the last Parliament, is free from any responsibility for the mistakes of the past.

April 27   . . . There has been a strike of dock labourers at Liverpool and Birkenhead all week, as the result of a grand scheme for ameliorating their conditions – less hours and the same pay, the whole agreed to by their representatives and described as the 'Dockers Charter.'

May 5   The above mentioned strike terminated last Monday, the men coming in to work on the agreed terms but refusing to work any overtime. The attitude of my fellow creatures is to me amazing. To me it seems that after this war the one thing needful is steady attention to the 'daily round – the common task' and yet apparently it is the one thing no one can do.

On Tuesday I went to Manchester to an excellent meeting of the local branch of the F.T.U., proceeding thence to London mainly in order to attend a meeting of the *Common Sense* directors on Wednesday and of the F.T.U. on Thursday. The newspaper is not going as well as I should like. There has been a big fall in the circulation since we raised the price to twopence.

At the F.T.U. we decided to open a campaign against the Imperial Preference proposals contained in the Budget. As Treasurer the burden of collecting money falls on me and I am now engaged in writing letters for that purpose to the 'assumed' Free Trade millionaires. I wonder what response will come.

May 23   Went to London on Saturday, returning on Tuesday evening. On Monday attended a great meeting at Albert Hall got up by Uncle Parmoor to protest against continuance of blockade and starvation of Central Europe. The hall was nearly full, probably 7000 present. I said a few words in support of Lord Beauchamp's Free Trade resolution and tho' my name was not on the bill and I supposed myself to be unknown I received a warm welcome from the meeting. The meeting was really a great success.

My main political interest at present is the Free Trade campaign just starting. I am Treasurer and am pleased to find money coming in more freely than I expected.

June 18   . . . Politically I am interested in an invitation to submit myself as candidate for the Louth division of Lincolnshire. I have been in communication with Mr. Wintringham the Lib. Assocn. chairman for about a month. The invitation came absolutely unsolicited and unexpected.

June 23   Last Thursday I went over to Leeds to attend Asquith's Free Trade meeting which took place in the Town Hall. The hall was very well filled – better than we expected – and Mr. A. made a good speech . . . Altogether a success. I said a few words at the end and subsequently was invited to stand for N.E. Leeds, so the impression cant have been altogether bad.

July 6   . . . Service to commemorate peace. I dont fancy any Liberals are very pleased with the peace which certainly contains nothing to cheer those who look for a new and Christian spirit in international relations. It is a great tragedy that in these last few years the Liberal element in English thought has lost its command of our Government mainly I fear through its own want of steadfastness and fatal compromising with enemies. A moral! Dont employ clever men of bad character, e.g. D.L.G. and W.L.S.C.

July 16 Since the last entry I have had an exciting and varied time. On Wednesday . . . I travelled to Louth in Lincolnshire to visit Mr. Tom Wintringham in order to decide whether I should or should not become Liberal candidate for that division. It was quite a pleasant visit, tho' strictly teetotal. On Thursday we motored round a lot of the division in a car driven by Sir Francis Bennett and in the evening met the executive committee who finally asked me to submit my name and this, after consulting E.L.H. in London, I agreed to do.

This was my first visit to Lincolnshire and I liked the country.

July 20 . . . Plenty of work as usual at business and the Dock Board which I have stirred up considerably since I have been out of Parliament.

Yesterday we had the official celebration of peace – a miserable affair so far as Liverpool is concerned. There is no dignity or moral elevation about our municipal life.

The Lord Mayor gave a garden party at Calderstones to which Anne and I went, meeting not many friends. Afterwards Alfred Holt entertained us to fireworks. Excellent fireworks but very poor company.

August 4 . . . There has been an anxious time since I last wrote in this book with labour disturbances. The men on the Dock Board floating plant going out on strike and trying to block the working of the docks by aid of the dock gatemen and tugboatmen. As Thomas Rome, the chairman, was away on his holidays, the labouring oar fell to me and we did settle the dispute after amicable negotiations on Monday July 28th sufficiently to procure the resumption of work and on Saturday we finally closed an agreement.

On that or the previous day the police, or about half of them, went on strike as a protest against the Police Bill which very properly deprives them of the right to strike. As a result the hooligans of the town burst out and looting was general in places such as London Road generally accessible to them. Not much damage at the docks. Soldiers are on duty and the great battleship, Valiant, is anchored off the Landing Stage, but as she is some 300 short of her complement (so I was told at the Dock Office) she is not very formidable as no one suggests using her big guns. The Tramway servants have all gone on strike and indeed the world seems mad, everyone thinking to remedy his own grievances by inflicting as much loss as possible on his neighbours – an operation which if everyone joins in must ruin all. . . .

On July 30th E. and I went to stay with Mr. Wintringham at Louth, when I was on July 31st adopted as Liberal candidate for that division of Lincolnshire – a very good first reception.

September 7 . . . Since I got back from Scotland I definitely fixed to sail for China etc. with Eliza and Grace in the Teiresias on November 8th for a trip of about 7 months. I wonder if it will come off or whether a political crisis which everyone seems to expect will intervene.

September 14 . . . Widnes election result announced on Friday. Arthur Henderson returned by nearly 1000 votes, a great slap in the face for the Government which had created the vacancy by making Willie Walker a peer. I dont like Henderson (whom the Liberals supported). He is vain and self seeking and at the critical moment in December 1916 it was he, as much as anybody, who enabled L.G. to overthrow Asquith by giving him Labour support.

Henderson is not to be trusted.

November 4 . . . On my return from Abernethy I almost at once left for Louth in Lincolnshire to commence my campaign as prospective Liberal candidate, staying there from Thursday, Oct. 23rd to Saturday, November 1st as guest of T. Wintringham. E.L.H. joined me on Tuesday 28th. On the whole a very successful series of meetings especially the meeting in Louth Town Hall at which Walter Runciman was principal speaker, said to have been the best on record out of election times.

1920

[Absent abroad when a vacancy occurred at Louth, Holt missed what, with hindsight, proved to be his best opportunity of returning to Westminster. Significantly, the apparent revival in the fortunes of independent Liberalism in the early months of 1919 was not maintained. Between April 1919 and the General Election of 1922 Louth was one of only three by-elections won by anti-Coalition Liberals. For the most part the Labour party was emerging as the government's most pressing challenger. Important developments for the Liberal party took place while Holt was out of the country. In February 1920 Asquith returned to parliament after winning the by-election in Paisley. But, as Holt recognised, this was probably not in the best interests of Liberalism for, in his late sixties, the former Prime Minister was but a shadow of his former self and gave neither lead, direction nor policy to those beneath him. Then in May the Leamington Conference of the National Liberal Federation revealed how deep were the divisions between the Asquithian and Coalition Liberals and ruled out any prospect of reconciliation for the forseeable future.

Apart from his continuing search for a parliamentary seat, Holt's attention turned increasingly to the contemporary industrial scene, characterised by mounting unrest between employers and labour.]

July 9 We got back from our trip [to the Far East] on June 19. . . .

The other misfortune [apart from the death of his Aunt Bessie] was the loss of the Louth seat where a bye-election occurred in early May owing to the death of the member and as I could not be run in my absence owing to my not being sufficiently known, Mr. Wintringham stood as Liberal candidate and brought off an excellent win by 2500 majority.

June taken up pretty fully in gathering up the reins of office at India Buildings and the Dock Office and in preparation for Grace's wedding.

July 23 . . . Yesterday Grace was married . . . Two Field Marshals at the wedding – Lords Methuen and Grenfell. Quite funny in view of my record as an anti-militarist. . . .

During the previous days when I was in London I had plenty of business etc. to attend to, including the affairs of *Common Sense* which is in a desperate position financially. On the Wednesday I addressed a meeting in Essex Hall on public economy and believe my speech was distinctly good and better than Simon's who followed . . . I went to an evening party at Lady Simon's for the Wee Frees. Asquith there, very polite, especially to Anne. Everybody very cordial towards me.

August 6 . . . Public affairs most disquieting. Ireland in a shocking state and more or less war in Poland, Mesopotamia and Syria. Government steadily sinking in public respect but no substitutes gaining favours.

September 9 . . . There is a strike of the printers etc. in Liverpool and Manchester with the result that there are no newspapers. Not a great loss. We could do without printing for many months. What would happen if the printers refused to print paper money?

September 19 . . . Last Monday at a meeting of the Liverpool Liberal Federal Council, preceded by a dinner paid for by myself, I was chosen President, i.e. titular leader, of the Liverpool Liberals, a position held by my father 40 years ago. It is supposed that the present Lord Mayor, Burton Eills, will be elected chairman as soon as he comes out of office, do the work and leave me with an honorary position, but I doubt it.

I made them a speech which was very well received. It was meant to be firm and conciliatory, enunciating and adhering to principles, asking for unity and deprecating quarrels about leaders who are really very worthless fellows (L.G. and H.H.A.)

That night I went up to London primarily to discuss the affairs of *Common Sense*, our excellent newspaper, but a financial failure. I fear its chances of survival are remote, however the rise in the cost of paper and printing has put all newspapers in difficulties.

September 23 . . . Everybody much agitated over the prospective strike by the colliers. The whole thing is utterly unreasonable. That a strongly organised body of men should hold up the whole community, exposing them to great discomfort and even starvation for the purpose of getting about 2/- per day extra pay for themselves is really outrageous. There is no sense of proportion in it, and greed and jealousy are the real motives of the miners, instilled I think by officials whose place and salary depends [sic] upon satisfying the extremists amongst their clientele. If shipowners did the same thing, how they would be execrated.

October 27 . . . On the 19th, Tuesday, I went to London returning the following day – business of the Free Trade Union. At the moment this is not going well. There is apathy on the subject as Ireland and domestic problems such as the coal strike divert public attention and we have a difficulty, largely personal, with the Manchester branch. . . .

Strike of miners started Oct. 18th and still goes on.

November 7 . . . On the Friday evening I addressed a small group at the Oxford University Liberal Club. It was not a success as those present wanted to hear about socialism and labour problems and I talked about Ireland, peace and finance.

November 21 . . . On Friday I went to Littleborough just beyond Rochdale staying with Gordon Harvey to address the Liberal Club there – quite a successful speech. It is pretty clear these people are thinking of me as a prospective candidate for the Royton division for which they asked me to stand in 1918 when it certainly would have been much better than Eccles, but I dont fancy anything at present unless it is specially good, like Louth.

November 29 . . . The next evening [November 25] Viscount Grey addressed a meeting at the Sun Hall on behalf of the League of Nations. . . .

Poor Grey is virtually blind. Can just see with a powerful magnifying glass, looks well and strong. He told me that during the whole time he was Ambassador at Washington he never saw President Wilson who was too ill to receive the diplomatic corps. What a state of affairs for a great country. They choose a dictator and he becomes a paralytic. Can't fulfil his duties, wont resign, can't be dismissed.

December 1 Last night dined as guest of Caledonian Assocn. Lord Derby in chair. He is really a good fellow, but the adulation of the local people is disgusting.

December 31 . . . My time fully taken up with work of which I have plenty, both in the office and outside. Bad trade and the absurd financial extravagance of the Government is bringing about considerable distress, but prices are falling steadily which should soon help matters particularly if wages can be put on a lower scale.

1921

[1921 saw no improvement in the fortunes of the Liberal party, although Holt himself was adopted as prospective parliamentary candidate for Rossendale in Lancashire. The government appeared most vulnerable to the charge of extravagant expenditure – a cry to which Holt was particularly sympathetic, believing as he always had done in the classic Liberal virtues of peace, retrenchment and reform.]

January 16 . . . Monday Jan. 10th I spoke at the Reform Club on 'What is Liberalism.' Rather over 100 people. Also a success.

Politics are becoming interesting. The financial situation is getting too serious and difficult for quackery and economic reality is beginning to assert itself. Trade is very bad, prices falling and unemployment is widespread, for which I see no remedy but lower wages, better work and lower prices. The great dole system is on its last legs as money cannot be found any longer for this expenditure – the taxpayer is at the end of his tether.

January 23 Quiet week at home except for a visit to London on Wednesday when I attended meetings of the directorate of *Common Sense* and of the Committee of the Free Trade Union. Also a lunch at the Savoy given by Sir H. Bell, Sir H. Leon and Hirst to Geo. Lambert who moved the economy resolution in H. of C.

January 30 . . . Trade shocking. No prospect of improvement without a drastic reduction in wages.

February 6 On Tuesday I attended, by invitation, a full mass in honour of the deceased Archbishop of Liverpool, Dr. Whiteside, in the Pro-Cathedral behind the Adelphi Hotel. The ceremony lasted two hours and except for a short address eulogizing the deceased was incomprehensible to me. I had never been to a Roman Catholic ceremonial before but this was worse than I could have supposed: tawdry splendour, bowing, scraping, changing clothes, lighting and extinguishing candles – the most miserable performance exactly like the Buddhist priests.

February 21 Rather a hard week. Federal Council on Monday to discuss the resolutions to be proposed at National Liberal Fedn. at Nottingham. On Tuesday spoke to the Fairfield Liberal Club, then travelled to London by the midnight train, went to meeting of directors of *Common Sense* and decided to wind it up as the financial position shows no sign of improvement. This is a tragedy and I am deeply sorry for Hirst who has conducted the paper splendidly. . . .

On Saturday went to Todmorden to address the annual meeting of the Sowerby Liberal Assocn.

A good attendance of about 100. There is a semi-socialist element attached to the Liberal party who believe that the State ought to support the unfortunate and incompetent. I dont!

February 27 . . . The meeting at Nottingham [of the National Liberal Federation] was unsatisfactory as no real discussion of the important subjects raised was allowed. Several unwise resolutions were passed, I am afraid under influence of a desire to bid against the Labour party for electoral support, and there was a general disregard of financial considerations which is very distasteful to me and does not augur well for the future of the country or the party. I spoke once or twice, but it was useless, especially in view of time limitations preventing a serious presentation of any argument.

March 6 . . . There have been curious election results during the week. The Labour party lost Woolwich to the Coalition although they put up Ramsay MacDonald, their ablest man. In fact I think he and Snowden the only really able men they have. He was beaten by a V.C. officer who had risen from the ranks. On the other hand Coalition lost Dudley – Sir A. Boscawen made Minister of Agriculture – and Kirkcaldy to the Labour party. One cant help regretting the absence of Free Liberalism from these fights.

April 10 [visiting Marseilles] . . . I saw such a collection of useless steamers as I have never seen or expect to see again – obsolete French vessels and hopeless Americans built of unseasoned wood and leaking so as to be unseaworthy (all bought by the French Government) and scarcely a decent ship in the whole harbour in which business was almost at a standstill.

April 17 We have had a period of great excitement. As a consequence of the decontrol by Government of the coal mines the miners ceased work on March 31st sooner than accept the modified rates of pay offered by the mine owners and after much negociation nothing has been agreed upon. Meanwhile their partners in the so-called Triple Alliance, the railwaymen and transport workers, were threatening to join in a general strike which many timorous people including the Government believe to be the prelude of a general revolution. However on Friday night for some reason not absolutely clear at present the two latter bodies broke away and have left the miners to fight single handed. As the proposed sympathetic strike would have been highly injurious to the interests of the railwaymen and transport workers it is very probable the leaders called off the strike because the followers would not obey. Evidently the solidarity of the trades unionists is a good deal damaged.

Wednesday and Thursday I spent in London for Free Trade Union and a very pleasant lunch with Wee Frees in H. of Commons.

April 24 . . . On Saturday I went to Bury to address the annual meeting of the Assocn. of Lancashire Liberal Clubs: a very good gathering of about 80 men from all parts of East Lancashire and they received me and my speech very kindly. It was a fine afternoon and the atmosphere was clear as the mills etc. were not working owing to the coal strike. That part of the world would be quite attractive if it were not for the murky pall which usually hangs over it.

The coal strike goes on and I dont think will be easily settled. There is a good deal of privation already and will be more very soon as nobody seems to have laid in any stock except the Dock Board who had almost 30,000 tons, 14 weeks consumption at the normal rate, which by economy could be made to last for 6 months. As there was imminent danger that some of this would be seized for the benefit of the less provident, we agreed to sell 6000 tons, 2500 of which to go to the Liverpool Corpn. who had only 3 weeks consumption in stock. No departure from the principle laid down in the parable of the wise and foolish virgins should ever be permitted. The only effect will be to encourage folly and discourage foresight and precaution. Those who wish to discourage folly should let fools drink the cup they have prepared to its last dregs.

May 8 The miners' strike has continued since the last entry without much inconvenience except the restriction on railway travelling and the fact that as manufactures are being stopped the cargo for the steamers is coming to an end.

The railway and transport workers have refused to join in the strike and in Liverpool the latter have handled foreign coals without much trouble tho' in Glasgow and London they have refused to do so.

May 22 The strike still drags on its weary course while work gets less and less. However the shortage of coal has its good side. The atmosphere is clearer and the flowers and plants cleaner and more flourishing than I have ever seen them before and we have had a spell of beautiful weather which is very good for people who are short of coal.

On Monday the 9th E.L.H. went up to London to attend Women's Liberal Federation meetings and lost her seat on the executive – disappointing but not surprising in view of her necessarily poor attendance.

June 23 I have been a good deal in London since the last entry with the result that my duties to this book have been neglected. Frequent railway journeys take up a lot of time and sap one's energies as well. Let us see what I can remember. . . .

Then there is the coal strike, still continuing, the miners having rejected the last very favourable offer made to them by the owners and the Government, the latter proposing to devote £10 millions of public money to ease the drop in wages. Quite unnecessary and most unfair to an already overburdened public.

There are now signs of a few men dribbling back to isolated mines and there is little doubt that the miners' resources are all but exhausted and credit is being refused them by the provision dealers, so I expect a break up of the strike before very long. A lot of harm has been done to trade and commerce but in some respects good, as merchants are enabled to sell off old stock without lowering their prices and there may well be a rather lucky liquidation of high priced goods. Coal must go down to something more nearly the prewar prices if the trade of the country is to flourish and so must other wages.

July 17 . . . On July 12th we had an evening party for Liberals – mostly young – to meet Mr. Asquith who had been dining with the Granards and was certainly affected by his drink. Mrs. A. was awful – covered with paint – a dreadful woman whom one is ashamed to see in the house. However some very nice people came – Beauchamp, who came early and helped us to receive with Lady Maclean, Sir C. and Lady Hobhouse, Sir J. and Lady Simon, McKinnonWood and his daughter, Lady Denman with gorgeous pearls. There was a good number of really young people and I gather Liberalism is quite flourishing at the Universities . . . Would that we could get rid of Mr. A. He must go before we succeed. An honest sober fellow like Maclean would do twice as well.

The coal strike terminated early this month on a muddled agreement which is hardly likely to give the cheap coal which is essential to industry.

July 24 I have had a very strenuous week as a result of London visit, endless business here which I have only just squared off and on the top of that political meetings to preach public economy. Tuesday Wavertree, Wednesday Breckfield, Friday Garston and Thursday at East Toxteth Committee to consider Eleanor Rathbone's candidature. This lady always plays for herself and yet can spoil every other person's chance.

July 31 . . . Nothing fresh in politics or commerce except that the attack on public expenditure is gaining force. I spoke at two meetings this week and had to miss a third. The financial estimate of the Government is a complete failure and I dont see how income and expenditure can be balanced. There is a good manifesto published by traders, merchants and manufacturers which has attracted much attention. All our firm signed it. Coal is steadily falling but I don't see the end. It seems impossible to give the miners the wages they want at the prices the consumers can afford.

We have just bought coals at Glasgow at 39/-per ton, thrice pre war price, less than half that of a year ago.

September 20 A busy time since I last wrote. The first week [of September] I spent in Liverpool doing some politics in addition to my business. One night I went to Manchester to meet the representatives of the Bury Liberal Assocn. as to a possible candidature there and on Saturday 10th Sept. I went to Rawtenstall to address the Rossendale Liberal Assocn. with the idea that they may ultimately ask me to represent them. I had a capital meeting and was much pleased with the spirit of the people and also with the character of the country. This would be a most convenient constituency. On the 11th I went to London and met Anne at Lowndes Square and on the next evening we crossed to Amsterdam . . . for an International Free Trade Congress convened by the Cobden Club. On the whole the Conference was a success in spite of the fact that the stupid French and Belgians refused to come and meet the Germans. . . .

November 1 Municipal elections. A good deal of interest as the position of Max Muspratt and his Coalition Liberals would be defined in the election. They openly supported the Conservative candidates against the Free Liberals, but their influence on the ordinary electors was small and the Liberal poll was quite as good as I expected. We again lost seats to the Nationalists in the city wards as we are bound to do and it will be a good thing to be definitely rid of that alliance. Sydney Jones lost his seat in Exchange Ward – rather a shock to serious minded citizens. The Liberal party must concentrate their efforts on the outer districts and rally the better class of citizen against the Irish-Labour efforts to exploit the ratepayer and the Tory dictatorship of Salvidge.

November 2 . . . Free Trade Union meeting in the afternoon. Resolved we could do nothing effective when the public attention is rivetted on Ireland and unemployment.

[late November] . . . On Saturday November 19 E.L.H., the two daughters and myself went by motor to Rawtenstall in Rossendale. We lunched with Lady Maden at Bacup, then attended the Liberal Council whom I addressed, after which I was adopted as prospective candidate. We talked and made ourselves pleasant and motored back, getting home about 9.30 – a long day. So now I am launched on a new constituency, the fifth I have wooed and though I think the chances of success are good I confess I dont like the job.

Politically the dramatic interest lies in the Irish question. What is the proposal to Ulster, rejected by Ulster, and what the Government will do we dont know, but the great Tory Conference in Liverpool has declared for a peaceful settlement.

But I suspect the real danger to the Government lies in the total failure of their finance.

December 11 On Monday I had to attend a meeting of the Liberal Federal Council – nothing of importance. On Tuesday I went to Rossendale and visited a Liberal Club in the evening at an outlandish place called Scoutbottom returning by motor from Ramsbottom, a 2 hours drive which brought me home at midnight. On Wednesday I went over to Bacup, dined at Lady Maden's and then addressed a public meeting, being supported by Lieut. Brown, Liberal candidate for Salisbury. Just a fair meeting, better in quality than numbers.

December 18 . . . In Parliament the Government's Irish policy has been ratified by an enormous majority in both Houses, but the Irish pseudo-Parliament (the Dail) is still debating the matter apparently with violent differences of opinion largely turning on personal questions.

1922

[In the event it was not Independent Liberalism, nor even some broad-based anti-Coalition alignment under a renegade Tory such as Lord Robert Cecil, which brought down the Lloyd George Government. At the famous Carlton Club meeting in October the rank and file of the Conservative party defied the advice of their leader, Austen Chamberlain, and voted to fight the next election under their own party colours. In the General Election which followed victory went to the Conservatives under Bonar Law. For both wings of the Liberal party, which continued to oppose one another, the result of the contest proved disappointing. Fielding over 330 candidates the Asquithian Liberals secured only 60 M.P.s, losing Sir Donald Maclean at South Midlothian. Their best results were almost always achieved in straight fights with Conservatives. Against Labour they did badly and in three-cornered contests they were beginning to look like the third party in a two party system. Holt's experience in Rossendale was typical and left him bemoaning the absence of proportional representation. Another worrying feature was the party's lack of a secure regional base.]

January 15 . . . On Monday I went to Rossendale and spent an hour or so in the Liberal Club at Stacksteads, making myself pleasant and motoring back from Ramsbottom so as to be in good time for the visit of the Japanese commercial mission to Liverpool next day.

January 29 . . . On Sunday E.L.H. and I went to London in order to attend the Free Liberal meeting at the Central Hall, Westminster, on Monday night. Lord Gladstone in the chair, Asquith and Grey the principal speakers, the latter particularly fine and very impressive in his denunciation of the unclean politics of the Coalition. The meeting was a great success and very stirring. . . .

On Saturday I went to Bolton to Asquith's meeting. The theatre was packed. Evidently a strong Liberal revival and a good speech too.

[March] I spent the first week after my return [from the U.S.A.] in clearing off arrears of work and then devoted several evenings to meetings in Rossendale where all seems to be going on well.

[June] On Saturday 24th I went to Rossendale in order to take part in a League of Nations meeting at Haslingden where I had the pleasure of meeting Major Halstead the Conservative candidate. Evidently quite a good fellow but no sign of Parliamentary talent.

July 6 . . . Politically events in Ireland have been the most striking, the last fortnight having witnessed the assassination of Sir Henry Wilson in London and the struggle in Dublin between the Government of the Free State and the out and out Republicans. The Irish are a curious people and the less the English have to do with them the better for the English. Above all the Irish should get no English money.

July 11 . . . They tell me Lord Robt. Cecil is to speak at a Liberal meeting at Chippenham. He is moving.

July 31 I addressed small gathering of Liberals at Reform Club on current politics. Good reception and fairly good report in the press.

August 3 . . . On Wednesday Aug. 2nd E.L.H. and I motored out to Walton Jail to take tea with Major and Mrs. McTier . . . when the Major (Governor) very kindly showed me over the prison. The place was beautifully clean and airy and there is nothing brutal about it though no doubt the life of the prisoners is miserably monotonous.

October 29 . . . The great event has been the break up of Lloyd George's Coalition Government and the formation of a purely Tory ministry under Bonar Law. This resulted from the fact that the Tory rank and file, contrary to the wishes of Balfour, Birkenhead and A. Chamberlain decided to withdraw from the Coalition. It is difficult to make out the exact reason but probably sheer distrust of L.G. personally and dislike of his methods were the real cause. To an observer it looks like a revolt of honest men against the rogues – some of them very clever.

The effect is that I am at once plunged into electioneering and yesterday went down to Rawtenstall and was there adopted as Liberal candidate for Rossendale.

November 26   . . . Well the election is over, the poll was on Wed. Nov. 15th and in Rossendale the result was:

Major Halstead	Conservative	12881
Mr G.W. Jones	Labour	11029
R.D.H.	Liberal	6327

This was very disappointing as throughout the election we had appeared to be doing well and certainly up to the very last moment thought we had done much better. All the signs seemed favourable. The Catholics of whom there are a good many decided to vote for the Labour party because I would not give them the pledges they desired in favour of their schools and some Wesleyan tee-totallers did likewise because I refused to promise all they wanted about temperance and I dont suppose I got much support from the teachers and other Government servants whose one idea of the issue at an election appears to be that they should extract a promise from the candidate that their salaries and wages should never be reduced. Finally it is alleged a good many Liberals voted Conservative to keep the Labour man out. It is impossible to say what all these things meant, but it was obvious at the count that while Bacup and Haslingden had given very fair support, the vote in Rawtenstall was dead against me. The organization in that borough was poor and there were no workers and our meetings were badly attended.

We stayed for the election at the Crown Hotel, Rawtenstall, an ordinary public house, where we were made extremely comfortable by Mr. and Mrs. Robinson (the landlord). The weather on the whole was fine and the election pleasant.

The general result is that the Tory Govt. gets a majority of 75 over all other parties combined of whom the Labour party is much the strongest – rather more than twice the size of either the Liberal or Lloyd George parties. Nevertheless the Tories have polled barely 40% of the total votes and have therefore but little moral authority. Nothing can be clearer than the urgency of Proportional Representation and without it I fear the Liberal party is doomed and men with views like my own are absolutely excluded from public life.

December 17   Another bad spell of Diary neglect. I have been hard at work since the election at my business and other things. . . .

But I have had to go to London once or twice and there were necessarily a lot of arrears of work. Besides business is not easy at present. The steamers are making some money, at any rate more than covering out of pocket expenses, but there is restlessness everywhere. The various steamship interests, both British and foreign, all seem to want more than they have got and I fear cast covetous eyes on the China trade which has been sensibly managed and has a good volume of business. It has been a constant difficulty to avoid any break up amongst the conflicting and jealous elements in our trade and how long this will continue reasonably peaceable I cant feel sure. All I know is that the duty of keeping the peace devolves largely on me.

The cost of shipbuilding has been enormous and even now is not a level equivalent to the earning power of the vessel when built, yet we must build to replace tonnage which is rapidly wearing out.

December 24 . . . On Tuesday I was chosen President of the National Reform Union in succession to my old friend Gordon Harvey who died in November. . . . On December 13th this body gave a dinner to Donald Maclean at Manchester at which I was asked to take the chair . . . I believe my remarks were acceptable and D.M. made a most admirable speech. It is a shame that such a man should have any difficulty in getting returned to Parliament. The N.R.U. has had a most honourable history. It began as an heir to the Anti-Corn Law League. Since its birth in 1866 it has continuously advocated Liberal reforms but independently of party leaders and caucuses. I think my selection for the Presidency is due to the wire pulling of Hirst, Molteno etc.

1923

[Liberals spent much time in 1923 grappling with the problem of reunion. Yet while most recognised this to be a political necessity, there were major difficulties at the levels of both personality and policy. In fact most of the enthusiasm for reunion came from the grass roots, while the leadership, particularly among Independent Liberals such as Asquith and John Simon, remained cool. Holt shared these misgivings, feeling particular outrage at Lloyd George's accumulated wealth, derived largely from the sale of honours. The obstacles in the way of reunion were only too apparent at the Annual Conference of the National Liberal Federation at Buxton in June. To Holt's satisfaction the Conference rejected the crucial amendment to a pro-reunion resolution, which called upon the leaders of Independent Liberalism to discuss the best means of promoting unity with the Lloyd Georgeites.

What no Liberal seemed able to achieve was done by a Conservative. When in the autumn the new Prime Minister, Stanley Baldwin, called another General Election on the specific issue of Protection, Liberals were able to reunite in defence of the hallowed doctrine of Free Trade. Though not all outstanding problems were fully resolved, the Liberal party could put forward a reasonably united front for the first time since 1916. Fielding more than 450 candidates the party enjoyed a partial renaissance. Liberals won 158 seats on a popular vote of nearly thirty per cent. Holt was narrowly defeated in North Cumberland in a straight fight with a Conservative. Once again, however, it was noticeable that Liberalism was still losing ground to Labour and its base in working-class support was dwindling.]

February 6 Went to Manchester in the afternoon to preside at a public meeting in the Memorial Hall called by the National Reform Union to declare Liberal policy on the occupation of the Ruhr by France. Earl Beauchamp, chief speaker, about 200 present and very successful. Passed our resolution demanding reference of Versailles Treaty etc. to the League of Nations with only two dissentients.

March 2 On Tuesday I went up to London to arrange the closing up of 63 Lowndes Square which I have sold . . . It is sad to have to give up the house and it is a great disappointment to Eliza and the girls, but with present taxation I cannot afford it. Such a nice house too. And to me it means the formal abandonment of all reasonable expectation of getting into Parliament.

March 18 . . . Public affairs are not going very well. The French occupation of the Ruhr has led to nothing except steadily increasing violence. How it will end no one can say but the chance of recovering any part of the cost of the war from Germany is steadily disappearing. There is a lot of talk about Liberal reunion mostly from the Lloyd George gang who are at present in the air. I dont want to see that lot back in the counsels of Liberalism for the evils of which we complain both at home and abroad are almost entirely due to L.G.'s personal policy. His has been a bad influence in public life – no real knowledge of history or political principle, vain, spiteful, treacherous, untrustworthy and dishonest, the man is evil. How can he live as we know he does live on any income he has honestly come by? What have been his transactions with the rich men who have received titles?

April 29 . . . On Wednesday 18th April Sir Donald Maclean came down and spent the night in order to help Liberalism the next day. At 2 p.m. on the Thursday we opened a Liberal bazaar at Birkenhead and in the evening had a small dinner at the Club and a meeting of the Federal Council and other workers. Successful and I hope some good result may follow in the strengthening of the Liberal cause.

May 28 . . . The sensation of the last ten days has been the resignation of Bonar Law – due to illness – and the reconstruction of the ministry with Stanley Baldwin as Premier. McKenna agrees to become Ch. of Exchequer on recovery from illness in three months time. This really is rather dreadful. I liked the man and thought well of him and to think he has ended thus. Men may change their political opinions and allegiance but they should get nothing for themselves out of their change.

June 3 On Wednesday I went to Buxton where E.L.H. met me. We stayed at the George Hotel, a moderate hostelry with nice servants. Jack Hobhouse turned up in the late afternoon and we devoted ourselves to the National Liberal Fedn. The most interesting part of the day's work was the discussion on Liberal reunion, which really means an enquiry as to whether Lloyd George is to be received back as a leader. There is no other difficulty. The general feeling was against his return and I trust the few remarks I contributed assisted in producing this result. At any rate our friends expressed themselves as highly pleased. . . .

The meetings were very well attended and a success but Asquith's speech tho' sound was stodgy. It is a pity he does not make himself more generally agreeable.

June 15 . . . I have been up [to London] for an odd day or two and seen some friends, mostly political.

Everybody is very cordial but I fear membership of H. of C. is very far off so far as I am concerned.

October 28 As I have often noted before this diary is kept in a most irregular manner. I always seem to be busy and unable to find time to write and yet it is difficult to say exactly how time disappears.

Last week was eventful at any rate for on Monday evening Asquith accompanied by his secretary Basil Herbert arrived in time for dinner . . . Mr. A. was in very good form and really friendly and human. . . .

The meeting held in the Stadium by Lime Street was crowded with an appreciative and attentive audience and Mr. A. made a speech which tho' hardly enthusing was thoroughly sound and well argued. It is a pity his great gifts lack the power of raising enthusiasm in the multitude. It is a pity he did not boldly say what General Smuts said the same day as to the French conduct in Germany.

November 4 I went up to London on Tuesday morning Oct. 30th to attend the banquet given by the Chamber of Shipping to the Colonial Premiers. I was seated between Bruce, P.M. of Australia, and Amery, first Lord of Admiralty. Bruce is a pleasant fellow, educated at Cambridge where he was in the boat but I did not think much of his brains and Massey, P.M. of N. Zealand seemed another poor thinker. They brought out the usual claims for assistance in raising the market price of what they sell. I responded to the toast of 'Overseas Trade' at the end of the evening and believe I made a good Free Trade speech.

Saw General Smuts on Oct. 31st on the subject of the export of fruit from S. Africa. A fine looking man with real power of statesmanship but perhaps a bit 'slim' as his detractors allege. Dined with Beauchamp to discuss the Free Trade Union and its future relation to Mond and the Lloyd George gang who want to pose as the defenders of Free Trade.

. . . Municipal elections in Liverpool on Nov. 1st ending in all parties retaining their seats except Labour lost one to the Irish who got Tory support. In view of Garston Housing scandal it was disappointing we gained nothing.

December 9 What events since the last entry! When Asquith was here Geoffrey Howard asked me if I would consider standing for North Cumberland, his old constituency, and I said yes, little dreaming the election would be over in six weeks. So on Saturday Novr. 10th I went to Carlisle to see the selection committee by appointment and it was then apparent that Mr. Baldwin meant to dissolve Parliament and ask for a mandate to introduce Protection. I was selected for recommendation to the executive on the following Saturday (Novr. 17th) and on that day I was adopted candidate and commenced the campaign with less than three weeks instead of the three years one had anticipated. The organisation was weak and there was no agent but there was a great body of volunteers and we procured an agent from London, S.A. Velden, who proved a great success. The local workers were splendid and spared themselves no exertion and I never took part in a better or more loyally fought election, but alas our hopes were dashed and I just failed to win.

Result – Hon. Donald Howard   9288
          R.D.H.   9070

This reduced the previous majority by about 50 votes. It was a great disappointment as we thought we had won. The result in the country was a complete smash for Protection, the Government majority of 75 becoming a minority of about 90. Amongst our friends elected are Hugh Rathbone and Sydney Jones for Liverpool, Geoffrey Howard, Luton, Leif Jones, Camborne, Arthur Hobhouse, Somerset, Seely, I. of Wight, Walter Rea, Bradford. Donald Maclean, Runciman and Molteno failed.

The question now is – what next? Conservatives about 260, Labour 190, Liberal 150. Baldwin must resign, I think, but who can form a Government? What a chance for a private member and how bitter to miss it.

December 30 . . . On Dec. 20th the Dock Board Election took place – the first contest for nearly 20 years and the first in which I have been a candidate. I was second in the poll with (I think) 1146 votes, the Chairman being first with five more. The six associated candidates were returned, the new comer, nominee of the sugar trade, being about 500 votes behind the lowest, Orme.

In politics nothing new. Baldwin has not resigned and awaits an adverse vote on the address, which he will get.

1924

> [The General Election of 1923 left the political situation confused, with no one party commanding an overall parliamentary majority. It was Asquith's decision that Labour, as the larger of the two free trade parties, should now have its chance to govern. In the House of Commons Austen Chamberlain pronounced what were prophetic words:
>
> '[Asquith] has taken his choice and he has by that choice constituted his own immortality. He will go down to history as the last Prime Minister of a Liberal administration. He has sung the swan song of the Liberal Party.'
>
> Accordingly, Ramsay MacDonald formed the first Labour government in the country's history. Several of Holt's radical colleagues from the days of the War were now members of the Labour administration, though he himself could never contemplate this transition.

During the months of Labour rule the Liberal party continued to fail in terms of both leadership and policy at a time when it was imperative to adopt a distinctive stance which would separate it from its opponents in the eyes of the electorate. It was clear that the reunion of the previous November existed in little more than name. When the government fell over its mishandling of the Campbell case and yet another General Election was held in October, Chamberlain's words seemed to be vindicated. Putting out only 340 candidates and mounting a singularly unimaginative campaign, the Liberal party was almost annihilated. Liberals won a mere forty seats on 18 per cent of the popular vote. Holt, beaten in a three-cornered contest in North Cumberland, certainly sensed that Liberalism was being squeezed out of the political landscape. Encouraged by Lord Beauchamp to believe that what was now needed was 'something like the moral fervour of Mr. Gladstone', Holt became involved in the party's enquiry into its electoral disaster.]

[early January] . . . I went to Carlisle for Saturday, Jan. 5th and was adopted as prospective Liberal candidate for N. Cumberland. Everybody very kind and enthusiastic, considering we did not win. So now I have to nurse a constituency for how long no one can tell. It is a bore and an objectionable expense but there is no other chance of getting in to Parliament and I certainly should like to be there. It is hard to bear this exclusion when one feels that one has the ability and experience to make some mark on that stage.

January 8 and 9 . . . The whole political position is very interesting. The Labour party are believed to be quaking in their shoes at the prospect of forming a Govt.

The European position is as bad as ever and the French are getting steadily worse in their treatment of Germany but now their exchange is crumbling rapidly and the franc today (January 14) is well over 90, perhaps 97, to the pound.

January 25 On Monday last, January 21st, the Baldwin Government was defeated on a vote of No Confidence and Ramsay MacDonald has become Prime Minister. The Cabinet includes two uncles – Parmoor and Sidney Webb – and is quite good. Indeed there is no reason why it should not be as efficient as its predecessor or more so. It hardly could be more inept than the Baldwin team. The greatest surprise is the inclusion of Chelmsford as First Lord of Admiralty. The public had no idea that he had Labour party leanings. I was at Winchester with him for 6 years and always kept above him. He was a regular Tory in those days.

There are a good many Cabinet Ministers with whom I used to co-operate in the Anti-Conscription fight. Some old Liberals such as Chas. Trevelyan and Noel Buxton and Arthur Ponsonby just outside the Cabinet.

April 13 . . . On Thursday 10th Dorothy and I went to Carlisle in the morning and thence to Kirkbride to open a small bazaar in the little Wesleyan Chapel getting back the same evening at 10.30. Rather a hard day but I think it was worth while as our people are working very hard and my presence is an encouragement.

June 3 . . . E.L.H. and I went to Brighton on Thursday May 22nd to attend the meetings of the National Liberal Fedn . . . I met Lloyd George for the first time since I lost my seat in Parliament. As might be expected from his nature he was quite civil and I believe I was likewise and as we met on a narrow stairway it was really a case of civility or gross rudeness. I dont like him.

Reception in the evening by Viscount Grey who made an excellent speech. Attended meetings next day and then heard Asquith at the public meeting in the evening. All went off well and the Liberal party appeared to be in good fettle.

June 22 . . . On Wednesday E.L.H. and I went to Carlisle by the morning train to attend an out door Liberal party at Longtown, given in the field of Mr. Ewart's farm, How End, and then to an evening meeting at Brampton, at both of which Geoffrey Howard spoke. Both were highly successful. Good of G.H. to come down seeing the Preference resolutions were to be discussed and divided upon that day but he had a pair. The majority against Preference on the first resolution was only six – too little to be pleasant.

July 27 . . . In public affairs the great question of the moment is the Conference in London on the subject of the Experts report on Germany's capacity to pay reparations and the question really is can the French be induced to allow Germany to pay or will they insist on so asserting their own power as to make it impossible for any persons to lend Germany money which is the foundation stone of the edifice of reparations.

I don't think there will be a general election this year and I don't particularly want one – too great a strain on one's finance. And I doubt if anyone else does.

August 4 . . . It is now announced that the Allied Governments have come to an agreement on the subject of Germany. We have now to see whether Germany will agree. And the Irish boundary question appears to be reaching a crisis with a possibility of a general election on the subject – a very favourable chance for Liberals and R.D.H.

September 1 . . . [Masterman] expects a general election in the winter either on Russia or Ireland and it is curious that on the first subject we are against the Government and on the latter with them. He thinks MacDonald no more honest than L.G. who we agreed was a rogue but I confess I am not so sure about this judgement of MacDonald.

Also we agreed that Percy Illingworth's death was the greatest misfortune that the Liberal party had suffered in recent years and that without his death L.G. could not have broken up the party. M. told me that L.G. had expressed the same opinion in private conversation.

October 12 . . . I had intended to stay [in Scotland] until this day week but the sudden general election has knocked that on the head and I had to leave on Friday, sleep that night at Glasgow and reach Carlisle at noon on Saturday. At two o'clock the Liberal Asscn. met and unanimously – indeed enthusiastically – chose me as candidate. I got here on Saturday night to pick up clothes and arrange a few affairs and go back tomorrow to start the campaign which ends on Oct. 29th.

The nominal cause of the election is the vote of H. of C. in favour of an enquiry into the dropping of a prosecution against one Campbell, an obscure person temporarily editing a Communist paper.

Why the Government should have objected it is difficult to understand unless it be that MacDonald really has told lies and certainly there is no obvious reason why they should dissolve sooner than accept the opinion of the majority of the House.

Perhaps Russia has more to do with it. The preposterous so-called Treaty could not have been defended and it may well be that an attempt to do so would have disclosed grave differences in their own ranks. Would Snowden have defended the loan?

November 10   The election took place on Wednesday, Oct. 29th and the result was an overwhelming victory for the Tory party who got 411 seats out of 615, the Liberals obtaining only 42. The Labour party lost 40 seats, their total result being 152. In North Cumberland a Labour candidate was brought out at the very last moment and the result was: Donald Howard 10,586, R.D.H. 6,821, B. Brooke (Labour) 2,125. It was most disappointing as we had improved our organization considerably and put in a lot of work and certainly our workers were in good spirits and supported us splendidly.

We had a pleasant contest and the weather was good which made getting about the country delightful . . . But the tide was altogether too strong. The Liberals were blamed on one side for putting the Labour party in office and on the other side for putting them out and they got no thanks for either action. MacDonald has behaved very badly and I now think Masterman was more right than I had supposed. MacDonald's conduct over the Zinovieff letter (or the alleged letter) is on any showing disgraceful and unworthy of a gentleman.

. . . On Monday 10th E.L.H. and I went up to London for a sudden call to a China Conference meeting which enabled us to attend an evening party at Lord Beauchamp's in Belgrave Square for the benefit of Liberal candidates. Asquith was guest of honour and spoke to us, as also L.G., badly received. There is no doubt in my mind that no party can include L.G. amongst its leaders and succeed. He is a rascal and liar and everybody knows it, but few dare say so.

November 30   . . . Two visits to Manchester, one on Tuesday for the N.R.U. and the other on Thursday to attend the Commission enquiring into the Liberal debacle at the election. The Commissioners, appointed by Asquith, were Donald Maclean, chairman, Godfrey Collins, now chief Liberal Whip, McCurdy and Sir Robert Hutchison, junior whip, the two latter being Lloyd Georgeites. I told these commissioners that in my view it was not organization which was wrong with the Liberal party: the organization is all right on paper, the trouble is that there are not live men filling the various places. The real causes of our disaster were three. First the political position brought about by our having infuriated the Tories by putting the Labour party in office in January and then infuriating the Labour party by putting them out in October. Both acts were right but neither act pleased anybody. Then we only had 340 candidates in the field which meant that we could not get a majority over both our opponents and therefore those who desired a stable government and an end to annual general elections were bound to vote Tory and finally I said no party could succeed if Lloyd George was reckoned one of their leaders. Seventy-five per cent of the country believe him to be a rogue and they are right. This puts Liberal candidates in an impossible position.

December 5 . . . Today I went over to Manchester where a special meeting of the N[ational] R[eform] U[nion] Committee met Lord Beauchamp at tea after he had opened a Liberal bazaar at Royton.

We had a good talk about politics and decided to invite Walter Runciman to lunch on Saty. Dec. 13th, which invitation was sent and accepted by telephone while we were waiting and talking. The Committee also adopted a manifesto on Liberal principles which I had drafted. Beauchamp thinks there is urgency to take the field. . . .

December 13 . . . On Thursday I went up to London . . . to dine with Sir Herbert Leon in his flat at 7 Cleveland Row . . . The party was in addition to the host, Sirs Hugh Bell, Ernest Benn, Chas. Seely, Messrs Molteno, Wedgwood Benn M.P., Hopkin Morris M.P., F.W. Hirst, A.J. Bonwick, Hugh Seely, Col. Kerr and myself – the common bond being detestation of Lloyd George.

. . . Then I returned by night train to Liverpool in order to preside at the lunch to Runciman given by the National Reform Union which was a great success. About 110 present – at only one week's notice, on a Saturday afternoon in Manchester. Walter made an excellent speech, as he generally does. The Liberal spirit is curiously good.

December 29 . . . We held a meeting of the Liberal Federal Council in the Reform Club to discuss the proposed Liberal Convention in London at the end of January and to nominate our delegates.

1925

[The General Election of 1924 produced a marked shift in the balance of power within the Liberal party. More than half of the forty Liberal M.P.s were former Coalition M.P.s or candidates. Asquith himself had been beaten and now went to the Lords as Earl of Oxford, while Lloyd George secured election as Chairman of the Parliamentary Party. Holt's sympathies, however, lay with the small group of nine M.P.s under Runciman who refused to accept Lloyd George. The ongoing question of Lloyd George's contribution to the party's finances continued to sour relations between the two factions, while another notable bone of contention was the Green Book, *Land and the Nation*, the report of a Land Inquiry Committee sponsored by Lloyd George.

It is interesting to note Holt's rather naive analysis of the party's problems. In his view party organisation was irrelevant and elaborate programmes unnecessary. All that was required was the reiteration of basic Liberal principles.]

[January] . . . On Wednesday [January 7] A.D.H. and I entertained Mr. and Mrs. Wedgwood Benn at Princes in Piccadilly and talked politics. He is a nice little chap, loathes L.G., as I do, because he too hates roguery and the dirty ways of the Welshman. . . .

The real disappointment is the collapse of the Liberal party and the feeling that there is no political career open to me or to my friends. I should have liked public life and I still believe that I could make a useful and influential Member of Parliament but there does not seem the smallest chance of getting elected unless I forswear some of the opinions which I believe to be right.

It is no use deluding oneself, I could not get a decent sized audience to listen to me in any place, except as candidate during an election, unless I was appearing as the satellite of some big politician. Nor is it easy to get one's opinions published in the public press.

January 18 I was in Carlisle on Monday 12th discussing whether I should go on as prospective candidate. It is mainly a question of whether the place will be satisfied with the amount of 'nursing' I can do. It is really impossible to spend weeks every year in a constituency and do something else really well.

On Saturday 17th attended a meeting at Manchester of the delegates from the Lancashire, Cheshire and N.W. Fedn. to the London Convention. Very large attendance. E.L.H. was with me. Tried unsuccessfully to get them to discard the idea of a programme.

January 27 . . . So Asquith becomes Earl of Oxford, a confession of failure and now the Liberal party will have to wrestle with Lloyd George's leadership. However much we may pretend, a peer never can be the de facto leader as the real decisions must be taken in H. of C. It is a horrid stroke of fate to find myself helpless.

February 8 On January 28th I went to London . . . to attend the great Liberal convention . . . Much pleasant and interesting talk about economic propaganda and how to get it to the people at a cost within our power. The great difficulty at present is to find the means by which to put an unattractive gospel before the people.

On Thursday January 29th E.L.H. and I attended the Convention . . . Nothing really important occurred, as might have been expected. Organization was discussed which is neither here nor there. In the afternoon we discussed an elaborate programme drawn up by Ramsay Muir and Co. against which I made the best protest I could and gained a great deal of sympathy, tho' I accepted defeat without attempting to take a vote. As time went on I think more and more people came to agree with my view that elaborate programmes do more harm than good and that the party ought not to be committed to anything but simple principles.

This evening I dined with the 'Weekly Westminster' crowd. I am a small shareholder in the venture which is no more successful than *Common Sense*. Ramsay Muir is the editor and is evidently heavily backed by the new Manchester school.

Afterwards there was a reception by Mr. and Mrs. Asquith at the National Liberal Club. . . .

Mr. A. said he heard I had been playing the rebel, so I said that I did not see what satisfaction there could be in taking a lot of time and trouble over political work if at the end one did not have the power to say what one thought right and he expressed entire agreement and he said he hoped in future to be in a position to do likewise.

On Friday January 30th we continued the Convention. In the afternoon there was a short discussion on Liberal leadership which we succeeded in terminating by pointing out that a leader always appoints himself. It is not a question of election, but of a man delivering a message which is acceptable to the followers. I told them that the leadership was determined by this – after the prophet has spoken will the people say 'This is the voice of a god' or 'Get thee behind me Satan' and this produced laughter.

In the evening a great demonstration at the Albert Hall with all the paraphernalia of reunion, L.G. walking in with Mrs. A. etc. Grey in the chair. Nobody really good except the representative of the young Liberals, Kingsley Griffith, who was certainly very eloquent.

[February 7] Dined at the annual Shipbrokers banquet. Amery chief guest, who made an extreme protectionist speech to the annoyance of many. Actually suggested a return to the Navigation Laws.

February 15 Have spent the last week in Liverpool, very quietly except for a wild outburst caused by my stating publicly at the Dock Board last Thursday what the Dock Board's views are on the subject of the Mersey Tunnel. The proposed branch to Wallasey is an absurd waste of money, apart from its objectionable position as regards the Alfred entrance, and would never have been agreed to by anybody who felt financial responsibility, but as the Government has agreed to provide most of the cost in order to relieve unemployment, nobody seems to care how much is spent. So far as I can see all the money spent in forcing works of doubtful utility in order to help the unemployed is making matters worse. Staving off the evil day generally does make the final catastrophe worse.

How true it is that 'Satan findeth mischief still for idle hands to do'.

March 1 . . . On Saturday . . . a meeting in Liverpool of the Lancashire, Cheshire and North Western Liberal Federation at which I was chosen one of the three representatives on the National Liberal Federation, Sir Arthur Haworth and Ramsay Muir being the others.

March 14 On Wednesday March 4th I was in London for the committee meeting of the Free Trade Union. Rather important because of the differences on this subject in the ranks of the Labour party. Afterwards I saw Lees Smith at the H. of Commons and had a friendly talk with him trying to persuade him and Lord Arnold or some other Free Trade Labour man to join the Committee. It was never intended that the F.T.U. should be a party organization but it is difficult to avoid this if some hold aloof.

I have done a good deal of political speaking at minor meetings: March 5 to Young Liberals at Manchester, March 12 likewise at Littleborough, March 13 Annual meeting of National Reform Union at Manchester with a dinner in the evening at which Beauchamp was the principal guest and made an excellent sensible speech. On March 9 we had a Liberal meeting here to consider what should be done and made no progress. What we are short of is somebody to get up and do it.

March 30 . . . In London I attended my first meeting of the National Liberal Federation Committee at which I was not tremendously impressed . . . I went again on the following Wednesday when Earl of Oxford and Lloyd George addressed us on the subject of the organiser and the money: not much done and I dont think the money scheme is making much progress.

April 4 E.L.H. and I went off to Carlisle to look after Liberalism in North Cumberland . . . Met the Executive Committee to discuss a new agent instead of that excellent fellow Velden who wishes to return South and has accepted the agency for Walter Runciman at Swansea.

Then on Monday I went to Brampton . . . and drove out in the afternoon to see the derelict collieries from Hallbankgate to Midgeholme. It is very sad to see the whole country side in failure, but I dont see how it can be helped. It is the inevitable result of the Trade Union policy of asking the same wages in good districts and in bad districts. The less well situated collieries with poor or broken seams must close down.

August 30 . . . On the Saturday evening I travelled to Perth joining E.L.H. there. The only other occupant of the dining car was Lord Haldane with whom I had a good talk particularly about the trouble in China. He has not a cheerful view of the public service, but I am not sure it is a wrong view. To my suggestions that we ought to have a first class minister in Peking or alternatively to send out a first class statesman from London he replied in both cases, 'Perhaps there is not such a man'.

September 6 . . . The seamen's strike in Australia and S. Africa goes on, and it is not a strike at all but a mutiny for the so called strikers are on articles. This disturbance was one of the reasons why I returned from Abernethy. I dont like leaving my partners alone to face all these disturbances and they are serious for us involving a considerable loss of money. It is remarkable how one's private affairs are affected by circumstances over which one has no control. Strikes in Australia, ferment of crude nationalism in China, the religious effervescence of the Wahabis stopping the pilgrimage to Mecca – all these things react unfavourably on my holidays and reduce my income.

September 13 On Tuesday morning I travelled up to London and thence by the Harwich boat to Amsterdam after an afternoon meeting on the subject of the strikes, or more properly mutinies, in Australia and South Africa. It really is extraordinary what people will do in pursuit of private gain. Here are the crews of ships who have signed an agreement to make a voyage to S. Africa or Australia and back, mostly decent men of good character and long service, who break their contracts, cause great loss to the people with whom they have made the contracts and intense discomfort and financial loss to the innocent passengers and owners of cargo. And all about £1 per month.

October 25 . . . Spent Wednesday in London partly for business and partly to attend the meeting of the N.L. Federation Committee. There is fresh trouble in front of the Liberal party over Lloyd George's preposterous Land policy, when what is really wanted is a period of sobriety and low taxation.

November 8 . . . The strike, i.e. mutiny, in Australia is just now collapsing – a most foolish performance involving the shipowners in substantial loss and probably bringing an immense amount of suffering to the house of every married sailor. It is extraordinary how blind men can be to their own interests when artful demagogues have suggested to them that they are ill treated.

November 22 . . . The event of last week was a visit to London with E.L.H. principally for meetings of Free Trade Union and Nat. Lib. Federation. It is very difficult to know what to make of the position of the former question. Continual nibblings with protection for lace and gas mantles but nothing serious attempted which makes it difficult to raise either money or energy in defence of the principle. At the N.L.F. the real question is the L.G. Land Campaign which seems likely to split the Liberal party. L.G. as usual tricky and dishonest.

November 29 On Monday E.L.H. and I went to Carlisle where we met Sir Donald Maclean . . . That evening we had meetings at Dalston and Wigton and the next night at Wetheral and Brampton. Quite good considering that there is no election in sight. . . .

On Tuesday I gave a lunch to meet Maclean, asking representatives from Cumberland constituencies in the hope of putting more life into them, especially Carlisle and Mid Cumberland.

Politically a split in the Liberal party which means a break with Lloyd George and his crew seems to be coming rapidly nearer. It really is hopeless trying to go on with a body of people whom nobody believes to be honest. That is the real crux of the matter. There can be no pleasant cooperation when you believe your allies are unmitigated rogues and they know you hold this opinion of them.

December 3 . . . On Tuesday night I went up to London partly to discuss evidence to be given before the Coal Commission on behalf of the shipowners and partly to attend another meeting of the N.L. Federation in connection with the Lloyd George Land policy. It appeared that there had been some discussion between L.G. and the Liberal Candidates Assocn. of which I am an absentee member, as a result of which L.G. has agreed to make his programme optional – in other words to scrap it.

December 13 . . . Went up to London that evening [December 10] in order to give evidence before the Coal Commission on behalf of the steam ship owners, jointly with Sir Ernest Glover. This was quite a pleasant experience and we seemed to be well received by all parties. I know so many of the people who are engaged in this sort of work that it is always a pleasant experience to meet them. For instance Herbert Samuel, the chairman of the Commission I knew very well in Parliamentary days and to a lesser extent Sir W. Beveridge, who used to be a Board of Trade official.

December 27 . . . Nearly had a row about Vivian Phillipps' speech at Hull concerning party funds and the Lloyd George fund. I trust the explosion will not be long delayed, no good can happen till we are rid of L.G. and all the stunt producers. . . .

Anne dined with me . . . and we went to 'Chauve Souris', a Russian ballet, artistic and grotesque. Russians dont appeal to me – nor any of their ideas.

1926

[The final rift between Asquith and Lloyd George came at the time of the General Strike in May, when the latter declared that he would not join the denunciation of the strike unless the government's conduct was also condemned. Holt was keen that the crisis should result in a complete split between the two wings of the party, but such an outcome was unlikely granted Lloyd George's continuing control over the party's finances. On 12 June Asquith suffered a stroke and in the weeks before his formal resignation in October the initiative passed progressively into Lloyd George's hands. By the end of the year, and much to Holt's disgust, Lloyd George had succeeded in capturing the party organisation and in removing entrenched Asquithians from its bureaucracy, in return for agreeing to underwrite the party financially. It was, thought Holt, an 'iniquitous deal.' In the meantime Holt had fought and lost a further by-election in Cumberland. His diary reveals a marked waning in his enthusiasm for the electoral fray.]

January 17 I have had two visits to London since I last wrote: on January 6th to attend a meeting of the Free Trade Union and on January 13th and 14th to attend meetings of the China and Australian Conferences and of the National Liberal Federation to consider the L.G. Land programme. Then on Friday the 15th I went up to Carlisle and held a meeting at Burgh that evening and spent the afternoon of the next day in discussing the Land programme and other things with the North Cumberland Liberal Assocn. There certainly is no desire for a radical alteration in the land system amongst the farmers of N. Cumberland.

February 1 . . . On Thursday evening I was obliged to go to London . . . which gave me a chance of attending Lord Oxford's gathering of Liberals on Friday afternoon. This was an appeal for funds for Headquarters and was quite interesting. Several people promised large sums but I did not as I have nothing much available in view of my other commitments. One of the sensations of the week has been Sir Alfred Mond's withdrawal from the Liberal party and entry into the Conservative ranks. I confess I am surprised. He seemed such a convinced Free Trader, but of course it was obvious from his career as a Coalitionist that personal ambition played a big part in his political conduct. At present the Liberal party offers no chance to the ambitious.

February 8 . . . My real object in going to London was to attend a meeting of the China Committee, a self appointed body with Lord Southborough for chairman whose object it is to advise the Govt how to handle the difficulty in China. The problem is intensely interesting and nobody has any real solution. The one point on which we are all agreed is 'Force is no remedy'. It is amusing to find Warren Swire an enlightened pacifist – very nearly a peace at any price man.

February 25 During the week after the previous entry there was nothing of any note except the annual meeting of the Ocean Steam Ship Company. It is really amusing to note how it is possible for the most important event of the year to appear unimportant. After all the O.S.S. Co. does mean to me and mine worldly prosperity, bread and butter, all the pleasures of life – Abernethy, politics and so on – and yet in one sense it appears a very unimportant thing and we take its affairs like a rainstorm. However, we had a fairly good account, much better than the shareholders expected and the meeting was quite a joyous occasion. Prospects for the next financial year are rather better. It is a great help that the difficulties in the Hedjaz have come to an end and that the pilgrimage is resumed. I find it impossible to avoid a quiet chuckle at the thought that a middle class English household in Liverpool has its material welfare seriously affected by the religious differences of Mahometans. The world is a funny place. The interdependence is much greater than most people suppose and it matters more to me and many most respectable fellow citizens how the Sultan of the Wahabis behaves than what happens in Football, Cricket or Golf matches, although no one would suspect this from reading the newspapers.

Then last week I attended the Liberal Convention in London to consider Lloyd George's land scheme. The Urban proposals on Wed. Feb. 17th went through with very little contention but the Rural proposals were seriously modified mainly as a result of the North Cumberland amendments. Lloyd George was in a conciliatory mood, his object being to fix himself upon us as Leader of the party and it was impossible to force a breach with him without putting oneself hopelessly in the wrong. The compromise resulted from an extremely amusing speech by Sir Harry Verney – he is a good and most delightful fellow.

. . . Went up to Carlisle on Monday March 1st speaking at Gilsland that night with Finney, ex-M.P. and prospective candidate for Hexham, and on Tuesday at

Low Row. The meetings were well attended seeing that there is no election in sight and we are keeping the Liberal party in N. Cumberland in good fettle. There is no desire for the Land programmes.

March 7 . . . Last night the paper announced that the French Government had fallen owing to the Chamber of Deputies rejecting the financial proposals necessary to balance their budget. The future of France seems full of danger as there can be only one end to the persistent refusal to pay the taxes necessary to meet the public expenditure and the position is curiously like that three or four years before their Revolution. It does not look as if either England or America would ever receive a halfpenny of the money lent to France.

March 14 . . . The League of Nations meeting at Geneva called to admit Germany seems to be nearing disaster. The French appear to be trying to place a satellite – Poland, Spain or even Brazil – on the Council as a permanent member as a set off to Germany and to this it appears that Austen Chamberlain has become a consenting party in spite of the fact that British opinion is almost unanimous in opposition to any proposal to make the entry of Germany into the League of Nations the subject of a bargain.

Sweden has held out single handed against the deal, sustained by the sympathy of most of the Northern people.

France is building up a terrible day of reckoning, making enemies of everybody.

March 19 . . . The Geneva meeting broke up on Tuesday night in complete failure, Brazil having vetoed the assignment of a permanent seat on the Council to Germany, everyone thinks at the instigation of France.

April 23 . . . This afternoon I went to Manchester to the annual meeting of the National Reform Union, only a small attendance but I made a fairly long speech in the hope of publication, mainly about national finance. I wish we could get more of the educated classes to take a burning interest in public affairs. And the hope of publication did not materialize.

May 8 . . . Now we are wrestling with a general strike. No Trade Unionist is to do any work and the whole activities of the community are to be held up until this particular section of manual workers are satisfied with the arrangements made for running the coal mines. So far the country has been very quiet and in Liverpool there has been but little difficulty – trams running, electric power stations working, some ships discharging by volunteer labour mainly food of which there is no scarcity. The greatest trouble is the railways which are hardly working at all but of course motor transport gets over a good deal of this difficulty.

May 16 . . . In the middle of the week the general strike was officially called off. It was a complete failure. It had not really terminated on Saturday as questions of reinstating the strikers or some of them were not settled and of course until the miners return to work and coal becomes plentiful most industries must go slow.

The dock labourers had only returned to work at Liverpool and Southampton. London, Birkenhead, Bristol Channel and Glasgow idle except for volunteer labour.

There has been no serious disorder.

May 21 Except for the coal strike work has gone on as usual and we are sending three ships to sea on tomorrow and Sunday with good, and in two cases, full cargoes. I dont expect any early end of the coal strike. The representatives of the masters and men are equally impossible and there is a complete absence of goodwill. This means that other business will gradually terminate.

May 31 . . . The coal strike is still dragging on, but it looks like a break and a settlement in some districts irrespective of any National settlement, and in my opinion no good will come about until negotiations are conducted in small areas instead of on these huge unwieldy scales.

June 6 . . . Coal strike still going on and people accommodating themselves to the circumstance. Some considerable importation of foreign coal on the quiet is helping to keep things going and may account for an improvement in the railway services.

On Wednesday evening I went up to London for an emergency meeting of the Committee of the N.L.F. to consider the Lloyd George position. Thanks to the publication of a letter from Lord Oxford terminating his political connection with L.G. on account of the latter's action during the general strike and his letters to the American press, there seems some chance of getting rid of the scoundrel but of course this cannot be done without something like a split in the Liberal party. However the unity since 1923 has been only superficial and an open split would be far better. The men L.G. brought with him from his Coalition days are joining the Tory party freely and he has very little following except what he buys with the great fund obtained by the sale of titles during his Premiership.

No party can succeed with L.G. as a leader – the distrust is too deep-seated.

June 24 . . . On Wednesday 16th June I went to Weston-super-Mare – a second rate seaside place – to the annual meeting of the National Liberal Fedn. Stayed at the Grand Atlantic Hotel – also second rate – but there was much pleasant company there. The meetings were successful in avoiding an open breach and it is pretty clear to me that the rank and file of the Liberal party do not desire a quarrel. They do wish for unity and they dont understand the great and real objections to Lloyd George which have never been stated in plain language so as to reach the rank and file. My impression is that whoever forces a quarrel will lose the day. Lord Oxford's illness brought on by worry forced him to be absent. L.G. turned up and had a rather lukewarm reception. Runciman was there at the beginning, sulked and went away – a foolish exhibition. John

Simon spoke twice and well, improving his position, while Charles Hobhouse who was there all the time made a great stride to the front. Viscount Grey spoke well at the evening meeting on Friday.

July 26 . . . The coal stoppage is still going on with very little sign – indeed no sign – of its coming to an end. In Warwickshire alone has there been any substantial return to work, a small return in Staffordshire and none elsewhere. One result is a great improvement in the country so far as cleanliness, gardens etc. are concerned, but the other is a general stoppage of business. Goods are not manufactured, particularly those such as iron and steel which require a great quantity of coal. A good deal of foreign coal is being imported so the railways are giving a full passenger service, very necessary in view of the holiday season but vexatious regulations about coal for domestic use make it difficult even for enterprising people to arrange their cooking etc.

However gas and electricity are going, but the coal used is costing at least double. It is a miserable affair largely due to the absurd hopes entertained directly after the war and the apparent inability of the wage earners or their leaders to accept the position that people cannot expect to be as well off after a devastating war as they were before.

August 1 . . . The coal strike no nearer an end, except in the sense that every day must bring a conclusion nearer. But there is no real willingness on any part to meet the views of others.

August 29 E.L.H. and I arrived home last night . . . I from Carlisle where I had just been adopted Liberal candidate to fight the bye-election caused by Donald Howard succeeding as Lord Strathcona on his mother's death. A beastly nuisance – 3 weeks hard work, £800 expense at least and in all probability another defeat. A jolly holiday interrupted too. The political situation is very difficult, and although the Government has given anything but satisfaction the dissension in the Liberal party has done a good deal to lower its vitality. I gather Lord Oxford is suffering from old age. The letter to L.G. in May was a terrible mistake unless it was to be followed up by further steps and a vigorous presentment of the real case for declining to deal with him. The difficulty for Lord Oxford is that L.G. has done nothing since 1923, when he was received back into the Liberal party, worse than the things he did before.

September 19 Got back today. The polling was on Friday and the declaration yesterday with the expected result. Graham (C) 8867, R.D.H. 6871, McIntyre (Labour) 2793. Of course we deluded ourselves into the belief that we were going to get much nearer although there was no solid foundation for that view. The Labour party were very disappointed with their poll as they expected 6000 when the count began. We had a lot of help from friends. Chas. Hobhouse gave 4 days, G. Howard, D. Maclean, H. Verney, Lord Beauchamp 2 each and there was a host of professional speakers. Chas. Roberts as President worked all the time and everything possible was done. Our party stuck together splendidly. We were fortunate in having very fine weather. . . .

After the election there was a violent attack upon me in Lloyd George's paper, the *Daily Chronicle*. It will do him the greater injury.

October 24 . . . I went up to London on Tuesday evening to attend a meeting of the Executive of the National Liberal Federation. The internal position of the Liberal party is very difficult as there are no central funds and in recent years the party has been led to look to Headquarters for its money. Ll.G. has offered to finance the rural constituencies. He has his great fund acquired by corruption when P.M. of a predominantly Tory coalition. What are we to do? The only salvation, to my mind, lies in the constituencies becoming independent financially and taking their own course.

Lord Oxford resigned the leadership of the Liberal party on Oct. 15th. In some ways a great figure, yet he succeeded to the leadership when the party was in overwhelming strength and he left it a ruin, sunk lower than any great party ever sank. It is impossible to acquit him of the major responsibility for this event. He trusted Ll.G. when he should have known that Ll.G. was not trustworthy, he surrounded himself with very inferior men and he ruined the whole party by the first coalition – an admission of weakness from which no recovery was possible for a generation. And he took Ll.G. back in 1923.

And yet difficult and even hopeless as the position is, there is no place for some of us except in a Liberal party. The Tories and the Labour are equally impossible. . . .

The coal stoppage goes on. There is a slow return to work, very slow. About 25% of the miners are back now, mainly in the Midlands. The weather has gone very cold – snow tonight – and it is hard when one can't burn fires freely or put on the central heating.

November 3 I was up in London on Thursday last to attend a lunch given by the Free Trade Union at the expense of F.H. Lambert of Penarth to Walter Runciman in order that W.R. should make a speech on Imperial Preference as a sort of counterblast to the visit of the Colonial Premiers. W.R. did it very well. . . .

The coal stoppage goes on. The men dribble back to work and as coal is very high in price those who are working are earning high wages. The end can hardly be far off, but the suffering and loss to the community is enormous. Had there been less political interference in the last 15 years and had these problems been left to a purely economic solution we should not have had a tenth of the trouble.

November 14 . . . Yesterday was my 58th birthday . . . Anyhow I have a lot to be thankful for and I hope I am thankful. Very good health, a comfortable fortune, the best wife in the world, three excellent and loving daughters, a very interesting business and a certain small position in public life. It is really far more than most and one ought to be very grateful, especially as I might add a great number of very kind friends.

November 21 Rather a hectic week. On Monday morning I went to Hull primarily to speak for the Liberal candidate at the bye-election . . . I had quite a good meeting but I doubt if my speech was very effective to an audience mainly of manual labourers. Got back on Tuesday at midday, spoke to the Young Liberals in the evening and went up to London by the night train to discuss the Lloyd George finance proposals at the executive committee of Nat. Liberal Fedn. I dont see how any bargain can be made with Ll.G. properly. First of all the money has been got by gross corruption in office and ought not to be touched and then it is utterly wrong for a political association to take money on terms. And one of the terms is that Vivian Phillipps is to be ejected from his position – not a condition I should accept. We adjourned consideration till next Wednesday but the position is terribly difficult as the money is badly needed and few have the courage to refuse it and take the consequences.

November 25   . . . On Wednesday I rushed up to London by the 9.45 and was 45 mins. late owing to fog. Attended the N.L. Fedn, or rather the administrative committee of the million fund, and witnessed the sale of the Liberal party to Lloyd George. I have done what I could to protest against it and when it was carried by 17 votes to 10 left the room in company with J.A. Spender, the President, Vivian Phillipps, Donald Maclean, A. Brampton, Sir F. Layland-Barratt, Lady Currie, Lady Violet B[onham]-Carter, F.C. Thornborough, A.E. Withy and J.E. Myers. It is disgusting and to think that Charles Hobhouse who has spoken as strongly as I have about Ll.G. (in private) has taken the lead in this iniquitous transaction.

December 12   . . . E.L.H. and I went up to London again on the morning of Wednesday, December 8th when I was entertained at dinner by the 80 Club as a recognition of my services to the party and the bye-election in Cumberland. Walter Runciman took the chair . . . It was all very flattering and I am told that I made a really good speech . . . I emphasized the necessity of making retrenchment, repayment of public debt and the conservation of the financial resources of the country the first care of the Liberal party and of all who desire to improve the condition of the people.

There is a scheme on foot for building 6 or 7 very fast steamers – 22 or 23 knots speed – to run between this country and Australia and the promoters offered the management to us. I saw them on Thursday and declined. It is impossible to believe in the scheme financially and it was evident that our reputation was to be used to induce investment. Moreover the whole scheme of our business life would have to be revolutionized.

I have omitted to record that the Coal Stoppage came to an ignominious end about a fortnight ago. The men have gone back on district agreements and in a short time things will be normal. Let us hope for quiet and real friendliness in industry.

December 21   I was in London on Wed. Dec. 15th to attend the Nat. Lib. Fedn. when the sale of the organization to Lloyd George was agreed upon by 18 votes to 14. The gift of Ll.G's money is said to be unconditional, which I disbelieve as there is nothing in writing and we are told that it imposes moral obligations upon us, in which case it is not unconditional. We shall see.

1927

[Lloyd George's domination of the party at least provided it with a sense of purpose which had been lacking for some years. The impact of his control emerged in several by-election gains from the Conservative government in 1927 and 1928, although the narrow loss at Westbury in June 1927 was a disappointment. But the party was moving in a direction of which Holt and many others disapproved. Dissident Liberals established the Liberal Council under the veteran, Lord Grey, and Holt declined to assist the Liberal Central Association. 'It is a great pity,' he wrote, 'that unity in the Liberal party should be frustrated by requiring members of that party to profess respect for a particular person.' Nonetheless Holt agreed to accept nomination once more as Liberal candidate for North Cumberland at the next General Election. At a political meeting in November he was questioned about his attitude towards the Liberal leader and only wriggled out of an awkward situation by stressing that, strictly speaking, there was no leader of the party at that time, merely chairmen in the two Houses of Parliament.

Unrest in Shanghai during the course of the year caused Holt considerable concern on commercial and financial grounds.]

January 30 I was in London on Wednesday, Jan. 19th when a majority on the National Liberal Federation Executive Committee agreed finally to sell the organization to Lloyd George: price was an undertaking on his part to put £300,000 in the hands of trustees to finance the next general election and to defray the expenses of headquarters in London to the tune of about £42,000 annually. Ll.G. attended himself and gave his own explanation.

£42,000 represents the interest on a million pounds and he is also financing the Land campaign and a Liberal Industrial Enquiry, both of which are costly, so that his capital sum cannot be much short of 2 million pounds – all this obtained by shameful corruption in office. Vivian Phillipps was required to resign his position as chairman of the organization committee and I imagine every Liberal who will not bow the knee to Ll.G. will be driven from official positions in the party. All of which is supposed to promote party unity and to my sorrow has had the support of Beauchamp and Charles Hobhouse. Well some of us must keep up our independence and see that some of the constituencies stand fast.

February 1 At 10.45 a.m. Mrs. Rome let the water into the Gladstone Dock and we shall never see the bottom again . . . Rome and I are the only persons alive who were members of the Works Committee of the M.D. and H.B. when the job was started. The first move was in 1905 when we started to get Parliamentary powers and the whole work has suffered greatly from delays, put in by want of financial courage against which Rome and I protested. These have doubled the cost besides depriving us of the earnings we should have got in wartime.

February 17 . . . On Saturday 12th I went to Carlisle and interviewed the Executive Committee of the North Cumberland Liberal Association and agreed to be their candidate again. This is a decision I have taken with some doubt, especially as E.L.H. is against it, but I do not like doing nothing in this present crisis and hardly feel equal to making a new start in a new district. There is a solid backing in N. Cumberland not to be thrown away lightly. Then I help Liberalism all over Cumberland by keeping the flame burning and Carlisle and Mid-Cumberland are not dead tho' I fear that in the West – Whitehaven and Workington – there is scarcely a glimmer. And finally as the adopted candidate of a live Association no one can impugn my claim to be a Liberal. . . .

On Monday 14th I went to Glasgow for political speaking . . . I had quite a nice afternoon meeting in the Liberal Club and then in the evening at Clydebank an extraordinary fine meeting of about 750 in the Town Hall who listened to me for 40 minutes with great attention.

Seeing that Clydebank is a hot bed of Socialism I was utterly astonished at the meeting. The people appeared to belong to the better class of artisan and the small shopkeepers. . . .

On Wednesday morning we appointed the new organizing committee of the Liberal party, unanimously, Sir Herbert Samuel chairman. It would have been impossible to have chosen anyone better as he has been out of all the party disputes. Rumour says Ll.G. is not pleased.

In the evening a banquet of the Chamber of Shipping. Baldwin chief guest. He delivered a dithyramb on the heroism of British seamen especially during the war – very poetical – but Mr. Justice Hill and I agreed that we learned nothing of interest. Froth-blowing !!

March 10 . . . On Saturday morning I went to Carlisle and addressed the annual meeting of the Liberal Assocn., spending the week end at Boothby with Charles and Lady Cecilia Roberts.

Very kind – but teetotalism with poor food and a hugger mugger household is hard to bear, but probably good for body and soul.

Went to Glasgow on Monday afternoon and spoke to the young Liberals of Pollok on Monday and to a Liberal meeting at Alva near Alloa on the Tuesday . . . I should judge that Major Donaldson was putting up a good fight in Clackmannan and East Stirling. He is very bitter against Ll.G. and no wonder. Scottish Liberalism was ruined in 1918 when 27 Liberal seats were sold by Ll.G. to the Tories thro' Geo. Younger. This is the reason why Ll.G. has now got 2 million pounds or more to spend on politics, which will never benefit him. . . .

The position in China still full of difficulty. The Cantonese undoubtedly gaining ground. The real point of interest now is whether they can shed their Bolshevist advisers and get on to a friendly footing with the European trading nations. It is all so unreal in many ways as Nationalism appears to be everywhere. So far as my political observation goes Nationalism generally means the uprising of the inferior civilisation against the superior. 'Good government is no substitute for self government' is quite true but it is a tragedy that self government so often means bad government. The phenomenon is much the same as that exhibited by the Labour party, which is fundamentally a class movement representing the wish of the manual workers when organized in Trade Unions to get the leading places in Government filled by 'our lot'. These people look on big places as perquisites in which all classes of the community should get their share. They do not conceive of the office as a trust to be held by the most competent man.

March 20 . . . Wednesday given to the National Liberal Federation. Nothing of importance except a vote on the appointment of Tweed as organizing secretary which was carried by a substantial majority mainly because Herbert Samuel recommended it. To my mind Tweed is quite untrustworthy as everybody who is in Ll.G's confidence is: honest men dont go into that stable.

March 27 On Monday we had a visit from Lord Thomson, a Labour peer, really a regular soldier taken into the Cabinet as Secretary of State for Air. The object of his visit was to speak at a League of Nations meeting at the Toxteth Congregational Church. It was a good meeting but the speech was not much. Quite a pleasant fellow with very little affinity to the Labour movement. . . .

I went to the Wellington Rooms on Thursday with the young people. It seemed a fair dance but the place is filthy and scarcely fit for gentle folk. It must be given up and I daresay I shall never go there again. It is painful to think of this collapse of Liverpool Society and to reflect on what the place was 30 years ago.

April 1 On Tuesday evening I went up to Carlisle and spoke at Ireby that night. The hall was packed – about 200 present – but I daresay an excellent entertainment – concert, ventriloquism etc – had as much to do with the audience as my eloquence . . . On Thursday travelled to Bolton where I opened a Liberal bazaar. A very good attendance and it is surprising how much money is raised at these East Lancashire bazaars. £1000 the first day and they were hoping to make £3500 in a four day sale.

There is no doubt the Liberal Party has been much encouraged by the results of the bye-elections at Leith and North Southwark, both of which they have won. It is a funny result that Wedgwood Benn joining the Labour party and resigning his seat in protest against Lloyd George getting a control of the Liberal party through his money should have enabled one of Ll.G's henchmen – Ernest Brown – to secure a considerable personal triumph.

Affairs in China are getting very bad. The Europeans have to evacuate the Yangtsze*[sic]* Valley and there is no doubt that the Cantonese revolution is for the moment definitely anti-foreign. While the disturbance is getting much worse in the North, matters are rather easier in the South and goods are going into consumption from Hong Kong more freely. Perhaps this is due to the agitation having moved North.

A deficit of about £36 millions announced in the finance of the year. Winston

Churchill will find himself in great difficulty with his Budget as any new taxes will be bitterly resented. What a chance the Liberals have if they will come out boldly as the champions of economy, the taxpayer and the consumer.

May 9 On Tuesday I went to Carlisle and addressed a good gathering at Wigton, I think to the general satisfaction. Since I last spoke in Cumberland we have had three political events. The Budget which is a sham of the worst type, the deficiency being made good by raiding the road fund (12 ms.), making payers of property tax pay three half yearly instalments in one year (15 ms.) and taking one month's credit from the brewers (5 m), which means a prospective deficit of 32 mills. next year. Then there is the Trade Union Bill – a foolish aggravation of ill feeling just when industrial relations seemed to be settling down and the proposal to give votes to women on the same terms as men. This is incorrectly but picturesquely described as votes for flappers and wont be popular with anybody. It is unanswerable as a matter of abstract justice but nobody wants this huge addition to the electorate.

May 23 . . . In spite of all the disturbances in China trade is still alive on a larger scale than anyone could have expected.

May 26 At the meeting of the Dock Board today Arthur Bibby moved and J.H. Beazley seconded my appointment as Chairman – carried unanimously. It is a great compliment, not only to myself but also to the family and the business. This is probably the most important public office out of London and the highest post which I could have hoped to attain after losing a career in Parliament . . . In the world at large the chairmanship of the Dock Board may not be a big thing, but in the vision of Liverpool as I knew it when I started on my career in business it was a very big thing.

June 17 . . . Today the result of the Westbury election was announced. The Conservative returned by about 150 votes – rather disappointing to our hopes. The Labour candidate was a bad third.

July 4 Went to Carlisle for Saturday to see the new agent . . . Had a pleasant and interesting talk with the Secretary of the Labour party who is a blacksmith at the Naworth Colliery. He was very friendly and volunteered the opinion that they ought to support me and put the Tory out. I think he felt it would be nice to win . . . He asked me if I was related to Holt of the Blue Funnel Line, so I said I was that man and he observed 'What strikes me about people like you is that you must know an awful lot of things and have to think about an awful lot of things.' Very nice.

July 12 . . . On Thursday I attended a lunch given in honour of Harcourt Johnstone for his gallant attempt at Westbury, John Simon in the chair. I met . . . Lady Oxford who was cordial and observed 'I like you – you hate Lloyd George so thoroughly.' But I dont think I do. I only regard him as a scoundrel.

July 19 Gladstone Dock opened. This day King George V and Queen Mary arrived at the Riverside Station from Edinburgh at 11.30 a.m. where they were received by a large party including myself as Chairman of the Dock Board and E.L.H. . . . The whole thing was a great success as I heard next morning from Lord Derby who most considerately wrote to me on the very evening that he had never known the King and Queen enjoy a ceremony more.

September 11 . . . The neighbourhood is changing so rapidly, nearly all the big houses gone and a new town of moderate 2 storey houses covering the place.

November 21 . . . On [November 9] Miss Margaret Beavan was elected Lord Mayor of Liverpool, the first woman to be so elected. I rather think the motive was to make a break as Fred Bowring during his two years term had spent money on a scale which would defy comparison by any possible successor and such expenditure would not be expected from a lady.

Next day I went to Carlisle speaking at Kingstown and Longtown that night and at Abbey Town and Silloth on Friday. Harcourt Johnstone came to help me. He speaks very well and I like him, but he is not our sort. Too fond of his bed for my taste. . . .

On Tuesday November 15th I went to London and attended a very pleasant dinner given by Sir Hugh Bell at the Reform Club to discuss the position of the Free Trade movement . . . It is a curious circumstance that while Free Trade is certainly gaining ground in acceptance intellectually amongst all who have international interests at heart, and very largely amongst foreigners, it is no longer an important electioneering issue here and is being stealthily undermined in practice by a Parliament which is in fact protectionist tho' elected for wholly different reasons.

December 18 . . . Another event of great public importance is the rejection by the House of Commons of the proposed new alternative Prayer Book. This was quite unexpected and has greatly upset the Church party who fondly believed that they had freed themselves from the control of Parliament while retaining the advantages of establishment. The real cause was an outburst of Protestant feeling at alterations in the Communion service and proposals for reservation of the sacrament. The meaning of the vote seems to me to be 'Parsons, remember the Church of England is a Protestant Church.' The parsons have forgotten the vast number of protestants who are outside the church.

1928

[The Lloyd Georgeite Liberal party continued to make progress in the course of 1928, but it was significant that Labour was the main beneficiary of the government's mounting unpopularity. In February the famous 'Yellow Book', *Britain's Industrial Future*, was published by Lloyd George's Liberal Industrial Inquiry, a body of politicians and economists which included Keynes, Ramsay Muir and Herbert Samuel. It marked a distinct movement towards interventionism in Liberal thinking. Holt clung to the hope that the traditional Liberal issue of Free Trade would be at the forefront of the next election campaign.]

January 8 . . . In the South of England there have been terrible floods through rain and melting snow and the houses near the Thames from Chelsea to the City have been flooded and some people drowned in their basements.

Yesterday we finished at India Buildings. I have worked there since Easter 1889 and the business of the Ocean Steamship Co. has been carried on there since its birth in 1865 . . . We start tomorrow in our new building.

[The India Buildings, erected in 1834 by George Holt, were so named because in that year the monopoly of the East India Company was finally abolished, enabling Liverpool merchants henceforth to trade freely with the Far East. The second India Buildings, into which the Ocean Steam Ship Company moved in 1928, was built on a site four times the size of the original. It was destroyed by fire bombs during the Second World War.]

January 22 On Thursday I was entertained by my Liberal friends at the Reform Club here to express their appreciation of my services as President of the Liverpool Liberal Federal Council on the occasion of my retirement made necessary by my appointment as Chairman of Mersey Docks and Harbour Board. A large attendance – Sir Ben Johnson in the chair, Vivian Phillipps came from London and spoke after Johnson in proposing my health. All far too flattering.

January 29 . . . Nothing startling in the great world. The trade with China still goes on remarkably considering the chaos in the government of that country. The Blue Funnel enterprise is flourishing and I only hope that we may [be] allowed 12 months at least without disturbance, or misfortune.

February 8 . . . On Monday I went to London for business next day and attended Lady Beauchamp's party for Liberal members of the two Houses of Parliament. L.G. was there but I did not come across him (intentionally). I saw a lot of friends and enjoyed myself a great deal, but what a horrible descent from the days when I first went to such parties 20 years ago. Cruel fate.

February 12 . . . The public event of the week has been the election at Lancaster where the Liberal candidate won the seat by a big majority. Lloyd George supported him heavily and was violently attacked by Lord Ashton, long the head of Liberalism in Lancaster, so that the election is very much a triumph for that dangerous man.

February 20 . . . The Earl of Oxford and Asquith died last week and has been buried today. He was a great figure in public life and had some very fine qualities of mind and heart. He was noble in his generosity to his associates and in not suspecting evil from them, but this was unfair to his followers who suffered because he allowed unworthy men – and in particular Ll.G. – to control affairs. I consider that he was a weak man in the management of affairs and easily imposed upon. He bore undeserved misfortune with great magnanimity. His greatest misfortune was his second marriage. Lady Oxford was not sympathetic to the backbone of Liberalism and her extravagance particularly with regard to money caused much scandal. It was shocking to have it announced only a few months ago that Lord Oxford was living on the charitable subscriptions of persons, many of whom were political opponents. However that is better than wealth acquired by the corrupt sale of titles. Lord Oxford's power of speech was remarkable – the fewest possible words in proportion to the meaning, most effective in Parliament but not on a popular platform.

April 10 . . . King Amanullah of Afghanistan took this occasion to visit Liverpool and on Thursday afternoon I had to help receive him and his party on arrival from Manchester via Port Sunlight at the Landing Stage. E.L.H. with me. The Queen very attractive and looks almost European. That evening a banquet at the Town Hall which was quite pleasant. Next morning I had to receive him at Gladstone Dock, when there was a deluge of rain which made it impossible to do anything but drive round in motor cars and then we all drove out to Aintree. The Grand National was a fiasco, only one horse out of 42 or more starters finishing the course without falling. Tipperary Tim, a rank outsider with a tube in his throat ridden by an embryo solicitor in Chester named Dutton.

April 23 [Business trip to Holland] I think our negotiations were successful – certainly we arranged all our difficulties with the Dutch with whom we are on cordial terms but the Germans are not pleasant: they want to get back their pre-war position which is impossible seeing that others, Scandinavians, Japanese etc. have partly filled it and cannot be driven out. One of the disgusting features of our Conference is that both the Germans and Scandinavians freely break their agreements if necessary to get business for their lines. . . .

Then on Monday April 30th I returned to London for a dinner given by Harcourt Johnstone at the Ritz Hotel to forward the Free Trade cause. Walter Runciman was the principal guest – a party of about 20. Next day a meeting of the Committee of F.T.U. when Beauchamp's resignation was accepted and Henry Bell elected his successor. I dont understand the inwardness of B's resignation. Time will show.

. . . I think it was on Wednesday May 2nd, I received an invitation to join the Board of Martin's Bank – really the old Bank of Liverpool founded by my grandfather and others, of which Uncle William and my father were in turn directors. With the consent of my partners I have accepted. This is one of the Liverpool institutions which it is important to keep alive as such and for that reason I gladly accepted. A year or two ago, thro' the friendliness of Walter Runciman, I was offered a seat on the board of the Westminster Bank which I declined as it was completely off my beat, but Martin's Bank is quite different.

June 8 . . . On the 1st of June I handed over to the Boy Scouts connected with Ullet Road Church as a loan a meeting room into which the old stable here has been converted. The Scout movement is doing a lot of good in teaching the boys self discipline and I am glad to be able to help it on.

September 8 . . . Plenty of work of course. Luckily everything is going on well at India Buildings and we are really making a little money, but could do with more.

November 2 . . . Municipal elections yesterday. Considerable gains to Labour party everywhere and particularly in Liverpool.

November 11 . . . [November 9] E.L.H. and I went to Manchester to the dinner of the N.R. Union at which of course I took the chair. J.M. Robertson, chief guest, made an excellent fighting Free Trade speech. We had a good assembly of fully 120 persons and the speech was very well received but there was only a poor report in the Manchester Guardian next day.

It is very disheartening work – this fight for Liberalism and the existence of the Liberal party.

November 25 . . . Free Trade is going to be a major issue at the election and evidently the Government is doing badly. They are unpopular because they have done nothing well.

December 21 . . . Spent an uneventful week in Liverpool. Daily round is quite sufficient for me with the Dock Board and the steamers which it is a satisfaction to record are doing quite well. It is remarkable how the China trade has kept up in spite of all the difficulties and these do seem to be lessening, tho' there can be no prospect of good government in China until the idea of honest and disinterested public service gets into the Chinese mind. This is an idea which has been prevalent in this country long enough to make everybody accept it as a commonplace even though in practice there may be failures, but in many countries it is quite unknown. Public service is simply a chance to feather your nest.

December 31 . . . End of 1928 – not a bad year. In spite of many difficulties especially in China our business has done well and we have made a better profit than for many years and the prospects look slightly better. . . .

In public matters we are all very anxious about the King who has been gravely ill since the latter half of November. There is still ground for hope but no one can be ill so long without great loss of strength. King George has been an admirable public servant. No more conscientious man in the country and he is widely and deeply respected.

1929

[By the end of the decade unemployment had become the country's most pressing social and economic problem. A special committee headed by Lloyd George, Seebohm Rowntree and Lord Lothian (Philip Kerr) produced the document 'We Can Conquer Unemployment' in March 1929. Calling for a massive programme of public works, the report formed the basis of the party's election campaign later that year. Trevor Wilson has written of this campaign: 'It is unlikely that the British electorate has ever been paid the compliment of a more far-sighted and responsible party programme.' Holt, on the other hand, was unimpressed. If Lloyd George's doctrine was Liberalism, it was not the creed with which Holt had been associated for the whole of his adult life. His career in the Liberal party effectively came to an end just as the party made its last significant attempt to regain power.]

January 27 . . . No great events in the world. Trade improving very slowly but there is a general feeling of encouragement. In China things are slightly improved but we are a very long way from a settled government. Nanking has very little real authority and the problems of disbanding the armies and keeping the ex-soldiers from brigandage seem almost insuperable, especially as the nominal government is in the hands of people with no real experience of administration, with no settled revenues and no body of honest officials to carry out their decrees.

February 4 . . . On Wednesday we had the annual meeting of Ocean S.S. Co.: a good year adding £90,000 to our carry forward after making full provision for everything. The managers at last got something for themselves above their minimum allowance – very useful, but half of it goes in taxation.

On Saturday I went to Preston to the annual meeting of the Lancashire, Cheshire and North Western Liberal Federation. Stanley of Alderley in the chair, Herbert Samuel chief speaker. A very good gathering with lots of spirit. I said a few words which were well received.

March 7 . . . The Government are getting very unpopular. They have done nothing well and if Liberals and Labour were united the Tories would have a terrible disaster. They have got their tails down. Mr. [C.P.] Williams says that is so as regards the H. of Commons and I do not think that any vote catching Budget can recover popularity for them. It is too late and every sensible man knows that their management of finance has been very bad. No good Budget can be proposed, tho' a specious one may be proposed, but I think people will see through it and that any attempt at vote catching will make things worse for the Government.

March 14 We went up to Carlisle as arranged and I had quite good little meetings on Monday and Tuesday returning here on Wednesday morning . . . I must go back to Carlisle tomorrow for two more meetings. It's terribly hard work with business and the Dock Board as well.

Lloyd George has made things very difficult for sober minded Liberals by a reckless promise to cure unemployment in 12 months. All sorts of public works financed by loan which will only add to the difficulties of all legitimate trade by enhancing prices and wages.

It is a terrible misfortune to have him on our side.

March 29 . . . on the Saturday night we had Donald and Lady Maclean to dinner. He was less opposed to Ll.G's promises than I expected. I find a strong feeling that Ll.G. has touched the popular imagination and that we ought not to throw cold water on his schemes, and of course if they can be switched off into a project for compelling the unemployed to work in exchange for their keep there may be a solid gain. . . .

On Tuesday I went to Leeds and spoke at a Liberal meeting for Free Trade and then next morning went to London partly to see friends with regard to the Australian trade and partly to attend a meeting of the Liberal and Radical candidates Assocn. on the subject of the Ll.G. pledge. This was expounded by a young man named Dr. Wallace. I was rather horrified by the type of man chosen as Liberal candidate – mostly professionals – no one of any standing so far as I can judge. Leif Jones, Chas. Roberts – not a candidate – Walter Rea, F. Murrell of Somerset and Harcourt Johnstone in the chair the only persons I knew out of about forty. Was glad not to stay long.

[On this note of disenchantment with the party with which he had for so long been associated, Holt's diary came to an abrupt end. He himself lived on until 1941 but never again stood as a parliamentary candidate. In the General Election of 1929 Holt came nearer to success than in all probability he had expected. The figures in North Cumberland were:

F.F. Graham	(Con.)	10,392
R.D. Holt	(Lib.)	9,661
C.A. O'Donnell	(Lab.)	3,092

But by this stage of his career Holt's attachment to the brand of Liberalism presented to the British electorate by Lloyd George was tenuous in the extreme.

There is no clear indication why the diary ends at this point. Possibly Holt, disappointed by his narrow failure to secure election yet reconciled now to the eclipse of his parliamentary aspirations, considered that his future career would not be of sufficient importance to warrant the diarist's pen. But just as probably, this ever cautious man, having filled up the second of the bound volumes in which the original manuscript diary is contained, decided that an appropriate point of finality had been reached.]

APPENDIX ONE

Biographical Notes

Agnew, Sir George (1852–1941). Liberal M.P. for Salford West 1906–18; High Sheriff of Suffolk 1922.

Allendale, First Baron (1829–1907). Wentworth B. Beaumont. Liberal M.P. for South Northumberland 1852–85 and for Tyneside 1886–92.

Allendale, Second Baron, First Viscount (1860–1923). Wentworth C.B. Beaumont. Liberal M.P. for Hexham 1895–1907; Liberal whip 1905–07; favoured temperance and free trade.

Amanullah, King of Afghanistan (1892–1960). Ruler of Afghanistan 1919–29. Lost his throne because he tried to modernise his backward state too quickly, the attempt to emancipate women being one of the most decisive causes of the revolution by which he was overthrown.

Amery, Leopold S. (1873–1955). Conservative M.P. for Birmingham South 1911–18 and Birmingham, Sparkbrook 1918–45; First Lord of the Admiralty 1922–24; Colonial Secretary 1924–29; Dominions Secretary 1925–29; Secretary for India 1940–45. Fellow of All Souls, Imperialist and follower of Joseph Chamberlain.

Anderson, William C. (1877–1919). Labour M.P. for Sheffield, Attercliffe 1914–18; chairman Independent Labour Party 1911–13 and Labour Party 1914–15. Victim of post-war influenza epidemic.

Arnold, Sydney, First Baron Arnold (1878–1945). Liberal M.P. for Holmfirth 1912–18 and Penistone 1918–21. Member of the Labour Party 1922–38; Paymaster General in Labour government 1929–31.

Ashton, Thomas G., Lord Ashton of Hyde (1855–1933). Liberal M.P. for Hyde 1885–86 and Luton 1895–1911. Remained a significant figure in Lancashire Liberalism after he left the House of Commons.

Asquith, Herbert Henry, First Earl of Oxford and Asquith (1852–1928). Liberal M.P. for Fife East 1886–1918 and for Paisley 1920–24. Home Secretary 1892–95; Chancellor of the Exchequer 1905–08; Prime Minister 1908–16. Leader of the Liberal Party 1908–26.

Asquith, Margot, Countess of Oxford and Asquith (1864–1945). Wife of above. Caustic and outspoken critic of Lloyd George. Jowett, Master of Balliol College, called her 'the best-educated ill-educated woman that I have ever met.'

Baddeley, Sir Vincent W. (1874–1961). Service in the Admiralty 1899–1935.

Baldwin, Stanley, First Earl Baldwin of Bewdley (1867–1947). Conservative M.P. for Worcestershire West 1908–18 and for Bewdley 1918–37. President of the Board of Trade 1921–22; Chancellor of the Exchequer 1922–23; Prime Minister 1923–24, 1924–29 and 1935–37; Lord President of the Council 1931– 35. Leader of the Conservative Party 1923–37.

Balfour, Arthur James, First Earl Balfour (1848–1930). Conservative M.P. for Hertford 1874–85, for Manchester East 1885–1906 and for City of London 1906–22. Host of ministerial offices before becoming Prime Minister (1902–05) in succession to his uncle, Lord Salisbury. Subsequently First Lord of the Admiralty 1915–16; Foreign Secretary 1916–19.

Baring, Sir Godfrey (1871–1957). Liberal M.P. for Isle of Wight 1906–10 and Barnstaple 1911–18.

Barlow, Sir John E. (1857–1932). Liberal M.P. for Frome 1892–95 and 1896–1918.

Bates, Col. C.L. Conservative candidate at Hexham in 1907 and January 1910.

Beauchamp, Seventh Earl (1872–1938). William Lygon. Lord President of the Council 1910 and 1914–15; First Commissioner of Works 1910–14. Considered resignation over British involvement in the First World War, but remained prominent in Liberal politics until his career was abruptly terminated by a homosexual scandal in 1931.

Beaumont, Wentworth H.C., Second Viscount Allendale (1890–1956). Liberal candidate at Hexham in 1918. Lord in Waiting 1931–32, 1937–45 and 1954–56.

Beavan, Miss Margaret (c.1876–1931). Coalition Liberal who joined the Conservatives in 1924. First female Lord Mayor of Liverpool (1927–28); described as the 'Mighty Atom' by Alderman Salvidge.

Beazley, James H. Member of the Mersey Docks and Harbour Board 1902–29.

Bell, Sir Hugh (1844–1931). Ironmaster. Father-in-law of C.P. Trevelyan. Financial backer of *Common Sense*.

Benn, Sir Ernest (1875–1954). Businessman and author.

Benn, William Wedgwood, First Viscount Stansgate (1877–1960). Liberal M.P. for Tower Hamlets 1906–18 and Leith 1918–27. Joined the Labour Party in 1928 and sat as M.P. for Aberdeen North 1928–31 and Manchester Gorton 1937–42. Secretary of State for India 1929–31 and for Air 1945–46.

Bennett, Sir Francis (1863–1950). Lincolnshire timber merchant. Son of Joseph Bennett, M.P.

Beveridge, Sir William (1879–1963). Academic and civil servant. Director of

Labour Exchanges 1909–16. Author of the Beveridge Report 1942. Liberal M.P. for Berwick-on-Tweed 1944–45. Baron 1946.

Bibby, Arthur W. (1846–1935). Chairman Bibby Steamship Co. Ltd. Member of the Mersey Docks and Harbour Board 1892–1900 and 1905–30. Chairman of same 1929–30.

Birrell, Augustine (1850–1933). Liberal M.P. for Fife West 1889–1900 and Bristol North 1906–18. President of Board of Education 1905–07; Chief Secretary for Ireland 1907–16. Resigned after the Easter Rising.

Bliss, Joseph (1853–1939). Liberal M.P. for Cockermouth 1916–18.

Bonham-Carter, Lady Violet (1887–1969). Baroness Asquith of Yarnbury (Life Peerage 1964). Never an M.P. but influential in Liberal politics over several decades. Daughter of Asquith, close friend of Churchill and ardent supporter of the League of Nations.

Bonwick, Alfred J. (1883–1949). Liberal M.P. for Chippenham 1922–24; Liberal whip 1924.

Booth, Sir Alfred Allen. Shipowner. Appointed by the government as chairman of the Liverpool Committee for the Coordination of the Naval, Civil and Military Requirements of the port.

Booth, Charles (1840–1916). Shipowner and writer on social questions. Partner in Alfred Booth and Co. Author of *Life and Labour of the People in London*, which gives a comprehensive and illuminating picture of London in the last decade of the nineteenth century.

Boscawen, Sir Arthur Griffith- (1865–1946). Conservative M.P. for Tunbridge 1892–1906, Dudley 1910–21 and Taunton 1921–22. Minister of Agriculture 1921–22; Minister of Health 1922–23.

Botha, General Louis (1862–1919). First Prime Minister of the Transvaal in 1906 under the new constitution and of the Union of South Africa in 1910.

Bowring, Sir Frederick. Served two terms as Lord Mayor of Liverpool 1925–27. His donations helped to extend the Walker Art Gallery.

Boyton, Sir James (1855–1926). Conservative M.P. for Marylebone East 1910–18; member of London County Council 1907–10.

Brady, Patrick J. (1868–1943). Nationalist M.P. for Dublin, St. Stephen's Green 1910–18; Senator in the Irish Free State 1927–28.

Brassey, Lord (1836–1918). Thomas Brassey. Liberal M.P. for Hastings 1868–86. Civil Lord of Admiralty 1880–84; parliamentary secretary to Admiralty 1884–85. Earl 1911.

Broadhurst, Henry (1840–1911). Liberal M.P. for Stoke-upon-Trent 1880–85,

Bordesley 1885–86, Nottingham West 1886–92 and Leicester 1894–1906. Supporter of Home Rule and Land Reform. Junior Minister in 1886. Retired from parliament in 1906, disappointed at not being offered office in the new Liberal government.

Brown, Lieut. A. Ernest (1881–1962). Liberal and later Liberal National M.P. for Rugby 1923–24 and Leith 1928–45. Secretary for the Mines 1932–35; Minister of Labour 1935–40; Scottish Secretary 1940–41; Minister of Health 1941–43; Chancellor of the Duchy of Lancaster 1943–45. Leader of the Liberal National Party 1940–45.

Bruce, Stanley M., First Viscount Bruce (1883–1967). Prime Minister of Australia 1923–29. Later High Commissioner in London.

Brunner, J.F.L. (1865–1929). Liberal M.P. for Leigh 1906–10, Northwich 1910–18 and Southport 1923–24.

Brusilov, Aleksei A. (1853–1926). Russian military commander. Launched major Russian offensive in 1916. Replaced by the Provisional Government in 1917.

Buller, Sir Redvers H. (1839–1908). British Commander in the Boer War until replaced by Lord Roberts.

Burke, Councillor Thomas. Metals and furs business in Liverpool. Nationalist councillor for the Vauxhall ward. Author of a *Catholic History of Liverpool*.

Burns, John, E. (1858–1943). Independent Labour M.P. for Battersea 1892–95 and Liberal M.P. for Battersea 1895–1918. Leader of the docks strike of 1889. First working man to sit in the cabinet. President of Local Government Board 1905–14; President of Board of Trade 1914. Resigned over British involvement in the First World War.

Buxton, Noel, First Baron Noel-Buxton (1869–1948). Liberal M.P. for Whitby 1905–06 and for Norfolk North 1910–18; Labour M.P. for Norfolk North 1922–30. Minister of Agriculture 1924 and 1929–30.

Cameron, Robert (1825–1913). Liberal M.P. for Houghton-le-Spring 1895–1913.

Campbell-Bannerman, Sir Henry (1836–1908). Liberal M.P. for Stirling Burghs 1868–1908. Chief Secretary for Ireland 1884–85; War Secretary 1886 and 1892–95; Prime Minister 1905–08. Leader of the Liberal Party 1899–1908.

Carpenter, Professor George (1865–1939). Theologian and zoologist.

Carson, Sir Edward (1854–1935). Conservative M.P. for Dublin University 1892–1918 and Belfast, Duncairn 1918–21. Solicitor-General 1900–05; Attorney-General 1915; First Lord of the Admiralty 1916–17; Minister without Portfolio 1917–18. Leader of the Irish Unionists 1910–21.

Cawley, Sir Frederick, First Baron Cawley (1850–1937). Liberal M.P. for Prestwich 1895–1918. Chancellor of the Duchy of Lancaster 1916–18.

Cecil, Lord Hugh, First Baron Quickswood (1859–1956). Brother of above. Conservative M.P. for Greenwich 1895–1906 and for Oxford University 1910–37.

Cecil, Lord Robert, First Viscount Cecil of Chelwood (1864–1958). Conservative M.P. for Marylebone East 1906–10 and Hitchin 1911–23. Minister of Blockade 1916–18; Lord Privy Seal 1923–24; Chancellor of the Duchy of Lancaster 1924–27. Son of Lord Salisbury. President of League of Nations Union 1923–45.

Chamberlain, Sir Austen (1863–1937). Liberal Unionist M.P. for Worcestershire East 1892–1914 and Conservative M.P. for Birmingham West 1914–37. Son of Joseph Chamberlain. Author of Locarno Treaties (1925). Chancellor of Exchequer 1903–05 and 1919–21; Secretary for India 1915–17; Minister without Portfolio 1918–19; Lord Privy Seal 1921–22; Foreign Secretary 1924–29; First Lord of the Admiralty 1931.

Chamberlain, Joseph (1836–1914). Liberal M.P. for Birmingham 1876–86 and Liberal Unionist M.P. for Birmingham West 1886–1914. Imperialist and Radical social reformer. President of Board of Trade 1880–85; President of Local Government Board 1886; Colonial Secretary 1895–1903.

Chaytor, A.H. Conservative candidate for Hexham in December 1910. Lost to R.D.H. by 790 votes.

Chelmsford, First Viscount (1868–1933). Frederic J.N. Thesiger. Viceroy of India 1916–21; First Lord of the Admiralty 1924.

Cherry, Richard R. (1859–1923). Liberal M.P. for Liverpool, Exchange 1906–09. Attorney-General for Ireland 1905–09; Lord Chief Justice of Ireland 1914–16.

Churchill, Winston L.S. (1874–1965). Conservative M.P. for Oldham 1900–04; Liberal M.P. for Oldham 1904–06, for North-West Manchester 1906–08, for Dundee 1908–22. Conservative M.P. for Epping 1924–45 and for Woodford 1945–64. President of Board of Trade 1908–10; Home Secretary 1910–11; First Lord of the Admiralty 1911–15; Chancellor of the Duchy of Lancaster 1915; Minister of Munitions 1917–19; Secretary for War 1919–21; Colonial Secretary 1921–22; Chancellor of the Exchequer 1924–29; Prime Minister 1940–45 and 1951–55. Leader of the Conservative Party 1940–55.

Clemenceau, Georges (1841–1929). Ubiquitous figure in the history of the French Third Republic. Prime Minister 1906–09 and 1917–20. The ferocity of his journalistic attacks brought him the sobriquet of 'The Tiger'.

Collins, Sir Godfrey (1875–1936). Liberal and later Liberal National M.P. for Greenock 1910–36. Liberal chief whip 1924–26; Scottish Secretary 1932–36.

Collins, Sir William J. (1859–1946). Liberal M.P. for St. Pancras West 1906–10 and for Derby 1916–18.

Courtney, Leonard H., First Baron Courtney of Penwith (1832–1918). Liberal M.P. for Liskeard 1871–85 and for Bodmin 1885–1900. Journalist, academic and politician. Deputy Speaker of Commons 1886–92. President of Liberal Foreign Affairs Committee set up in 1912. Zealot for proportional representation. Married Kate Potter, sister of R.D.H.'s mother.

Cowans, General Sir John (1862–1921). Quartermaster General.

Cripps, Alfred S., Second Baron Parmoor (1882–1977). Barrister brother of Sir Stafford Cripps. Conservative candidate for Buckinghamshire, Wycombe 1906.

Cripps, Sir C.A., First Baron Parmoor (1852–1941). Conservative M.P. for Stroud 1895–1900, for Stretford 1901–06 and for Wycombe 1910–14. Lord President of the Council (Labour) 1924 and 1929–31; Leader of the House of Lords 1929–31.

Crompton, Albert. Manager Ocean Steamship Company 1882–1901.

Cronje, General Piet (1835–1911). Played a leading role in both Boer Wars. Enjoyed a striking success in the first part of the war of 1899, repulsing Lord Methuen's attempt to relieve Kimberley.

Crosthwaite, Arthur. Stockbroker (G.A. Tinley and Co.). Lord Mayor of Liverpool 1900–01.

Czernin, Count Otokar. Austrian foreign minister and author of the peace initiative of 1917. He had been a member of the Archduke Franz Ferdinand's circle, after whose assassination he said 'My sun went down with the Archduke.'

Davies, Maurice Llewellyn. Manager of the Ocean Steamship Company 1895–1913.

Dawes, James A. (1866–1921). Liberal M.P. for Walworth 1910–18 and for Southwark South East 1918–21.

Derby, Seventeenth Earl of (1865–1948). Edward G.V. Stanley. Conservative M.P. for Westhoughton 1892–1906. Postmaster General 1903–05; Director General of Recruiting 1915–16; Secretary for War 1916–18 and 1922–24; Ambassador to France 1918–20. Long-time arbiter of Conservative politics in Lancashire.

Devonport, First Viscount (1856–1934). Sir Hudson E. Kearley. Liberal M.P. for Devonport 1892–1910. Food Controller 1916–17.

Devonshire, Eighth Duke of (1833–1908). Spencer Compton Cavendish. Liberal M.P. for North Lancashire 1857–68, Radnor 1869–80 and North-East Lancashire 1880–85. Liberal Unionist M.P. for Rossendale 1885–91. War Secretary 1866 and 1882–85; Postmaster-General 1868–71; Chief Secretary for Ireland 1871–74; Secretary for India 1880–82; Lord President of the Council 1895–1903.

Dilke, Sir Charles W. (1843–1911). Liberal M.P. for Chelsea 1868–86 and for

Forest of Dean 1892–1911. President of Local Government Board 1882–85. Advanced Radical whose career was ruined after he was cited as co-respondent in the Crawford divorce case, 1885–86.

Donaldson, Major E.J. Liberal candidate for Glasgow Hillhead 1922 and 1923 and for Clackmannan 1924 and 1929..

Eills, Burton W. (d. 1936). Ship chandlery merchant and Liberal politician. Lord Mayor of Liverpool 1919–20.

Elibank, Master of, First Baron Murray of Elibank (1870–1920). Liberal M.P. for Midlothian 1900–05, for Peebles and Selkirk 1906–10 and for Midlothian 1910–12. Liberal Chief Whip 1910–12.

Emmott, Alfred, First Baron Emmott (1858–1926). Liberal M.P. for Oldham 1899–1911. First Commissioner of Works 1914–15.

Evans, Edward (1846–1917). President of the Liverpool Liberal Federal Council from 1889 and chairman of the National Liberal Federation from 1894.

Ewart, Sir John S. (1861–1930). Served in South African War and entered the War Office in 1902. Adjutant-General to the forces and second military member of the Army Council 1910–14. G.O.C.-in-C. Scottish Command 1914–18.

Falconer, James (1856–1931). Liberal M.P. for Forfarshire 1909–18 and 1922–24.

Fernie, David. Member of the Mersey Docks and Harbour Board 1889–1903.

Finney, Victor H. (1897–1970). Liberal M.P. for Hexham 1923–24.

Fischer Williams, Sir John (1870–1947). International lawyer. British legal adviser, Reparations Commission 1929–30.

Fisher, John A. 'Jackie', First Baron Fisher (1841–1920). First Sea Lord 1904–10 and 1914–15, when he resigned over differences with Churchill relating to Dardanelles Campaign.

Forwood, Sir William (1840–1928). Shipowner and Conservative member of Liverpool City Council for 58 years. Lord Mayor 1903. Co-founder of Liverpool's Overhead Railway.

France, Gerald A. (1870–1935). Liberal M.P. for Morley 1910–18 and for Batley and Morley 1918–22.

Franklin, Sir G. (1853–1916). Director of National Telephone Company. Served on several government committees. Lord Mayor of Sheffield 1897–98.

Franz Ferdinand, Archduke (1863–1914). From 1896 heir to the Austrian Empire. His assassination by a Bosnian nationalist helped precipitate the First World War. Ironically he favoured internal autonomy for the subject nationalities of the Empire.

Odyssey of an Edwardian Liberal 111

French, General Sir John, First Earl of Ypres (1852–1925). Commander-in-Chief British Expeditionary Force 1914–15; C-in-C Home Forces 1915–18; Lord Lieutenant of Ireland 1919–21.

Geddes, Sir Eric C. (1875–1937). Conservative M.P. for Cambridge 1917–22. First Lord of the Admiralty 1917–19; Minister without Portfolio 1919; Minister of Transport 1919–21. Chairman of Committee to advise the Chancellor of the Exchequer on national expenditure 1921 (the 'Geddes Axe').

Lloyd George, David, First Earl Lloyd George of Dwyfor (1863–1945). Liberal M.P. for Caernarvon Boroughs 1890–1945. President of Board of Trade 1905–08; Chancellor of Exchequer 1908–15; Minister of Munitions 1915–16; Secretary for War 1916; Prime Minister 1916–22. Leader of the Liberal Party 1926–31.

Lloyd George, Margaret (1866–1941). First wife of above.

Gilmour, Sir John (1876–1940). Conservative M.P. for Renfrewshire East 1910–18 and Glasgow, Pollok 1918–40. Conservative whip 1913–15 and 1919; Scottish Secretary 1924–29; Minister of Agriculture 1931–32; Home Secretary 1932–35; Minister of Shipping 1939–40.

Gladstone, Sir Herbert J., First Viscount Gladstone (1854–1930). Liberal M.P. for Leeds 1880–85 and Leeds West 1885–1910. Liberal Chief Whip 1899–1905; Home Secretary 1905–10. First Governor-General of South Africa 1910–14. Prominent in Liberal Party organisation 1919–24. Son of W.E. Gladstone.

Glover, Sir Ernest W. (1864–1934). Worked at Ministry of Shipping from its formation.

Glynn, Walter. Member of Mersey Docks and Harbour Board 1876–1905.

Graham, Sir (Frederick) Fergus (1893–1978). Conservative M.P. for Cumberland North 1926–35 and for Darlington 1951–59.

Grenfell, Francis W., First Baron Grenfell (1841–1925). Field Marshal. Service in Africa 1874–92. Commander-in-Chief Ireland 1904–08.

Grey, Sir Edward, First Viscount Grey of Fallodon (1862–1933). Liberal M.P. for Berwick-on-Tweed 1885–1916. Foreign Secretary 1905–16. At the outbreak of European War in 1914 he noted, 'The lights are going out all over Europe. We shall not see them again in our life'.

Griffith, Frank Kingsley (1889–1962). Liberal M.P. for Middlesbrough West 1928–40. County Court Judge 1940–56.

Gulland, John W. (1864–1920). Liberal M.P. for Dumfries Burghs 1906–18. Government Chief Whip 1915–16.

Gwynne, Stephen L. (1864–1950). Journalist and author. Irish Nationalist M.P. for Galway City 1906–18.

Haldane, Richard Burdon, First Viscount Haldane of Cloan (1856–1928). Liberal M.P. for Lothian East 1885–1911. War Secretary 1905–12; Lord Chancellor 1912–15 and (Labour) 1924.

Halstead, Major David (1861–1937). Conservative M.P. for Rossendale 1922–23.

Hamilton, Lord George (1845–1927). Conservative M.P. for Middlesex 1868–85 and for Ealing 1885–1906. Secretary for India 1895–1903. Chairman Mesopotamian Commission of Enquiry 1916–17.

Hampson, Robert A. (1852–1919). Conservative Leader of Liverpool Council 1901–02; Lord Mayor 1903–04.

Harcourt, Lewis, First Viscount Harcourt (1863–1922). Liberal M.P. for Rossendale 1904–17. First Commissioner of Works 1905–10 and 1915–16; Colonial Secretary 1910–15. Son of Sir W. Harcourt.

Harcourt, Sir William (1827–1904). Liberal M.P. for Oxford 1868–80, for Derby 1880–95 and for Western Monmouthshire 1895–1904. Solicitor-General 1873–74; Home Secretary 1880–85; Chancellor of the Exchequer 1886 and 1892–95. Leader of Liberal Party 1896–98.

Harris, Sir Percy A. (1876–1952). Liberal M.P. for Harborough 1916–18 and for Bethnal Green South-West 1922–45. Liberal Chief Whip 1935–45; Liberal Deputy Leader 1940–45. Member of London County Council 1907–34 and 1946–52.

Harvey, A. Gordon C. (1858–1922). Liberal M.P. for Rochdale 1906–18. President of National Reform Union at time of death.

Haworth, Sir Arthur A. (1865–1944). Liberal M.P. for Manchester South 1906–12. Junior Lord of the Treasury 1912.

Hedges, Alfred Paget (1867–1929). Liberal M.P. for Tonbridge 1906–10.

Hemmerde, Edward G. (1871–1948). Liberal M.P. for Denbigh East 1906–10 and for Norfolk North West 1912–18. Labour M.P. for Crewe 1922–24. A lawyer, he was speaking in the Commons, pleading for the fair treatment of Germany, when his chambers at the Inner Temple were bombed.

Henderson, Arthur (1863–1935). Labour M.P. for Barnard Castle 1903–18, Widnes 1919–22, Newcastle East 1923, Burnley 1924–31 and Clay Cross 1933–35. President of Board of Education 1915–16; Paymaster-General 1916; Minister without Portfolio 1916–17; Home Secretary 1924; Foreign Secretary 1929–31. Chairman of the Labour Party 1908–10 and 1914–17.

Herbert, J. Basil (1899–1972). Private Secretary to Asquith 1923–25. County Court Judge 1959–71.

Higginbottom, Samuel W. (1853–1902). Conservative M.P. for Liverpool, West Derby 1900–02.

Hirst, Francis W. (1873–1953). Editor of the *Economist* until 1916. Launched the weekly *Common Sense* in October 1916. Outspoken representative of laissez-faire, anti-war Liberalism. Contemporary of John Simon and F.E. Smith at Wadham College, Oxford.

Hobhouse, Sir Arthur L. (1886–1965). Liberal M.P. for Wells 1923–24.

Hobhouse, Sir Charles (1862–1941). Liberal M.P. for Devizes 1892–95 and for Bristol East 1900–18. Chancellor of the Duchy of Lancaster 1911–14; Postmaster General 1914–15.

Hobhouse, Sir John R. (1893–1961). Partner Alfred Holt and Co. 1920–57; Chairman Liverpool Steam Ship Owners Association 1941–43; Pro-Chancellor Liverpool University 1948–57.

Hobhouse, Stephen. Quaker. Imprisoned for conscientious objection in 1917, but released after several months of campaigning. His mother was a sister of R.D.H.'s mother.

Hogge, James M. (1873–1928). Liberal M.P. for Edinburgh East 1912–24. Joint Chief Whip of Independent Liberals 1919–23. Journalist and social investigator.

Holt, Alfred (1829–1911). Uncle of R.D.H. Founder of Ocean Steamship Co. Resigned as Chairman of Mersey Docks and Harbour Board 1890.

Holt, Anne (1899–1980). Daughter of R.D.H. Historian.

Holt, Eliza (1868–1951). Wife of R.D.H. Née Wells.

Holt, Elizabeth 'Betty' (1875–1947). Sister of R.D.H. Married Edward S. Russell.

Holt, George (1825–1896). Uncle of R.D.H.

Holt, George (d.1916). Son of Alfred Holt. Cousin of R.D.H. Manager of Ocean Steamship Co. 1895–1912.

Holt, George (1790–1861). Grandfather of R.D.H. and founder of family's fortunes. Asked on several occasions to stand for parliament. Unitarian and promoter of middle-class education.

Holt, Grace (1898–1972). Daughter of R.D.H. Married Anthony Methuen, Fifth Lord Methuen.

Holt, Lawrence (1882–1961). Brother of R.D.H. Manager of Ocean Steamship Co. 1908–53; Senior Partner Alfred Holt and Co. 1941–53. Lord Mayor of Liverpool 1929–30.

Holt, Lawrencina 'Lallie' (1845–1906). Mother of R.D.H. and sister of Beatrice Webb. Married Robert Holt in 1867.

Holt, Mary 'Molly' (1889–1955). Sister of R.D.H. Married John H. Russell.

Holt, Philip (1876–1958). Brother of R.D.H. City Councillor 1918–21.

Holt, Robert D. (1832–1908). Father of R.D.H. Leader of Liverpool Liberal Party 1879–89. First Lord Mayor of Liverpool 1892–93.

Holt, William D. (1823–1887). Uncle of R.D.H. Active in local politics in 1860s and 1870s.

Hopkin Morris, Sir Rhys (1888–1956). Liberal M.P. for Cardiganshire 1923–32 and for Carmarthen 1945–56.

Horne, F. Liberal candidate for Ludlow and Barkston Ash at successive elections between 1903 and 1910.

Howard, Donald S.P., Third Baron Strathcona and Mount Royal (1891–1951). Conservative M.P. for Cumberland North 1922–26. Junior Minister 1934–39.

Howard, Geoffrey W.A. (1877–1935). Liberal M.P. for Eskdale 1906–10, Westbury 1911–18 and Luton 1923–24. Liberal whip 1911–18; Parliamentary Private Secretary to Asquith 1908–10.

Hughes, John W. Member of Mersey Docks and Harbour Board 1888-1917.

Hughes, Sir Thomas (1838–1923). Conservative leader of the Liverpool City Council 1898–99. Long serving chairman of the Watch Committee and the Licensing Committee.

Hutchison, Sir Robert, First Baron Hutchison (1873–1950). Liberal and later Liberal National M.P. for Kirkcaldy Burghs 1922–23 and for Montrose Burghs 1924–32. Liberal Chief Whip 1926–30. Paymaster General 1935–38.

Illingworth, Percy H. (1869–1915). Liberal M.P. for Shipley 1906–15. Government Chief Whip 1912–15.

John, Edward T. (1857–1931). Liberal M.P. for Denbighshire East 1910–18. Joined the Labour party in July 1918.

Johnson, Sir Benjamin (1865–1937). Leader of Liverpool Liberal Party 1910. Paternalistic employer and owner of dyeworks.

Johnstone, Harcourt (1895–1945). Liberal M.P. for Willesden East 1923–24, for South Shields 1931–35 and for Middlesbrough West 1940–45. Liberal whip 1931–32. Junior minister 1940–45.

Jones, C. Sydney (1872–1947). Liberal M.P. for Liverpool West Derby 1923–24. Lord Mayor 1938–42. Director of Ocean Steamship Company. Treasurer and Pro-Chancellor of Liverpool University.

Jones, Sir (Henry) Haydn (1863–1950). Liberal M.P. for Merioneth 1910–45.

Jones, Leif S., First Baron Rhayader (1862–1939). Liberal M.P. for Westmorland North 1905–10, for Rushcliffe 1910–18 and for Camborne 1923–24 and 1929–31.

Kenworthy, Joseph M., Tenth Baron Strabolgi (1886–1953). Liberal and (after 1926) Labour M.P. for Hull Central 1919–31. Labour Chief Whip in House of Lords 1938–42.

Keynes, John Maynard (1883–1946). Economist. Principal Treasury representative at Paris Peace Conference 1919. Highly critical of Versailles Treaty. Returned to Treasury in 1939. Played a leading part in the Bretton Woods Conference of 1944 which led to the creation of the International Monetary Fund and the World Bank.

Kitchener, Horatio Herbert, First Earl Kitchener of Khartoum (1850–1916). C-in-C. South Africa 1900–02 and in India 1902–09. Consul-General Egypt 1911–14. Secretary for War 1914–16. Drowned on way to Russia.

Klein, Dr. L. de Beaumont Minister at Ullet Road Unitarian Church until 1903, where R.D.H. worshipped. Previously Minister at Renshaw Street Unitarian Chapel.

Lambert, Francis H. (1867–1929). Free trader, prominent in Welsh Liberal politics.

Lambert, George, First Viscount Lambert (1866–1958). Liberal M.P. for South Molton 1891–1924 and 1929–31; Liberal National M.P. for South Molton 1931–45. Civil Lord of Admiralty 1905–15.

Lambert, Richard C. (1868–1939). Liberal M.P. for Wiltshire North 1910–18.

Lansdowne, Fifth Marquis of (1845–1927). Henry C.K. Petty-Fitzmaurice. Viceroy of India 1888–94; War Secretary 1895–1900; Foreign Secretary 1900–05; Minister without Portfolio 1915–16. Author of the famous call for a negotiated settlement to the War in 1917.

Law, Andrew Bonar (1858–1923). Conservative M.P. for Glasgow, Blackfriars 1900–06, for Camberwell 1906–10, for Bootle 1911–18 and for Glasgow Central 1918–23. Colonial Secretary 1915–16; Chancellor of Exchequer 1916–19; Lord Privy Seal 1919–21; Prime Minister 1922–23. Leader of the Conservative Party 1911–21 and 1922–23.

Law, Hugh A. (1872–1943). Irish Nationalist M.P. for Donegal West 1902–18. Member of Dail Eireann 1927–32.

Lawrence, Sir E. Durning (1825–1909). Liberal Unionist M.P. for Truro 1895–1906.

Layland-Barratt, Sir Francis (1860–1933). Liberal M.P. for Torquay 1900–10 and for St. Austell 1915–18.

Lees-Smith, Hastings B. (1878–1941). Liberal M.P. for Northampton 1910–18.

Odyssey of an Edwardian Liberal

Joined Labour Party 1919. Labour M.P. for Keighley 1922–23, 1924–31 and 1935–41. Postmaster General 1929–31; President of Board of Education 1931. Leader of H.M. Opposition and Acting Chairman Parliamentary Labour Party 1940–41.

Leon, Sir Herbert (1850–1926). Liberal M.P. for Buckingham 1891–95.

Lewis, Sir (John) Herbert (1858–1933). Liberal M.P. for Flint Boroughs 1892–1906, for Flintshire 1906–18 and for University of Wales 1918–22. Junior minister 1905–22.

Lothian, Eleventh Marquis of, Philip H. Kerr (1882–1940). Private Secretary to Lloyd George 1916–21. Chancellor of the Duchy of Lancaster 1931. Resigned from government over Ottawa Agreements. Ambassador in Washington 1939–40. Prominent appeaser.

McArthur, Charles (1844–1910). Liberal Unionist M.P. for Liverpool, Exchange 1897–1906 and for Liverpool, Kirkdale 1907–10. President Liverpool Chamber of Commerce 1892–96.

McCallum, Sir John M. (1847–1920). Liberal M.P. for Paisley 1906–20.

McCurdy, Charles A. (1870–1941). Liberal M.P. for Northampton 1910–23. Coalition Liberal Chief Whip 1921–22.

McDonald, John A. Murray (1854–1939). Liberal M.P. for Bow and Bromley 1892–95, for Falkirk Burghs 1906–18 and for Stirling and Falkirk Burghs 1918–22.

MacDonald, James Ramsay (1866–1937). Labour M.P. for Leicester 1906–18, for Aberavon 1922–29, for Seaham 1929–35 and for Scottish Universities 1936–37. Prime Minister and Foreign Secretary 1924; Prime Minister 1929–35; Lord President of the Council 1935–37. Chairman of the Labour Party 1912–14; Leader of the Labour Party 1922–31; Leader of the National Labour Party 1931–37.

Macdonnell, Antony P., First Baron Macdonnell (1844–1925). Indian Civil Service; Under-Secretary of State for Ireland 1902–08, his term of office ending in controversy. Chairman of the Royal Commission on the Civil Service.

McKenna, Reginald (1863–1943). Liberal M.P. for Monmouthshire North 1895–1918. President of Board of Education 1907–08; First Lord of Admiralty 1908–11; Home Secretary 1911–15; Chancellor of Exchequer 1915–16. Offered the Exchequer by Bonar Law in 1922.

McKinley, William (1843–1901). Twenty-fifth President of the United States, 1897–1901. Shot by an anarchist early in his second term.

McKinnon-Wood, Thomas (1855–1927). Liberal M.P. for Glasgow, St. Rollox 1906–18. Scottish Secretary 1912–16; Chancellor of Duchy of Lancaster 1916.

Maclay, Sir John P., First Baron Maclay (1857–1951). Minister of Shipping 1916–21.

Maclean, Sir Donald (1864–1932). Liberal M.P. for Bath 1906–10, for Selkirk and Peeblesshire 1910–18, for Midlothian and Peeblesshire South 1918–22, and for Cornwall North 1929–32. Chairman Parliamentary Liberal Party 1919–22; Acting Leader of the Liberal Party 1919–20; President National Liberal Federation 1922–25. President of Board of Education 1931–32. Father of the notorious spy.

Maden, Lady. Widow of Sir J.H. Maden (1862–1920), the latter having been Liberal M.P. for Rossendale 1892–1900 and 1917–18.

Mann, Tom (1856–1941). Trade Union leader and syndicalist. Active in the Liverpool strikes of 1911–12. Four times a parliamentary candidate.

Mason, James F. (1861–1929). Conservative M.P. for Windsor 1906–18.

Massey, William F. (1856–1925). Leader of New Zealand Conservative Party. Prime Minister 1912–25.

Massingham, Henry W. (1860–1924). Editor *Daily Chronicle* 1895–99, resigning because of the unpopularity of his opposition to Boer War. Editor of the *Nation* 1907–23. Supported Lansdowne in 1917 and joined Labour Party in 1923.

Masterman, Charles F.G. (1874–1927). Liberal M.P. for West Ham North 1906–11, for Bethnal Green South-West 1911–14 and for Manchester, Rusholme 1923–24. Chancellor of the Duchy of Lancaster 1914–15.

Melly, Florence E. (1856–1928). Daughter of George Melly. Liberal member of Liverpool Education Committee.

Methuen, Field Marshal Lord (1845–1932). Commanded First Division in South Africa 1899–1902. G.O.C.-in-C. South Africa 1908–12.

Middlebrook, Sir William (1851–1936). Liberal M.P. for Leeds South 1909–22.

Molteno, Percy A. (1861–1937). Barrister and shipowner. Liberal M.P. for Dumfriesshire 1906–18. Helped found Royal Institute of International Affairs.

Molyneux, Richard F. (1873–1954). Brother of Fifth Earl of Sefton. Served in Boer War, and in France 1914–15.

Mond, Sir Alfred M., First Baron Melchett (1868–1930). Liberal M.P. for Chester 1906–10, for Swansea 1910–18, for Swansea West 1918–23 and for Carmarthen 1924–26. Joined Conservative Party because he disagreed with Lloyd George's Land Policy. Conservative M.P. for Carmarthen 1926–28. First Commissioner of Works 1916–21; Minister of Health 1921–22. Chairman of I.C.I. from 1926.

Morley, John, Viscount Morley of Blackburn (1838–1923). Liberal M.P. for Newcastle-upon-Tyne 1883–95 and for Montrose Burghs 1896–1908. Chief Secretary for Ireland 1886 and 1892–95; India Secretary 1905–10 and 1911; Lord

President of the Council 1910–14. Resigned over British entry into First World War.

Morrissey, John W.T. First Liverpool socialist to be elected to a public position (Public Auditor) in 1900. Labour councillor 1905–08. Teetotaller and pacifist.

Mounsey, Edward (d.1903). Baptist and chartered accountant. Unpaid elected rate-payer, with responsibility for checking the accounts of Liverpool corporation.

Muir, J. Ramsay B. (1872–1941). Academic and writer. Liberal M.P. for Rochdale 1923–24. Chairman National Liberal Federation 1931–33. Professor of Modern History at University of Liverpool 1906–13 and at University of Manchester 1913–21.

Murrell, Frank (1874–1931). Liberal M.P. for Weston-super-Mare 1923–24.

Muspratt, Sir Max (1872–1934). City councillor in Liverpool 1903. Liberal M.P. for Liverpool Exchange Jan. – Dec. 1910. Lord Mayor 1917; Leader of Coalition Liberals on City Council from 1918. Joined Conservative Party 1926. President Federation of British Industries 1926.

Nicholson, Sir Charles N. (1857–1918). Liberal M.P. for Doncaster 1906–18.

Northcliffe, First Viscount (1865–1922). Alfred C. W. Harmsworth. Journalist and newspaper proprietor. Owner of the *Daily Mail* and *The Times*, which he used to criticise Asquith, Kitchener, Haldane and others during the War.

Nuttall, Harry (1849–1924). Liberal M.P. for Stretford 1906–18. Import and export merchant.

Orde-Powlett, William G.A., Fifth Baron Bolton (1869–1944). Conservative M.P. for Richmond (Yorkshire) 1910–18.

Orme, Edward B. Member Mersey Docks and Harbour Board 1919–37.

Paget, General Sir Arthur H.F. (1851–1928). Commanded British forces in Ireland 1911–14. Prominent role in Curragh Incident of March 1914. Special mission to the Balkans 1914–15.

Paton, Alexander A. (d.1934). Cotton-broker. Attached to British Embassy, Washington 1915–18.

Phillipps, H. Vivian (1870–1955). Liberal M.P. for Edinburgh West 1922–24. Private Secretary to Asquith 1917–22. Liberal Chief Whip 1923–24. Chairman Liberal Party Organisation 1925–27.

Ponsonby, Arthur, First Baron Ponsonby of Shulbrede (1871–1946). Liberal M.P. for Stirling Burghs 1908–18; Labour M.P. for Sheffield, Brightside 1922–30. One of the founders of the Union of Democratic Control 1914. Chancellor of Duchy of Lancaster 1931. Leader of Labour Party in House of Lords 1931–35. Resigned from Labour Party 1940.

Potter, Richard. Whig M.P. for Wigan 1832–39. Favoured removing bishops from House of Lords. Great-grandfather of R.D.H.

Power, Admiral Sir Lawrence (1864–1927). Rear-Admiral 1916; Vice-Admiral 1920.

Price, Charles E. (1857–1934). Liberal M.P. for Edinburgh Central 1906–18.

Primrose, Sir Henry W. (1846–1923). Chairman Board of Inland Revenue 1899–1907. Member of the Royal Commissions on Civil Service (1912) and the Railways (1913).

Pringle, William M.R. (1874–1928). Liberal M.P. for Lanarkshire North West 1910–18 and for Penistone 1922–24. Chairman Liberal and Radical Candidates Association 1924–28.

Rathbone, Eleanor (1872–1946). Independent M.P. for Combined English Universities 1929–46. Liverpool's first female councillor 1909–34. President National Union for Equal Citizenship 1919–29.

Rathbone, Herbert R. (1862–1930). Lawyer and Liberal city councillor. Lord Mayor of Liverpool 1913–14. Active in fields of education and nursing.

Rathbone, Hugh R. (1862–1940). Liberal M.P. for Liverpool, Wavertree 1923–24. Member Mersey Docks and Harbour Board 1905–33. President of the Council and Pro-Chancellor, Liverpool University 1918–24.

Rawlinson, John F.P. (1860–1926). Conservative M.P. for Cambridge University 1906–26.

Rea, Russell (1846–1916). Liberal M.P. for Gloucester 1900–10 and for South Shields 1910–16.

Rea, Sir Walter, First Baron Rea (1873–1948). Liberal M.P. for Scarborough 1906–18, for Bradford North 1923–24 and for Dewsbury 1931–35. Junior minister 1915–16 and 1931–32. Liberal Chief Whip 1931–35.

Rendall, Athelstan (1871–1948). Liberal M.P. for Thornbury 1906–22 and 1923–24. Joined Labour Party 1925. Member of Fabian Society.

Rhodes, Cecil J. (1853–1902). Imperialist. Became Prime Minister of Cape Colony in 1890, but his backing of the Jameson Raid in 1895 led to his resignation.

Rigg, Richard (1877–1942). Liberal M.P. for Appleby 1900–05. Mayor of City of Westminster 1939–40.

Roberts, Charles H. (1865–1959). Liberal M.P. for Lincoln 1906–18 and for Derby 1922–23. Junior minister 1914–16. Chairman Cumberland County Council 1938–58.

Roberts, First Earl (1832–1914). Frederick Roberts. Restored the British

120   *Odyssey of an Edwardian Liberal*

position in the Boer War and returned to become Commander-in-Chief of the British Army. Led campaign for national service before the First World War.

Robertson, John M. (1856–1933). Liberal M.P. for Tyneside 1906–18. Junior minister 1911–15. Author of *The Political Economy of Free Trade* (1928).

Robertson, Sir William 'Wully' (1866–1933). Chief of the Imperial General Staff 1915–18. Rose from private to become Field Marshal. Enjoyed increasingly acrimonious relationship with Lloyd George over conduct of the War.

Roch, W.F. (1880–1965). Liberal M.P. for Pembrokeshire 1908–18.

Rome, Thomas. Member of Mersey Docks and Harbour Board 1893–1938; Chairman 1919–27.

Rose, Sir Charles D. (1847–1913). Liberal M.P. for Newmarket 1903–10 and 1910–13.

Rosebery, Fifth Earl of (1847–1929). Archibald P. Primrose. Lord Privy Seal and First Commissioner of Works 1885; Foreign Secretary 1886 and 1892–94; Prime Minister 1894–95. The end of his premiership saw the Liberal Party in disarray. Thereafter, though his return to high office was often predicted, he pursued an increasingly independent line.

Rowntree, Benjamin Seebohm (1871–1954). Philanthropist and chocolate manufacturer, famous for his social surveys of York.

Royden, Sir Thomas (1871–1950). Conservative M.P. for Bootle 1918–22. Shipowner.

Runciman, Sir Walter, First Baron Runciman (1847–1937). Liberal M.P. for Hartlepool 1914–18. Shipowner and insurance broker.

Runciman, Walter, First Viscount Runciman of Doxford (1870–1949). Liberal M.P. for Oldham 1899–1900, for Dewsbury 1902–18, for Swansea West 1924–29, for St. Ives 1929–31 and (as a Liberal National) for St. Ives 1931–37. President Board of Education 1908–11; President Board of Agriculture 1911–14; President Board of Trade 1914–16 and 1931–37; Lord President of Council 1938–39. Head of famous mission to Czechoslovakia 1938.

Russell, E. Stanley (d.1917). Husband of Betty Holt.

Rutherford, Sir William W. (1853–1927). Conservative M.P. for Liverpool, West Derby 1903–18 and for Liverpool, Edge Hill 1918–23. Member of Liverpool City Council 1895–1912; Lord Mayor 1903.

Salvidge, Archibald T. (1863–1928). President Liverpool Constitutional Association 1919–28. Alderman and the powerful 'boss' of local party organisation, famous for his brand of Tory Democracy.

Samuel, Herbert L., First Viscount Samuel (1870–1963). Liberal M.P. for

Cleveland 1902–18 and for Darwen 1929–35. Chancellor of Duchy of Lancaster 1909–10; Postmaster General 1910–14 and 1915–16; President Local Government Board 1914–15; Home Secretary 1916 and 1931–32. Chairman Liberal Party Organisation 1927–29. Liberal leader in House of Commons 1931–35 and in House of Lords 1944–55.

Seely, Sir Charles (1859–1926). Liberal Unionist M.P. for Lincoln 1895–1906; Liberal M.P. for Mansfield 1916–18.

Seely, Sir Hugh, First Baron Sherwood (1898–1970). Liberal M.P. for Norfolk East 1923–24 and for Berwick-on-Tweed 1935–41. Junior minister 1941–45.

Seely, Sir John E.B., First Baron Mottistone (1868–1947). Conservative M.P. for Isle of Wight 1900–04; Liberal M.P. for Isle of Wight 1904–06 and 1923–24, for Liverpool, Abercromby 1906–10 and for Ilkeston 1910–22. Secretary of State for War 1912–14, resigning over Curragh Incident.

Sefton, Sixth Earl of (1871–1930). Osbert Cecil Molyneux. Master of the Horse 1905–07.

Seymour, Sir Edward H. (1840–1929). Admiral of the Fleet. Served in Crimea and China. Commanded International Naval Brigade during Boxer Rising 1900.

Shaw, Sir T.F. Charles E. (1859–1942). Liberal M.P. for Stafford 1906–10.

Shortt, Edward (1862–1935). Liberal M.P. for Newcastle-on-Tyne 1910–18 and for Newcastle-on-Tyne West 1918–22. Chief Secretary for Ireland 1918–19; Home Secretary 1919–22. President British Board of Film Censors 1929–35.

Simon, Sir John A., First Viscount Simon (1873–1954). Liberal M.P. for Walthamstow 1906–18 and for Spen Valley 1922–31; Liberal National M.P. for Spen Valley 1931–40. Barrister and Fellow of All Souls. Attorney-General 1913–15; Home Secretary 1915–16 and 1935–37; Foreign Secretary 1931–35; Chancellor of Exchequer 1937–40; Lord Chancellor 1940–45. Leader of Liberal National Party 1931–40.

Smith, Frederick E., First Earl of Birkenhead (1872–1930). Conservative M.P. for Liverpool, Walton 1906–18 and for Liverpool, West Derby 1918–19. Barrister. Solicitor-General 1915; Attorney-General 1915–19; Lord Chancellor 1919–22; Secretary for India 1924–28.

Smith, Sir Swire (1842–1918). Liberal M.P. for Keighley 1915–18.

Smuts, General Jan C. (1870–1950). South African soldier and politician. Became a fervent supporter of Britain after Boer War. Served as Minister of the Interior and of Defence under Botha after 1910. Prime Minister 1919–24 and 1939–48.

Snowden, Philip, First Viscount Snowden (1864–1937). Labour M.P. for Blackburn 1906–18 and for Colne Valley 1922–31. Chancellor of the Exchequer 1924 and 1929–31; Lord Privy Seal 1931–32.

Southborough, First Baron (1860–1947). Francis J.S. Hopwood. Permanent Secretary, Board of Trade 1901–07, Permanent Under-Secretary for Colonies 1907–10; Civil Lord of Admiralty 1912–17. Investigated Austrian peace proposals 1917. Chairman Indian Franchise Committee 1918–19 and many other committees.

Spencer, Fifth Earl (1835–1910). John P. Spencer. Lord-Lieutenant of Ireland 1868–74 and 1882–85; Lord President of the Council 1880–83 and 1886; First Lord of Admiralty 1892–95.

Spender, John A. (1862–1942). Editor *Westminster Gazette* 1896–1922. Biographer of Asquith.

Stanley of Alderley, Fifth Baron (1875–1931). Arthur L. Stanley. Liberal M.P. for Eddisbury 1906–10.

Stevens, Marshall (1852–1936). Conservative M.P. for Eccles 1918–22.

Stoddart, Wilfred B. (1871–1935). Merchant and shipowner. Liberal member of Liverpool City Council. Played football for an England team 1897.

Taylor, Austin (1858–1955). Conservative M.P. for Liverpool, East Toxteth 1902–06; Liberal M.P. for Liverpool, East Toxteth 1906–10. Shipowner and member of Liverpool City Council.

Taylor, Theodore C. (1850–1952). Liberal M.P. for Radcliffe-cum-Farnworth 1900–18. Advocate of profit sharing.

Thomas, James H. (1874–1949). Labour M.P. for Derby 1910–31; National Labour M.P. for Derby 1931–36. Colonial Secretary 1924 and 1935–36; Lord Privy Seal 1929–30; Dominions Secretary 1930–35. Resigned in 1936 because of budget leak.

Thomson, Sir Graeme (1875–1933). Entered Admiralty 1900. Director of Shipping 1917–19.

Thomson, Baron, of Cardington (1875–1930). Christopher Birdwood Thomson. Labour peer and Secretary for Air 1924 and 1929–30.

Thornborough, F.C. Seven times a Liberal parliamentary candidate between 1918 and 1931 without success. A staunch Asquithian, he nonetheless received the 'Coupon' in 1918, which he refused to use.

Timmis, Henry S. Member Mersey Docks and Harbour Board 1904–42.

Toulmin, Sir George (1857–1923). Liberal M.P. for Bury 1902–18.

Townshend, Major-General Charles V.F. (1861–1924). Commanded the Mesopotamian forces 1914–16 and surrendered at Kut-el-Amara on 29 April 1916 after a siege of nearly five months.

Trevelyan, Sir Charles P. (1870–1958). Liberal M.P. for Elland 1899–1918;

Labour M.P. for Newcastle-on-Tyne Central 1922–31. President of Board of Education 1924 and 1929–31. Junior minister 1908–14, when he resigned in protest at British involvement in the War.

Trotsky, Leon (1879–1940). Leading Russian Revolutionary figure. Negotiated the Treaty of Brest-Litovsk in 1918. His policy of permanent revolution was rejected by Stalin and he was exiled in 1929. Assassinated in Mexico in 1940.

Tweed, Colonel Thomas F. Leading Liberal organiser in Manchester in 1923 when the party made spectacular gains in the city. General Secretary Liberal Summer Schools 1921–27; Organising Secretary of the Land and Nation League from 1926.

Verney, Sir Harry C.W. (1881–1974). Liberal M.P. for Buckingham North 1910–18. Junior Minister 1914–15.

Walker, William H., First Baron Wavertree (1856–1933). Conservative M.P. for Widnes 1900–19.

Walters, Sir J. Tudor (1868–1933). Liberal M.P. for Sheffield, Brightside 1906–22 and for Penryn and Falmouth 1929–31. Paymaster General 1919–22 and 1931.

Watson, Dr. Robert Spence (1837–1911). Political, social and educational reformer. President National Liberal Federation 1890–1902. President of Peace Society.

Webb, Beatrice (née Potter) (1858–1943). Fabian diarist. Author of noted Minority Report on Poor Law 1909. Sister of R.D.H's mother.

Webb, Sidney J., First Baron Passfield (1859–1947). Labour M.P. for Seaham 1922–29. President of Board of Trade 1924; Colonial Secretary 1929–31; Dominions Secretary 1929–30. Member London County Council 1892–1910. Husband of above.

West, Sir Algernon (1832–1921). Private Secretary to W.E. Gladstone 1868–72. Chairman Board of Inland Revenue 1881–92.

Weston, Colonel John W. (1852–1926). Independent Conservative M.P. for Kendal 1913–18 and Conservative M.P. for Westmorland 1918–24. In 1913 he refused to include tariff reform in his election programme. Though he was the official nominee of the local Conservative Association, the party's National Union withdrew their support after he had been nominated. Chairman Westmorland County Council 1908–26.

Whetham, W. Cecil D. (1867–1952). Independent candidate for Cambridge University 1918. Husband of R.D.H's sister Kitty.

White, Sir George S. (1835–1912). Served in Indian Mutiny and Afghan War. Commander-in-Chief India 1893–97. In command in Natal during South African War 1899–1901. Field Marshal 1903.

Whitehouse, John H. (1873–1955). Liberal M.P. for Mid-Lanark 1910–18. Parliamentary Private Secretary to Lloyd George 1913–15. Founder of the Ruskin Society.

Whiteside, Thomas (1857–1921). Fourth Catholic Bishop of Liverpool (1894) and first Archbishop 1911–21. In politics a Unionist.

Whittaker, Sir Thomas P. (1850–1919). Liberal M.P. for Spen Valley 1892–1919.

Wiles, Thomas (1861–1951). Liberal M.P. for Islington South 1906–18. Member of London County Council 1899–1907.

Williams, Christmas P. (1881–1965). Liberal M.P. for Wrexham 1924–29.

Wilson, Sir Henry H. (1864–1922). Director of Military Operations 1910–14; G.O.C. Eastern Command 1917–18; Chief of the Imperial General Staff 1918–22; Field Marshal 1919. Became Unionist M.P. for North Down in 1922 but was assassinated later that year.

Wilson, John W. (1858–1932). Liberal M.P. for Stourbridge 1895–1922.

Wilson, William Tyson (1855–1921). Labour M.P. for Westhoughton 1906–21. Labour Chief Whip 1919.

Wilson, Woodrow (1856–1924). Twenty-eighth President of United States 1913–20. His famous 'Fourteen Points' of January 1918 were intended to provide the basis of peace with Germany.

Wintringham, Thomas (1867–1921). Liberal M.P. for Louth 1920–21.

Wise, George (1856–1917). Protestant crusader and Liverpool councillor 1903–06.

Wortley, Henry Bell (d.1919). Manager Ocean Steamship Company 1908–19.

Younger, George, Viscount Younger of Leckie (1851–1929). Conservative M.P. for Ayr Burghs 1906–22. Chairman Unionist Party Organisation 1917–23.

APPENDIX TWO

R.D. Holt's Electoral Career

1903	By-election: Liverpool West Derby	W.W. Rutherford (Con) R.D. Holt (Lib)	5455 3251
1906	General Election: Liverpool West Derby	W.W. Rutherford (Con) R.D. Holt (Lib)	5447 3600
1907	By-election: Northumberland Hexham	R.D. Holt (Lib) C.L. Bates (Con)	5401 4244
Jan.1910	General Election: Northumberland Hexham	R.D. Holt (Lib) C.L. Bates (Con)	5478 4417
Dec.1910	General Election: Northumberland Hexham	R.D. Holt (Lib) A.H. Chaytor (Con)	5124 4334
1918	General Election: Eccles	M. Stevens (Co.Con) R.D. Holt (Lib)	15821 3408
1922	General Election: Rossendale	D. Halstead (Con) G. Jones (Lab) R.D. Holt (Lib)	12881 11029 6327
1923	General Election: North Cumberland	D.S.P. Howard (Con) R.D. Holt (Lib)	9288 9070
1924	General Election: North Cumberland	D.S.P. Howard (Con) R.D. Holt (Lib) B. Brooke (Lab)	10586 6821 2125
1926	By-election: North Cumberland	F.F. Graham (Con) R.D. Holt (Lib) H.W. McIntyre (Lab)	8867 6871 2793
1929	General Election: North Cumberland	F.F. Graham (Con) R.D. Holt (Lib) C.A. O'Donnell (Lab)	10392 9661 3092

APPENDIX THREE

Holt Durning Family
Simplified Family Tree

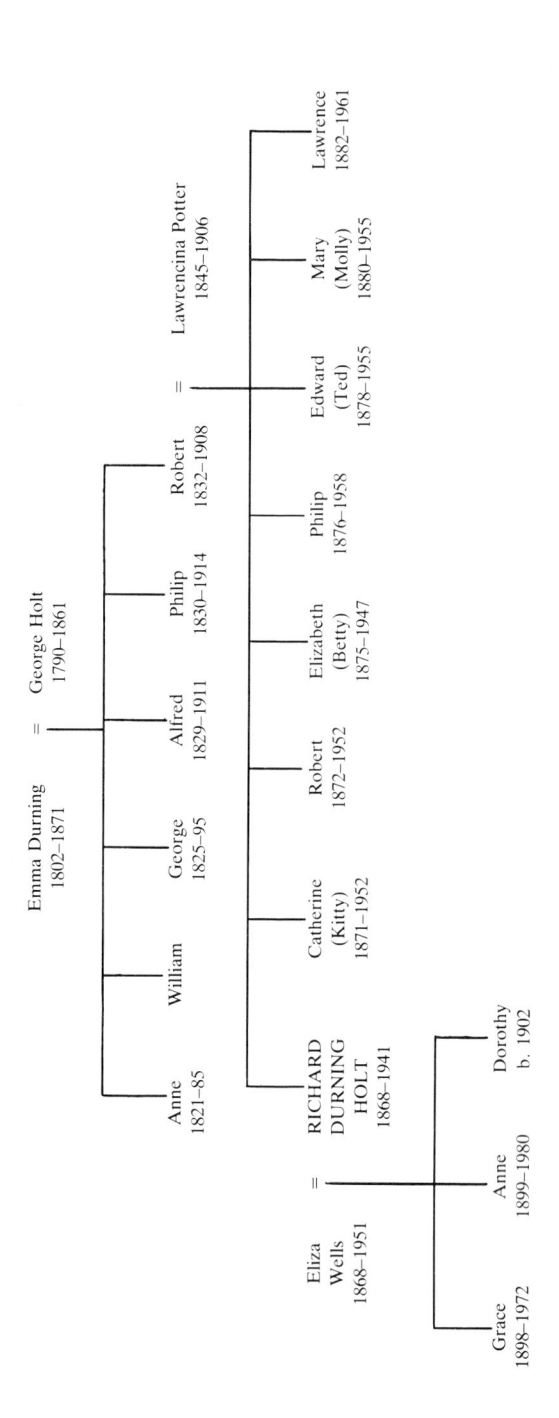

Emma Durning 1802–1871 = George Holt 1790–1861

- Anne 1821–85
- William
- George 1825–95
- Alfred 1829–1911
- Philip 1830–1914
- Robert 1832–1908

Robert 1832–1908 = Lawrencina Potter 1845–1906

- Catherine (Kitty) 1871–1952
- Robert 1872–1952
- Elizabeth (Betty) 1875–1947
- Philip 1876–1958
- Edward (Ted) 1878–1955
- Mary (Molly) 1880–1955
- Lawrence 1882–1961

Eliza Wells 1868–1951 = RICHARD DURNING HOLT 1868–1941

- Grace 1898–1972
- Anne 1899–1980
- Dorothy b. 1902

INDEX

(page numbers in bold type refer to the Biographical Notes)

Abbey Town 98
Abercromby (Liverpool) 14
Abernethy ix, x, 35, 38, 44, 60, 65, 85, 88
Achilles 43
Adelphi Hotel (Liverpool) 68
Afghanistan 100
Agnew, Sir George 31, **104**
Aintree 100
Air raids xxii, 40, 43, 49–52, 54
Albany Road (Liverpool) 15
Albert Hall (London) 63, 84
Albert sills (Birkenhead) xiv
Alcinous 32
Alexandra, Queen 13
Alfred Holt and Co. xiii, xiv, xxi, 27, 29, 40, 43; *see also* Ocean Steam Ship Company and Blue Funnel Line
Algeria 40
Allendale, First Baron 18, **104**
Allendale, Second Baron 18, 24, 28, **104**
Alloa 95
Alva 95
Amanullah, King 100, **104**
America 19, 45, 49, 55, 73, 89
American Red Cross 53
Amery, L.S. 77, 84, **104**
Amsterdam 71, 86
Anderson, W.C. 61, **104**
Anfield (Liverpool) 5
Anti-Corn Law League 75
Antilochus 40
Armageddon 28
Armistice (1918) 58
Arnold, S., First Baron Arnold 48, 51, 60, 61, 85, **104**
Ashton, T.G., Lord Ashton of Hyde 48, 99, 104
Asquith, H.H., First Earl of Oxford and Asquith xix, xx, xxii–xxv, 1, 11, 23, 26, 30, 31, 38, 39, 41–43, 46–48, 51–57, 61–63, 65, 66, 70, 71, 73, 75, 77, 78, 80–85, 87, 88, 90–92, 99, 100, **104**
Asquith, Margot 54, 70, 84, 97, 99, **104**
Asquith Coalition xviii, 36, 38, 42, 44–46, 59, 92
Association of Lancashire Liberal Clubs 69
Australia xiv, 43, 45, 77, 85, 86, 93
Austria 32, 35, 45, 58, 61
Avening 2
Avonmouth 56

Bacup 72, 74
Baddeley, Sir Vincent 45, **105**

Baghdad 48
Baldwin, S., First Earl Baldwin 75–79, 95, **105**
Balfour, A.J., First Earl Balfour 6, 12–14, 16, 18, 23, 31, 34, 52, 54, 74, **105**
Balkans 27
Bank of Liverpool 100
Bank rate 32
Baring, Sir Godfrey 57, **105**
Barlow, Sir John 48, **105**
Bates, Col. C.L. 18, **105**
Beauchamp, Seventh Earl 48, 54, 60, 63, 70, 76, 77, 79, 81, 82, 85, 91, 94, 100, **105**
Beaumont, W.H.C., Second Viscount Allendale 58, **105**
Beavan, Margaret 98, **105**
Beazley, J.H. 97, **105**
Belgium 26, 32, 52
Belgrave Square (London) 81
Bell, Henry 100
Bell, Sir Hugh 68, 82, 98, **105**
Bell, Sir T. 57
Benn, Sir Ernest 82, **105**
Benn, W.W., First Viscount Stansgate 82, 83, 96, **105**
Bennett, Sir Francis 64, **105**
Beveridge, Sir William 87, **105–6**
Bibby, A.W. 97, **106**
Birkenhead xiv, 27, 63, 76, 90
Birkenhead, Earl of *see* Smith, F.E.
Birmingham xvi, 51
Birrell, A. 44, **106**
Biscay, Bay of 43
Bliss, J. 51, **106**
Blockade 46
Blue Funnel Line x, xiii, xxi, 97, 99
Boer War xv, xxv, 1–8; peace settlement 8
Bolsheviks; Bolshevists 54, 59, 95
Bolton 73, 96
Bonham-Carter, Lady Violet 93, **106**
Bonwick, A.J. 82, **106**
Booth, Sir Alfred 24, 62, **106**
Booth, Charles 12, **106**
Boothby 95
Bootle 61
Boscawen, Sir A. Griffith- 69, **106**
Botha, General L. 22, 38, 39, **106**
Bowring, Sir Frederick 98, **106**
Boxer rebellion 1–3
Boy Scouts 100
Boyton, Sir James 26, **106**
Bradford 78

127

Brady, P.J. 26, **106**
Brampton 80, 85, 86
Brampton, A. 93
Brassey, Lord 9, **106**
Brazil 89
Breckfield 71
Bridges, Mrs 54
Brighton 79
Bristol 55
Bristol Channel 90
British and Foreign Unitarian Association 56–58
Broadhurst, H. 10, **106–7**
Brooke, B. 81
Brown, Lieut. A.E. 72, 96, **107**
Brown's Buildings (Liverpool) 4
Brownlow Hill (Liverpool) 7
Bruce, S.M. 77, **107**
Brunner, J.F.L. 48, 51, **107**
Brunner, J.W.W. 51
Brusilov, A.A. 50, **107**
Buckingham Palace 27, 59; Conference (1914) 31
Budget (1909) 19, 20, 46
    (1914) xxvi, 29, 30, 42
    (1915) 40, 41
    (1919) 63
    (1927) 97
    (1929) 102
Bulgaria 45, 58, 61
Buller, Sir Redvers 1, 2, **107**
Bullock, Colonel 46
Burgh 87
Burke, Councillor T. 5, **107**
Burns, J.E. 31, **107**
Bury 69, 71
Buxton 75, 76
Buxton, N., First Baron Noel-Buxton 48, 79, **107**
By-election, West Derby (1903) xv, 9, 10
    Norwich (1904) 12
    Hexham (1907) xvi, 17, 18
    South Westmorland (1913) 28
    Widnes (1919) 65
    Louth (1920) 65
    Paisley (1920) 65
    Dudley (1921) 69
    Kirkcaldy (1921) 69
    Woolwich (1921) 69
    Hull (1926) 92
    North Cumberland (1926) 87, 91, 92
    Clackmannan (1927) 95
    Leith (1927) 96
    North Southwark (1927) 96
    Westbury (1927) 94, 97
    Lancaster (1928) 99
    East Toxteth (1931) xxi
    Wavertree (1935) xxii

Cadogan Place (London) 42
Cairngorms ix
Calchas 49
Calderstones (Liverpool) 64
Caledonian Association 67
Cambrai 51
Cambridgeshire 3
Camborne 78
Cameron, R. 10, **107**
Campbell, Dr. 14
'Campbell Case' (1924) 79, 81
Campbell-Bannerman, Sir Henry 1, 2, 4, 8, 14, 16, 38, 39, **107**
Canterbury, Archbishop of (R.T. Davidson) 22
Cape Colony 5
Carlisle 77, 79, 80, 83, 85–88, 91, 95–98, 102
Carlton Club meeting (1922) 72
Carmarthen xviii
Carpenter, Professor G. 11, 62, **107**
Carson, Sir Edward 31, 41, 52, **107**
Casualties (1914–18 War) xviii, 34–38, 40, 43–45, 50, 55, 56, 58, 61
Cawley, Sir Frederick, First Baron Cawley 39, **107**
Caxton Hall (Westminster) 11
Cecil, Lord Hugh 23, 51, **108**
Cecil, Lord Robert 52, 72, 73, **108**
Central Hall (Westminster) 73
Chamberlain, Sir Austen 54, 72, 74, 78, 79, 89, **108**
Chamberlain, J. xv, xvi, xxii, 9, 11, 12, **108**
Chatham 57
Chathill 37
Chaytor, A.H. 21, **108**
Chelmsford, First Viscount 79, **108**
Chelsea 99
Cherry, R.R. 16, **108**
Chester ix, 100
Chesterfield 4, 6
China 1–3, 14, 21, 40, 65, 75, 85, 88, 95–97, 99, 101, 102
'Chinese slavery' xvi, 13
Chippenham 73
Church Stretton 10, 13
Churchill, W.L.S. 12, 15, 22, 23, 28, 31, 38, 64, 96–97, **108**
Clackmannan 95
Clemenceau, G. 61, **108**
Cleveland Row (London) 82
Clydebank 95

Index 129

Cobden Club 71
Collins, Sir Godfrey 51, 81, **108**
Collins, Sir William 51, 52, **108**
Colombo 35
Comédie Française 16
Committee on Admiralty Expenditure 42, 45, 55
Committee of Imperial Defence 27
Committee on Medical Re-examination 50
Committee on Postal Servants' Grievances 25, 26, 28, 29, 31
Common Sense 46, 52, 63, 66, 68, 84
Connaught Rooms 62
Conscientious objectors 51
Conscription xix, xxv, 28, 36, 39–44, 53, 55, 57, 79
Constitutional crisis (1911) xvii, 20
Corbridge 36
Corn Exchange (Liverpool) 24
Coronation (1911) 22, 25
Courtney, L.H., First Baron Courtney 3, 9, 10, 16, 22, 34, 40, 47, **109**
Covent Garden (London) 54
Cowans, General Sir John 28, **109**
Crawford xvii
Crewe 43
Cripps, A.S., Second Baron Parmoor 16, 23, **109**
Cripps, Sir C.A., First Baron Parmoor 16, 63, 79, **109**
Crompton, A. 5, **109**
Cronje, General P. 1, **109**
Crosthwaite, A. 4, **109**
Crown Hotel (Rawtenstall) 74
Croxteth Gate (Liverpool) 37, 50
Croxteth Park (Liverpool) ix
Cumberland xx, xxi, 75, 77, 79, 81, 85–87, 89, 93–95, 97, 103
Cunard Co. 9
Curragh Mutiny (1914) 30
Currie, Lady 93
Customs and Excise Committee 20–22, 25
Czernin, Count O. 54, **109**
Czolgosz 5

Daffodil 56
Dalston 86
Dardanelles 37, 39
Davies, M.L. xiv, 5, **109**
Dawes, J.A. 26, **109**
Denman, Lady 71
Derby 6, 55
Derby, Seventeenth Earl of 13, 67, 98, **109**
Deucalion 26
Devonport, First Viscount 43, **109**

Devonshire, Eighth Duke of 12, **109**
Devonshire Road (Liverpool) 1
Dilke, Sir Charles 9, **109–10**
Dock Board Bill 13, 32
Donaldson, Major E.J. 95, **110**
Doncaster 60
Doxford 37
Dublin 32, 44, 73
Dudley 69
Dundee 43, 49
Dutton (jockey) 100

Earle Road (Liverpool) 15
East India Company 99
East Toxteth (Liverpool) xxi, 8, 71
Easter Rising (1916) 44
Eccles xx, 58–60, 62, 67
Eccleston Square (London) 47
Edge Hill (Liverpool) 14, 15
Edinburgh 17, 98
Edmondson, Captain 44
Education Bill (1870) 6
  (1902) 6, 8, 9, 11
  (1906) 17, 18
Edward VII 4, 8, 13, 20
Edwards, Johnny 56
Eills, B.W. 66, **110**
Elder Dempster Shipping Lines xxi, 37
Elibank, Master of 24, **110**
Embankment (London) 40
Emden 35
Emigration Bill (1918) 56
Emmott, A., First Baron Emmott 12, **110**
Essex 50
Essex Hall (London) 53, 54, 66
Evans, E. 12, 15, **110**
Ewart, Sir John 31, **110**
Exchange (Liverpool) 3, 71
Exchange Hotel (Liverpool) 6, 16

Fairfield 68
Falaba 37
Falconer, J. 39, **110**
Falkland Islands 36
Fenchurch Street (London) 49
Fermanagh 32
Fernie, D. 11, **110**
Finney, V.H. 88, **110**
First World War ix, xvii–xxiv, xxvi, 30, 32–58, 78, 91
Fischer Williams, Sir John 40, **110**
Fisher, J.A., First Baron Fisher 38, **110**
Flanders 39
Flynn, Captain 40

130 Index

Food shortages 45, 48, 49, 53, 63
Food taxes 8, 27; *see also* Imperial Preference, Protection and Tariff Reform
Forwood, Sir William 12, **110**
France 32, 35, 43, 45, 48, 51, 55, 56, 76, 89
France, G.A. 18, 26, **110**
Franklin, Sir G. 42, **110**
Franz Ferdinand, Archduke 32, **110**
Free Liberals 66, 69, 71, 73, 75
Free Trade xvi, xix, xxi, xxiii, 9, 11–13, 28, 41, 43, 45, 48, 63, 75, 77, 85, 88, 98, 100, 101, 103
Free Trade Union xviii, xxii, 47, 63, 67–69, 72, 77, 84–87, 92, 100
Freemasonry xv
French, General Sir John 27, 28, 31, **111**

Gallipoli 41
Galway 24
Garston (Liverpool) 71, 77
Gas Bill (1918) 55
Geddes, Sir Eric 54, **111**
General Election (1900) ('Khaki Election') 1, 3
(1906) xvi, xxii, 14, 16
(January 1910) 20
(December 1910) 21
(1918) ('Coupon Election') xx, 59–61
(1922) xxiii, 65, 72, 74
(1923) xxiii, 75, 78
(1924) 79–82
(1929) xx, xxiii, xxiv, 103
(1931) xxi
General Strike (1926) 87, 89, 90
Geneva 89
George, David Lloyd, First Earl Lloyd George of Dwyfor xix, xx, xxii-xxvi, 1, 19, 21, 23, 25, 29, 41, 42, 44–48, 52–55, 57, 59, 61, 64–66, 72–77, 79–88, 90–99, 101–3, **111**
George, Margaret Lloyd 62, **111**
George V 21, 22, 23, 25, 27, 59, 97–98, 101
George Holt and Co. ix
George Hotel (Buxton) 76
German Spring offensive (1918) 55, 56, 61
Germany xviii, 32, 34, 38, 47, 48, 50, 52, 57–59, 61, 76, 79, 80, 89
Gilmour, Sir John 26, **111**
Gilsland 88
Gladstone, Sir Herbert xv, 73, **111**
Gladstone, W.E. xxii, xxv, 13, 79
Gladstone Dock (Liverpool) 94, 97, 100
Glasgow 3, 26, 49, 70, 71, 80, 90, 95
Glover, Sir Ernest 37, 87, **111**
Glynn, W. 13, **111**

Gorton (Manchester) 58
Gough, General 55
Graham, Sir Fergus 91, 103, **111**
Grand Atlantic Hotel (Weston-super-Mare) 90
Grand National 100
Great George Division (Liverpool) 3
Greece 41
Greenhead 29
Grenfell, F.W., First Baron Grenfell 66, **111**
Grey, Sir Edward, First Viscount Grey of Falloden 1, 2, 23, 34, 56, 67, 73, 80, 84, 91, 94, **111**
Griffith, F.K. 84, **111**
Guildhall (London) 28
Gulland, J.W. 56, **111**
Gwynne, S.L. 24, **111**

Haldane, R.B., First Baron Haldane of Cloan 85, **112**
Hallbankgate 85
Halstead, Major D. 73, 74, **112**
Haltwhistle 28, 36
Hamilton, Lord George 12, **112**
Hampshire 44
Hampson, R.A. 12, **112**
Harcourt, L., First Viscount Harcourt 25, **112**
Harcourt, Sir William 1, **112**
Harris, Sir Percy 57, **112**
Harvey, A.G.C. 31, 58, 67, 75, **112**
Harwich 86
Haslingden 73, 74
Haworth, Sir Arthur 84, **112**
Haydon Bridge 24, 36
Hedges, A.P. 54, **112**
Hedjaz 88
Heligoland 34
Hemmerde, E.G. 52, 53, **112**
Henderson, A. 61, 65, **112**
Herbert, J.B. 77, **112**
Herdman, G. 45
Hexham xvi, xix, 17, 18, 20, 22, 24, 28, 35–37, 39, 42, 43, 47, 48, 52, 53, 57–59, 88
Higginbottom, S.W. xv, 9, **113**
Hill, Mr. Justice 95
Hirst, F.W. 10, 46, 47, 57, 68, 75, 82, **113**
Hobhouse, Sir Arthur 20, 78, **113**
Hobhouse, Sir Charles 42, 48, 53, 61, 70, 91, 93, 94, **113**
Hobhouse, Sir John 76, **113**
Hobhouse, P. 56
Hobhouse, S. 44, **113**
Hobson, J.A. xxvi
Hogge, J.M. 57, **113**
Holland x, 37, 38, 59, 100

Holt, Alfred xiii, 10, 62, **113**
Holt, Anne xiv, 1, 60, 64, 71, 72, 92, **113**
Holt, Dorothy xiv, 37, 58, 72, 79, 92
Holt, Eliza ('E.L.H.') ix, x, xiv, xvi, 2, 10, 13, 14, 16–20, 22–25, 27, 36, 37, 41–45, 47, 48, 50, 53, 58–60, 62, 64, 65, 70, 72, 73, 76, 79–81, 83, 85, 86, 91–93, 95, 98, 101, **113**
Holt, Elizabeth ('Betty') 7, 17, 20, **113**
Holt, George (d.1896) 11, 62, **113**
Holt, George (d.1916) xiv, 5, **113**
Holt, George (d.1861) ix, 99, 100, **113**
Holt, Grace ('G.D.H.') xiv, 1, 23, 43, 47, 49, 50, 58, 60, 62, 65, 66, 92, **113**
Holt, Lawrence 7, 8, 20, 24, 50, **113**
Holt, Lawrencina ('Lallie') xiii, 16, 17, **113**
Holt, Mary ('Mollie') 7, 8, 20, **114**
Holt, Oliver ix
Holt, Philip ix, 20, 37, 44, 45, **114**
Holt, Robert ix, xiii, xv, xvi, xix, xxi, 13, 18–20, 66, 100, **114**
Holt, William 15, 100, **114**
'Holt Cave' xxvi, 30, 31
Home Rule 7, 20, 24, 25, 28, 32, 34, 45, 57
Home Rule Bill 25, 28, 29, 35
Hong Kong 96
Hope, S. ix
Hope Hall (Liverpool) 7
Hopkin Morris, Sir Rhys 82, **114**
Horne, F. 13, **114**
House of Commons Committee on Expenditure (1917) 50
Howard, D.S.P., Third Baron Strathcona and Mount Royal 75, 78, 81, 91, **114**
Howard, G.W.A. 77, 78, 80, 91, **114**
Hughes, J.W. 13, **114**
Hughes, Sir Thomas 15, **114**
Hull 62, 87, 92
Hunter, Dr. 11
Hutchison, Sir Robert, First Baron Hutchison 81, **114**
Hyde Park (London) 50
Hyde Park Corner (London) 49
Hydropathic Hotel (Hexham) 18, 24, 43, 53

Illingworth, P.H. 80, **114**
Imperial Preference 9, 63, 80, 92; *see also* Food taxes, Protection and Tariff Reform
India 22
India Buildings (Liverpool) 45, 66, 99, 101
Indian cotton duties xix
Influenza epidemic (1918) 53, 58, 60
International Free Trade Congress 71
Ireland xv, 30, 31, 45, 49, 55, 56, 66, 67, 72, 73, 80

Iris 56
Isle of Man xv
Isle of Wight 78
Italy 51

Jacks, Mr. 11
Japan 12
John, E.T. 48, **114**
Johnson, Sir Benjamin 99, **114**
Johnstone, H. 97, 98, 100, 103, **114**
Jones, C.S. 71, 78, **114**
Jones, G.W. 74
Jones, Sir Haydn 51, **114**
Jones, L.S., First Baron Rhayader 39, 43, 48, 50, 51, 53, 56, 57, 62, 78, 103, **114–15**
Junior Reform Club 7
Jupp, Mr. 11

Kenworthy, J.M., Tenth Baron Strabolgi 62, **115**
Kerr, Colonel 82
Keynes, J.M. xxv, 98, **115**
King's Liverpool Regiment ('Liverpool Pals') ix, 35
Kingstown 98
Kingsway Hall (London) 47
Kirkbride 79
Kirkcaldy 69
Kirkdale (Liverpool) 3
Kitchener, H.H., First Earl Kitchener of Khartoum, 1, 4, 8, 34, 37, 44, **115**
Klein, Dr. L. 4, 10, 11, **115**
'Knock-out blow' xix, 46, 51, 53
Kut-el-Amara 44

Labour Representation Committee xxiv
Ladysmith 2
Laertes 37
Lake District 43
Lambert, F.H. 92, **115**
Lambert, G., First Viscount Lambert 52, 68, **115**
Lambert, R.C., 47, 48, **115**
Lancashire 61, 69
Lancaster 99
Land and the Nation 82
Land Campaign 29, 86–89, 94
Lansdowne, Fifth Marquis of 18, 46, 51, 52, 54, 57, **115**
Lansdowne Letter xix, 46, 51
Law, A. Bonar xx, 45, 72, 73, 76, **115**
Law, H.A. 10, **115**
Lawrence, Sir E. Durning 16, **115**
Layland-Barratt, Sir Francis 93, **115**
Le Cateau 34
League of Nations 62, 67, 73, 76, 89, 96

League of Young Liberals 56
Leamington 65
Leeds 63, 103
Lees-Smith, H.B. 44, 85, **115–16**
Leicester 7
Leicester Square (London) 54
Leith 96
Lemberg 35
Leon, Sir Herbert 68, 82, **116**
Lewis, Sir Herbert 10, **116**
Liberal Candidates Association 87
Liberal Convention (1925) 82–84, 88
Liberal Council 94
Liberal Federal Council 6, 8, 12, 66, 68, 72, 76, 82, 99
Liberal Imperialists xxv, 1, 8
Liberal Industrial Enquiry 94
Liberal Nationals xxi
Liberal Party, decline of xx, xxii–xxvi, 60, 61, 72, 78, 79, 83, 88, 92
Liberal reunion xxiii, 75, 76, 79, 84, 90, 91
Liberal summer schools xx
Liberal Unionists 6
Liberal Yellow Book 98
Licensing Bill (1904) 13
Liège 34
Lime Street (Liverpool) 77
Limehouse 46
Lincolnshire 61, 63–65
Lister Drive (Liverpool) 24
Littleborough 85
Liverpool ix, x, xiii–xvi, xxi, xxii, 2, 3, 7, 10, 11, 13–17, 21, 24, 26–28, 31, 35–37, 41, 43, 45, 48, 50, 53, 58, 61–64, 66, 70–73, 77, 78, 82, 84, 88–90, 96–98, 100, 101
Liverpool Cathedral 2, 13
Liverpool City Council xiii
Liverpool Daily Post 12
Liverpool District Missionary Association 62
Liverpool Echo 32
Liverpool Street Station (London) 40
Liverpool Town Hall 4, 10, 13, 100
Lloyd George *see* George
Lloyd George Coalition xix, 47, 53, 59, 61, 65, 69, 72–74, 82, 88, 90, 92
Lloyd George Political Fund xx, 75, 76, 82, 85, 87, 90, 92–95
Local Legislation Committee 21, 22
London 10, 11, 13, 19–22, 25, 26, 28–30, 32, 35–46, 48, 50, 52–55, 60, 63, 66–68, 70, 71, 73, 77, 82–84, 86–88, 90, 92–94, 97–100
London Road (Liverpool) 64
Longtown 80, 98
Lothian, Eleventh Marquis of 101, **116**

Louth 61, 63–65, 67
Low Hill (Liverpool) 15
Low Row 89
Low Wood 43
Lowndes Square (London) 45, 46, 62, 71, 76
Ludlow 13
Lusitania 38
Luton 78

McArthur, C. 12, **116**
McCallum, Sir John 26, **116**
McCrie, N. 17
McCurdy, C.A. 81, **116**
McDonald, J.A.M. 39, **116**
MacDonald, J.R. 10, 47, 61, 69, 78–81, **116**
MacDonnell, A.P., First Baron MacDonnell 30, **116**
McKenna, R. 10, 31, 39, 40, 56, 60, 61, 76, **116**
McKinley, President William 5, **116**
McKinnon-Wood, T. 25, 48, 51, 61, 70, **116**
Maclay, Sir John, First Baron Maclay 54, **117**
Maclean, Sir Donald 56, 61–63, 71, 72, 75, 76, 78, 81, 86, 91, 93, 102, **117**
McTier, Major 73
Maden, Lady 72
Madrid 59
Mafeking 2
Manchester 60, 63, 66, 67, 71, 75, 76, 81–83, 85, 89, 100, 101
Manchester Guardian 101
Mann, T. 21, **117**
Marconi Scandal 46
Marseilles 69
Martins Bank xxi, 100
Mary, Queen 22, 23, 27, 97–98
Mason, J.F., 56, 57, **117**
Massey, W.F. 77, **117**
Massingham, H.W. 10, **117**
Masterman, C.F.G. 10, 80, 81, **117**
Mecca 85
Mediterranean 44, 54
Melly, Florence 3, **117**
Melly, P. 45
Memorial Hall (Manchester) 76
Mersey Docks and Harbour Board xxi, 11, 14, 15, 62, 64, 69, 78, 84, 94, 97–99, 101; Docks and Quays Committee of, 11, 62
Mersey Tunnel 84
Mesopotamia 66
Messines 49
'Methods of barbarism' (in the Boer War) 4
Methuen, Field Marshal Lord 66, **117**
Middlebrook, Sir William 39, **117**
Middlesbrough 29

Index   133

Midgeholme 85
Midland Hotel (Manchester) 59
Midlothian 72
Military Service Bill (1918) 55
Minchinhampton 2
Minimum Wage 2
Molteno, P.A. 31, 51, 61, 75, 78, 82, **117**
Molyneux, R.F. 9, **117**
Mond, Sir Alfred, First Baron Melchett 47, 77, 88, **117**
Mons 34
Morel, E.D. xxvi
Morley, J., Viscount Morley of Blackburn 1, **117–18**
Morrissey, J.W.T. 15, **118**
Mounsey, E. 2, **118**
Muir, J.R.B. 83, 84, 98, **118**
Municipal elections (Liverpool): (1900) 3; (1901) 5; (1902) 8; (1903) 11; (1904) 14; (1905) 15; (1906) 17; (1921) 71; (1923) 77; (1928) 101
Murrell, F. 103, **118**
Muspratt, Sir Max 71, **118**
Myers, J.E. 93

Nanking 102
Nation, The xix, 48
National Government (1931) xxii
National Insurance Bill (1911) 21–24
National Liberal Club 23, 39, 40, 62, 84
National Liberal Federation 2, 4, 6, 7, 11, 55, 65, 68, 75, 76, 79, 84–87, 90, 92–94, 96
National Reform Union 75, 76, 81, 82, 85, 89, 101
National Register Bill (1915) 39
National Telephone Company 42
Naval Estimates (1909–10) 19
Naval Prize Bill (1911) 23
Naval Review (1911) 23
Naworth Colliery 97
New Century Society 5, 6, 8
'New Liberalism' xxii
'New Right' xxv
New York 40, 59
New Zealand 77
Newcastle-upon-Tyne 29, 56
Nicholson, Sir Charles 31, 39, 48, 60, **118**
Non-ferrous Metals Bill (1917–18) 52, 53
North Sea 44
Northampton 44
Northcliffe, First Viscount 38, 45, 51, 53, **118**
Northern Liberal Federation 24, 29
Northumberland xvi, 17, 18, 29
Norwich 12
Nottingham 68

O'Donnell, C.A. 103
Ocean Steam Ship Co. x, xiii, xvi, 1, 5, 12, 25, 99; Annual Meeting of (1895) xiv; (1902) 7; (1912) 25; (1914) 30; (1916) 43; (1917) 47; (1926) 88; (1929) 102; *see also* Alfred Holt and Co. and Blue Funnel Line
Old Kent Road (London) 40
Oldbury 61
Orange Order xv
Orde-Powlett, W.G.A., Fifth Baron Bolton, 26, **118**
Orme, E.B. 78, **118**
Ottawa 46
Oxford, Earl of *see* Asquith, H.H.
Oxford Movement 6
Oxford University x, xiii, 67

Paardeberg 1
Pacific Ocean xiv
Paget, General Sir Arthur 30, **118**
Paisley 65
Palestine 61
Paris 16, 35
Parliament Act (1911) 21–23, 25, 35
Parmoor, Baron *see* Cripps
Paton, A.A. 9, **118**
Peace terms (World War I) xix, xx, 46, 47, 51–53, 61, 63, 64
Pekin 3, 85
Penryn xxi
Perth 85
Philharmonic Hall (Liverpool) 7, 11, 12, 15
Phillipps, H.V. 87, 93, 94, 99, **118**
Piccadilly (London) 83
Poland 66, 89
Police Bill (1919) 64
Political Economy Club 9
Pollok 95
Ponsonby, A., First Baron Ponsonby of Shulbrede 52, 79, **118**
Port Sunlight 100
Portbury by Avonmouth 56
Potter, R. 57, **119**
Power, Admiral Sir Lawrence 57, **119**
Prague x
Prayer Book 98
Preston 36, 102
Primrose, Sir Henry 30, **119**
Princes Park (Liverpool) 1
Pringle, W.M.R. 48, 51, 56, 57, **119**
'Pro-Boers' 1

Propert, Captain 37
Proportional Representation xx, 47, 48, 50, 73, 74
Proportional Representation Society 47
Protection xxi, xxii, 14, 75, 78, 84; *see also* Food taxes, Imperial Preference and Tariff Reform
Protestantism xiv, xv, 3, 4, 12, 14
Prudhoe 36
Prussia 35

Ramsbottom 72, 73
Rathbone, Eleanor 71, **119**
Rathbone, Herbert R. 5, 8, **119**
Rathbone, Hugh R. 78, **119**
Rawlinson, J.F.P. 49, **119**
Rawtenstall 71, 72, 74
Rea, R. 10, 39, **119**
Rea, Sir Walter, First Baron Rea 62, 78, 103, **119**
Recruitment (1914–15) 36, 37
Reduction of Armaments Committee (1909) 19
Reform Club 5–7, 10, 13, 68, 73, 82, 98, 99
Rendall, A. 51, **119**
Reparations 80
Representation of the People Act (1918) ('Reform Bill'), 47–51
Rhodes, C.J. 2, 8, **119**
Rigg, R. 3, **119**
Ritz Hotel (London) 100
Riverside Station (Liverpool) 98
Roberts, C.H. 48, 91, 95, 103, **119**
Roberts, First Earl 1, 4, **119–20**
Robertson, J.M. 43, 48, 53, 61, 101, **120**
Robertson, Field Marshal Sir William, 54, **120**
Roch, W.F., 57, **120**
Rochdale ix, 57, 67
Rome, T. xxi, 11, 62, 64, 94, **120**
Rose, Sir Charles 3, **120**
Rosebery, Fifth Earl of xxi, 1, 4, 6–8, **120**
Rossendale 67, 71–74
Rothbury 36
Rotunda 13, 16
Rowntree, B.S. 101, **120**
Royal Commission on the Civil Service 26, 30, 36, 41
Royal Institution (Liverpool) 62
Royden, Sir Thomas 37, 40, 61, **120**
Royton 58, 67, 82
Ruhr 76
Rumania 45, 46
Runciman, Sir Walter, First Baron Runciman 48, 54, 62, **120**
Runciman, Walter, First Viscount Runciman of Doxford xx, 16, 18, 21, 37, 41, 51–54, 56, 61, 62, 65, 78, 82, 85, 90, 92, 93, 100, **120**
Russell, E.S. 35, **120**
Russia 12, 32, 35, 39, 48, 50, 51, 80, 81
Russo-Japanese War 12, 13
Rutherford, Sir William xv, xvi, **120**

St. George's Hall (Liverpool) 11, 37
St. John's Gardens (Liverpool) 13
St. Margaret's Church (Westminster) 59
St. Paul's Cathedral 40
Salisbury 72
Salisbury, Third Marquis of 1
Salvidge, A.T. xiv, xv, 5, 9, 12, 72, **120**
Samuel, H.L., First Viscount Samuel, x, 10, 26, 42, 50, 56, 57, 61, 62, 87, 95, 96, 98, 102, **120–21**
Sandhills (Liverpool) 3
Savoy Hotel (London) 68
School Board 3
Scotland 3, 20, 23, 39, 58, 65, 80
Scoutbottom 72
Second World War xxv, 99
Seely, Sir Charles 51, 82, **121**
Seely, F. 48
Seely, General 48
Seely, Sir Hugh, First Baron Sherwood 82, **121**
Seely, Sir John, First Baron Mottistone 14, 16, 24, 27, 28, 31, 78, **121**
Sefton, Sixth Earl of 9, **121**
Servia 32, 35
Settlingstones 24
Seymour, Sir Edward 3, **121**
Shaftesbury Avenue (London) 54
Shanghai 94
Shaw, Sir Charles 51, **121**
Sheffield 42
Shipping Controller 60
Shortt, E. 48, 50, **121**
Shropshire 13
Silloth 98
Simon, Sir John xxi, xxv, 41–43, 47, 48, 50, 53, 61–63, 66, 70, 75, 90–91, 97, **121**
Simon, Lady 62, 66, 70
Singapore xiv
Sloane Court (London) 20
Smith, F.E., First Earl of Birkenhead 23, 74, **121**
Smith, Sir Swire 48, **121**
Smuts, General J.C. 77, **121**
Snowden, P., First Viscount Snowden 61, 69, 81, **121**
Social reform xvi, xxii, xxv, 21
Socialism xxii, xxv, 12, 15, 31, 47, 67, 68, 95

Index   135

Somerset 78
Somme 45
South Africa xvi, 2, 3, 5–7, 13, 38, 39, 77, 85, 86
South Africa Conciliation League 7
South West Africa 38, 39
Southampton 90
Southborough, First Baron 88, **122**
Southwark 96
Southwark, Bishop of (H.M. Burge) 54
Sowerby 68
Spain 89
Speaker's Conference 48
Spencer, Fifth Earl 13, **122**
Spender, J.A. 93, **122**
Sports ix, xvii, 5, 38, 88
Stacksteads 73
Staffordshire 91
Stanley of Alderley, Fifth Baron 102, **122**
Stanley, F. ix
Stevens, M. 60, **122**
Stirling 95
Stoddart, W.B., 53, **122**
Streatham (London) 51
Strikes 21, 24, 26, 27, 31, 63, 64, 66, 67, 69–71, 85, 86, 90–93; *see also* General Strike
Submarines 37, 38, 40, 48, 49, 51
Sun Hall (Kensington, Liverpool) xvi, 15, 67
Swansea 85
Sweden 89
Swire, W. 49, 88
Syria 66

Tariff Reform xvi, 9, 12, 15, 18, 28, 46; *see also* Food taxes, Imperial Preference and Protection
Taylor, A. 12, 16, **122**
Taylor, T.C. 48, **122**
Teiresias 65
Temple (London) 52
Temple Station (London) 49
Thames 40, 99
Theseus 38
Thomas, J.H. 43, **122**
Thomson, Sir Graeme 54, **122**
Thomson of Cardington, First Baron 96, **122**
Thornborough, F.C. 93, **122**
Tientsin 3
Tigris 44
Timbuctoo 59
Timmis, H.S. 38, **122**
Todmorden 68
Tory Democracy xiv, xvi, 9
Toulmin, Sir George 48, **122**
Townshend, Major-General C.V.F. 44, **122**

Toxteth Congregational Church 96
Trade Union Bill (1927) 97
Trade Union Congress 52, 53
Trade Unions 32, 69, 85, 89, 96
Trevelyan, Sir Charles 16, 28, 47, 50, 54, 79, **122–23**
Troilus 35, 43, 49
Trotsky, L. 54, **123**
Turkey 58
Tweed, Colonel T.F. 96, **123**
Tyrone 32

U.S.A. *see* America
Ullet Road (Liverpool) ix, x, 8, 17, 19, 36, 59
Ullet Road Unitarian Church x, 11, 100
Ulster 25, 30, 31, 72
Unemployment xxv, 24, 72, 84, 101–3
Union of Democratic Control xxvi
Unitarianism xiii, 6, 11, 17, 59

Valiant 64
Velden, S.A. 78, 85
Verney, Sir Harry 88, 91, **123**
Versailles 54
Versailles, Treaty of 76
Victoria, Queen 4, 5

Walker, W.H., First Baron Wavertree 65, **123**
Walker Art Gallery (Liverpool) 11
Wallace, Dr. 103
Wallasey 56, 84
Walters, Sir Tudor 57, **123**
Walton Jail (Liverpool) 73
War Aims debate (1917) 52
Warsaw 39
Warwickshire 91
Washington (U.S.A.) 67
Water Supplies Protection Bill (1910) 20
Waterloo Station (London) 40
Watson, Dr. R.S. 2, **123**
Wavertree (Liverpool) xxii, 12, 71
'We Can Conquer Unemployment' (1929) 101
Webb, Beatrice xiii, xiv, xvii, xviii, xxi, xxv, xxvi, 10, 16, 18, 28, **123**
Webb, S.J., First Baron Passfield xiv, xxvi, 2, 10, 79, **123**
Wee Free Liberals *see* Free Liberals
Wellington Rooms (Liverpool) 96
Welsh Disestablishment Bill (1912) 25, 28, 29, 35
West, Sir Algernon 54, **123**
West Derby (Liverpool) xv, xvi, 14, 15, 16
Westbury 94, 97
Westminster xvi, xx, xxi, xxiii, 16

Westminster Abbey 22
Westminster Bank 100
Westmorland 3, 28
Weston, Colonel J.W. 28, **123**
Weston-super-Mare 90
Wetheral 86
Whetham, W.C.D. 60, **123**
White, Sir George 2, **123**
Whitehall Court (London) 37
Whitehaven 95
Whitehouse, J.H. 43, **124**
Whiteside, T. 68, **124**
Whittaker, Sir Thomas 39, **124**
Widnes 65
Wigton 86, 97
Wiles, T. 48, **124**
Wilhelm II, Kaiser 59
Williams, C.P. 102, **124**
Williams, W.L. xviii
Wilson, Sir Henry 73, **124**
Wilson, J.W. 39, 42, 48, 60–62, **124**
Wilson, W.T. 26, **124**
Wilson, President Woodrow 38, 47, 61, 67, **124**
Winchester xiii, 79

Windermere 19
Windhoek 38
Windsor 5
Wintringham, T. 63–66, **124**
Wise, G. 3, 12, **124**
Withy, A.E. 93
Women's National Liberal Federation 62, 70
Women's Suffrage 25, 48, 97
Woolwich (London) 69
Worcester 54
Workington 95
World War I *see* First World War
World War II *see* Second World War
Wortley, H.B. 56, **124**
Wye 56

Yangtze Valley 96
Younger, G., Viscount Younger of Leckie 95, **124**

Zambesi 5
Zeebrugge 56
Zeppelins 40, 43
Zinoviev Letter 81